D0880691

The Harpsichord Owner's Guide

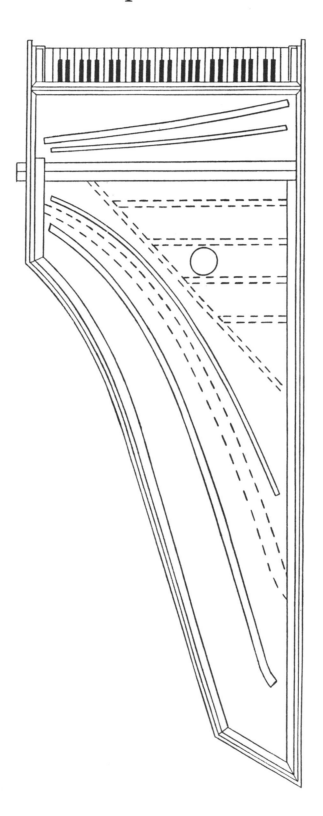

The Harpsichord Owner's Guide

A Manual for Buyers and Owners

by Edward L. Kottick

Drawings by Richard Masters

Photographs by T. Jorgensen

The University of North Carolina Press

Chapel Hill and London

786.23
K848h

LIBRARY
ATLANTIC CHRISTIAN COLLEGE
WILSON, N. C.

© Copyright 1987

The University of North Carolina Press

All rights reserved

Manufactured in the United States of America

Library of Congress Cataloging-in-Publication Data

Kottick, Edward L.

  The harpsichord owner's guide.

  Bibliography: p.

  Includes index.

  1. Harpsichord—Maintenance and repair.

I. Title.

ML652.K67 1987   786.2'3   87-4981

ISBN 0-8078-1745-7

To David J. Way, for what he taught me and

for what he made me learn by myself

JAN 5 1989

Music 24.77

88- 1715

Contents

Preface

For many years, the only maintenance manual available to the harpsichord owner has been a little booklet by Frank Hubbard, *Harpsichord Regulating and Repairing* (Boston: Tuner's Supply, 1963). Although an excellent and succinct aid, it was written for piano technicians, who were just beginning to come across examples of that new (old?) keyboard instrument, and had no idea what to do with all those jacks, plectra and pedals. Furthermore, although Hubbard did talk about the early modern harpsichord, the instrument to which he mainly addressed himself was the *revival* harpsichord, the twentieth-century harpsichord built prior to 1950 or so. This breed of instrument, to be described more fully later on, typically had a massive frame, a thick soundboard, a heavy keyboard, leather plectra and pedals for changing registers. Thus, it was quite different in appearance, action and sound from the classically-oriented harpsichords we normally see these days.

Two other builders have written privately published manuals on the maintenance of their own instruments: William Dowd, *A Short Maintenance Manual for William Dowd Harpsichords* (Boston: William Dowd, 1984); and Eric Herz, *Maintenance and Tuning of Harpsichords* (Cambridge, Mass.: Eric Herz, 1976). There is a great deal of useful information in these manuals, but, like Hubbard's booklet, they are necessarily aimed at a limited clientele.

There is no book, then, that explains in detail how to buy, fix, and maintain a harpsichord. This work is intended to fill that gap. Something like it should have been written years ago, or so say those who play harpsichords, who have built them from kits, those who buy my harpsichords, the customers of other makers, and the harpsichord makers themselves. Its contents will not transform anyone into a harpsichord technician, but it will certainly give players and owners information that will help them keep their harpsichords operating efficiently and in good repair. And, although it will not make harpsichord experts of prospective buyers, it will help them make more informed choices.

The audience addressed by this book is represented by a prototype. A fine harpsichordist, and a friend of many years, the instrument she owns was made by a builder who had a double standard. When he sold a harpsichord to a "name" performer, his efforts were of high quality; but for my friend, a "nobody," his work was slipshod. After years of fighting her instrument (and returning it to the builder for repairs that were charged for, but not done), she brought it to me. It took me three solid days to put it into the condition it should have been in when it first left the builder's shop (he had never even installed the buff stop!); moreover, I insisted that she work along with me. When we were finished, she discovered that she had a fairly decent harpsichord after all—it had just never been put into playing shape. During this process my friend learned a great deal about harpsichord maintenance, and at that moment the idea of writing this book was born.

Many people contributed to this book, both directly and indirectly. Before all others I must acknowledge my debt to my wife Gloria, herself a writer of some repute, who is my first reader and my severest critic. Whatever the merits of this book, they would be far fewer without her help. I owe special thanks to harpsichord builder Robert Greenberg, who gave me encouragement and sympathetic help early in this project, when both were sorely needed. One of the first readers of the manuscript, his valuable suggestions improved it significantly. Also, he shared with me his knowledge of the foibles of crow quill. My sincerest thanks also to John Bennett, who has helped me out on many occasions with his intimate and sophisticated knowledge of voicing.

Sheridan Germann, my mentor in the history of harpsichord decoration, gave the manuscript a close reading, and contributed much to its final form. R. K. Lee also made many useful comments and was particularly helpful to me in sorting out the history of the harpsichord early in

this century. Thomas Parsons read the manuscript with great care, and his helpful remarks saved me from making many wrong and wrong-headed statements. Laura Biklé put my prose through a fine-tooth comb and tried to convince me to remove from it all that was ungrammatical, unnecessary, unclear, and uncouth. Glenn Giuttari (Harpsichord Clearing House) was most supportive of this project and contributed some excellent ideas. Iowa City harpsichord builders John Fix and Peter O'Donnell also read the manuscript, and each contributed something of value. My thanks also to William Dowd and Eric Herz, both for their encouragement and for sharing with me the maintenance manuals they have prepared for the owners of their instruments. David Way (also known as D. Jacques Way), one of the last readers, provided me with many pages of voluminous comments. The book has been much improved by them and undoubtedly would be even better had I heeded them all.

To all these people I express my most profound gratitude.

If this book succeeds in clarifying some of the mystery of the harpsichord, much of that success is owed to its illustrator, Richard Masters, and to its photographer, Tom Jorgensen. Their work has illuminated the instrument's spatial concepts in ways far superior to mere words. I am indebted to them both for their skill and their dedication.

Finally, I want to convey my appreciation to the University of Iowa for awarding me a research assignment for the fall of 1985,

thereby giving me the opportunity to write the first draft of this book.

The reader should be aware of some conventions that have been adopted in this book. Octave designations are those usually employed for the harpsichord, and run from the "c's" to the "b's:" middle c′ is as notated, the octave below is c, the octave above is c″, and so on. Thus, the lowest note on a French harpsichord is FF; the note an octave higher is F, the next is f, then f′, f″, and f‴. The choir of strings that sound at normal pitch are the 8′ strings (the terminology is derived from the length of organ pipes); those an octave higher than normal pitch are the 4′ strings; an octave lower, 16′. Accordingly, a harpsichord disposed 2 × 8′, 1 × 4′ has two sets of 8′ strings and one set of 4′ strings.

Historically, Italian, Spanish and South-German harpsichords followed a Southern tradition of building, while Flemish and eighteenth-century French and English conformed to a Northern practice (this will all be described in chapter 2). Reference to a Southern influence can mean either a specific Italian trait, or a more general Southern characteristic in which Italian harpsichords share. The meaning should be clear from the context.

There are two final thoughts with which I would like to conclude this preface. First, I am aware that I could be accused of a bias, since I am an agent for D. Jacques Way and Zuckermann Harpsichords. I have been associated with the company for years and have built many instruments from Zuckermann kits. But I have also completed a number of instruments from Hubbard parts, and I have designed and built my own instruments as well. If I have a prejudice, it is toward builders whose instruments do not work or that fall apart.

Second, in this book I adhere to the convention of the generic use of the words "he" and "him" to mean "he" or "she" and "him" or "her." This usage is clear and correct, and ordinarily I would not take the trouble to call attention to it. In this case, however, I want to emphasize the fact that there are many talented builders, some among the best we have, who are women (Diane Hubbard and Lynette Tsiang are but two who come to mind). Although they need no apology from me, I would not want any one of them to feel that I had thoughtlessly slighted them.

The Harpsichord Owner's Guide

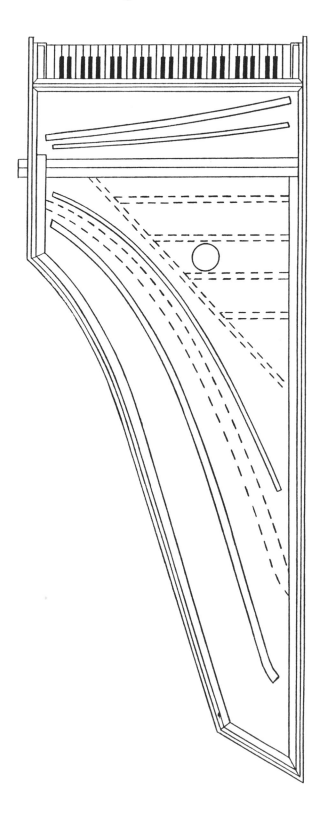

Introduction

Like the early music movement of which it is a part, the harpsichord seems to be here to stay. Twenty-five years ago few people had even seen a harpsichord; today almost every college and university music department in the United States and Canada owns at least one. High schools, churches, theaters, baroque ensembles, orchestras, opera companies, and museums use them, and private ownership grows at an ever-expanding rate.

Despite this activity, acquiring a harpsichord is often approached haphazardly. A symphony orchestra acquires the largest harpsichord it can find, erroneously equating size with loudness. The music department of a small college is advised to buy a complex double-manual harpsichord, although a modest single-manual instrument might better meet its needs. A student purchases an unsuitable instrument because his teacher plays one just like it. A professional uses a second-rate harpsichord because he falsely believes it to be more stable than others. For most people, buying a harpsichord involves a bewildering number of choices, with no place to turn for reasoned and unbiased information.

It is precisely those things that this book hopes to offer to the buyer—information and a basis for reasoned judgement. The book describes the workings of the instrument, provides information about its history, and discusses the pros and cons of the various shapes, forms and national styles of all the instruments called harpsichords. There are few products in this world whose history must be understood before a buyer is capable of making an informed choice, but the harpsichord is one of them. As closely as modern harpsichords seem to follow their antique ancestors, there are sometimes vast differences between harpsichords that builders are making today and those they made 250 years ago. Not that these differences are bad—it *is*, after all, 250 years later; but a prospective harpsichord buyer must be aware of what he thinks he is getting. If it was ever true that a little learning is a dangerous thing, it is in buying a harpsichord; and if ever one was served by a historical perspective, technical information, and a fount of knowledge, it is, again, in buying a harpsichord.

A harpsichord cannot be maintained by someone who does not understand how it works. That is easy to say—it would help us keep almost anything in operating shape if we knew how it worked. Fortunately, the harpsichord is nowhere near as complex as the internal combustion engine, or even the fortepiano. The harpsichord has a simple mechanism that operates on readily understood mechanical principles with which we all deal on a daily basis: friction, leverage, and gravity. Once these principles are grasped, problems can be isolated and solutions found. A sticking key, for example, is sticking because it is binding at one or more of several points—a matter of friction, in other words. It is then a simple matter to take the proper screwdriver, remove the name batten, extract the key, and ease the sticking. To some this may seem daunting, but the alternative is to do nothing and put up with the sticking key for six months of the year, if not forever.[1]

The harpsichord owner may feel that he is not treated fairly. With a piano, the technician does whatever adjusting is necessary when he comes on his semiannual tuning visit, but the harpsichord owner is expected to do his own maintenance. The piano owner is not asked to understand *his* action, so why the harpsichord owner? The piano owner is not asked to regulate *his* instrument, so why the harpsichord owner? The piano is a lot more complicated, but that is not the real reason; an understanding of its action is certainly not beyond the ken of a determined amateur. No, the real reason is that there is practically nothing you can do to the harpsichord's action that will seriously damage it. The mysterious soul of the instrument, which you would rightly fear tampering with, does not reside in its moving parts. The piano's action, on the other hand, is loaded with hidden *"kaboom switches"*—switches which, when pressed at the wrong time, cause the product to explode

with a loud *"kaboom."*[2] The piano owner *needs* to call on that specialist. You, the harpsichord owner, do not. As in olden days, the harpsichordist services his own instrument, and that puts him in a fortunate position. Unlike the poor piano owner, the harpsichord owner can *always* have a well-tuned, beautifully functioning and reliable instrument in front of him.

The ability to respond to the instrument's mechanical problems is important. Thus, these pages tell you how to replace a broken plectrum, how to free a sluggish tongue, how to replace a string, and what to do when your dampers no longer damp. But regular, preventive maintenance is also necessary; it is the only way that a harpsichord can be kept in first-class playing condition. Accordingly, this book also deals with the minutiae of voicing the plectra, adjusting the registers, regulating the key dip, and tuning. It does not treat matters that require dismantling parts of the instrument, nor (with one exception) does it tell you how to repair your instrument if its structural integrity is compromised.

This book hopes to help a great deal, but it cannot supply the skills of the professional harpsichord technician. Nevertheless, nothing described herein is beyond the capability of the average harpsichord owner (except those of you who have nine thumbs and cut yourself on the electric can opener every time you feed the cat; there *is* a limit!). If you have the digital dexterity to play the harpsichord you should be able to cut a plec-

trum, even if it takes ten tries, as long as you are shown *how* to do it.

Let me digress for a moment to present my qualifications and explain how I intend showing you how to do these tasks. I have built a respectable number of harpsichords (twenty-five at this writing), both from parts supplied by kits and from "scratch." As an agent for D. Jacques Way and Zuckermann Harpsichords, I have overseen the building of many more. Other instruments I have made include clavichords, fortepianos, guitars, lutes, citterns, vihuelas, gambas, psalteries, and fiedels. I have done considerable repair work and have sometimes rescued harpsichords from almost certain death. But this is a hobby, more a labor of love, which I pursue in my spare time. Otherwise, I am a professor of musicology at The University of Iowa, where I teach courses in music history and do research in the acoustics of the harpsichord. Thus, with an average output of two instruments a year (and falling), and with a full-time teaching job to occupy me, I do not consider myself a professional builder; on the other hand, with all that experience behind me I can scarcely be called an amateur.

It is this combination of knowledge and attitude that defines my approach in this book. I do not always tell you how the professional does it; or, if I do, I may tell you another way as well. I realize that most of you have neither the skills nor the specialized tools of the professional. Your situation is probably more like that of the friend I mentioned in the Preface. Replacing her first broken plectrum, she put the jack assembly on her breadboard, picked up her voicing knife, and tried to make the new plectrum look like the one next to it. You cannot develop the skills of a professional voicer if you only carve a plectrum once or twice a year, but you *can* learn to cut a workable quill, and that should be your aim.

Time is the enemy of the professional builder. When he strings an instrument, for example, he has to make loop after loop, in the most efficient way possible. The same is true of every other operation he does. But this is *not* true of the harpsichord owner, who needs to make only *one* serviceable string loop, and who cares little if it takes five minutes rather than thirty seconds. Done in a manner the professional might never consider, the object is success rather than speed. Anyone who has ever struggled with replacing a plectrum or a broken string knows what I mean.

All the harpsichords now in existence could be divided into three groups: the antique instruments, built between the sixteenth and the beginning of the nineteenth centuries; the harpsichords built between 1890 and about 1950, which are now known as revival instruments; and the modern harpsichords, those built since 1950. This book deals with the instruments of this last class, the harpsichords built along the classical lines of the antiques.

The line of demarcation between revival and modern harpsichords is not always clear. Some early modern harpsichords have revival elements—pedals, bushed keyboards, brass registers, or complicated adjusting mechanisms, for example. Many revival harpsichords were produced well after 1950, and some are still being made. This book may be of limited use to you if you own a revival harpsichord. Those instruments owed much to piano technology, and everything was made adjustable, sometimes whether it needed to be or not. Furthermore, the instruments all used leather plectra (although many have been converted to Delrin). Leather required a precise setting to pluck properly. Compared to the traditional crow quill, leather was less forgiving of the constant shifting of case and strings caused by normal variations in temperature and humidity. Thus, micrometer-like adjustment mechanisms were virtual necessities on these instruments, which were far more complex than the classical models.

So, be warned! The instructions given herein for easing a sticking key may not work on an old Sperrhake; and without prior knowledge and a specialized tool, even something as straightforward as removing a jack from one of those little blonde Wittmayers can do irreparable harm—those jacks could, and *did*, go *kaboom*! if they were pulled out without first releasing a little spring whose purpose was to keep the jack tight in its register slot.[3]

Back in 1969 Wolfgang Zuckermann wrote that "most people approach a harpsichord with caution, the way they do a vicious dog."[4] Unfortunately, this attitude still seems to prevail—people still think that the harpsichord is full of *kaboom* switches. In truth, there is practically nothing you can do in the course of the normal maintenance described in this book that will damage your instrument. Putting your fist through the soundboard will damage your harpsichord, and so will spilling your martini into the gap (no, I am not making these up). But a broken plectrum, tongue, jack, or string (placing the tuning hammer on a tuning pin is, to many people, suspiciously close to tinkering with a *kaboom* switch) is easily replaced and ridiculously inexpensive. So I hope you will read on, and take your tools in one hand and your courage in the other. Your harpsichord is one of the most glorious music-making devices created by man. It deserves to be put into the best possible condition, and it deserves to be kept there.

A moment ago the names of harpsichord-builders Sperrhake and Wittmayer were mentioned, and during the course of these chapters the names of other builders, past and present, will be seen. But note that these names appear only to make a point. Many of those who have read the manuscript of this book have urged me to provide a list of modern builders. I cannot do this. First of all, I know many builders, but I do not know them all—and there would be no way to make provision for builders who arrive on the scene after publication of this book. I would hate to think that some builder might be thought more or less of, even if by one person, simply because his name did or did not appear between these covers. Second, there are some builders—autodidacts, self-proclaimed geniuses—whom I could not in good conscience recommend even by the simple act of setting down their names.

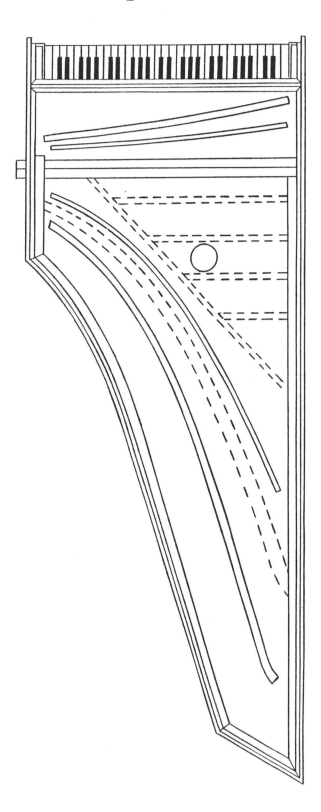

Chapter 1   How the Harpsichord Works

Explaining how the harpsichord works seems simple. A key is pressed. The back of the key rises, pushing up a jack from which protrudes a plectrum. The plectrum plucks the string, which vibrates. These vibrations are transmitted to the soundboard. In turn, the soundboard vibrates, radiating sound throughout the room and to the listener.

Obviously these few words of explanation beg the question. Although it may be convenient to think of the harpsichord in such elemental terms, it is not a straightforward tone generator. It is a complex mechanism, designed to convert mechanical energy into pressure waves, which, in turn, are transmitted to people's ears through a gaseous medium composed mostly of nitrogen and oxygen. Thus, it is a sound-producing device that must be considered mechanically, acoustically, and physiologically. Although we do not know nearly enough about it, we do have more information than those few opening sentences give us. Nevertheless, all the topic headings needed for a detailed discussion of how the harpsichord works are present in that opening paragraph, and it is by means of these key words—keyboards, jacks, strings, soundboard, room, and listener—that this chapter will proceed.

KEYBOARD

A keyboard begins with a keyframe—literally a "frame" of wood, with two end pieces and usually three cross pieces. The middle crosspiece is the balance rail. Balance pins are driven into it, and a cloth or felt bushing (balance punching) is placed on each pin. These are the fulcrums on which the keys pivot. The backs of the keys rest on the padded back rail (Figure 1-1). The fronts of the keys may or may not contact the front rail, depending on the way in which the action is stopped.

A key needs to be guided at two points, or else it will swivel like a compass needle. The balance pin provides the first point, and the second can be either at the head of the key or at the rear. The English seem to be the only ones who provided a guide pin that operated in a hole drilled under the head of the key (Figure 1-2). Rear guides can be either guide pins that run through holes in the backs of the keys (as on the upper manuals of French harpsichords (Figure 1-3), pins that run between the backs of the keys (as on many bentside spinets, Figure 1-4), or they can be rack guides (as on Italian and Flemish harpsichords). A rack guide consists of another rail, called the rack, fastened upright to the rear of the back rail. Slots are cut into the rack, and a metal

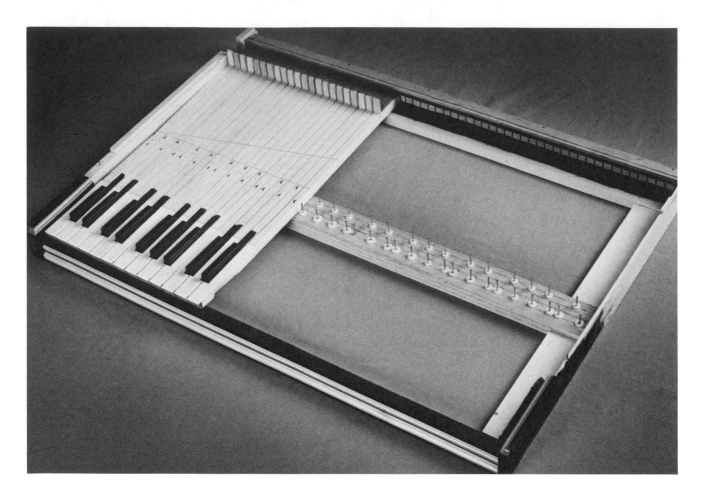

FIGURE 1-1.
Typical keyframe.

pin or a slip of wood, bone, or plastic, protruding from the back of each key, is inserted into the slot and is guided by it (Figure 1-5).

The dip of the keys, that is, the distance they descend when pressed down in playing, is a crucial element of regulation, affecting both the player's comfort as well as his ability to perform rapid passage work. Key dip is set according to one of the three ways in which the action may be halted: by head stop, rack stop, or jackrail stop. In the first, normally found on Italian and English harpsichords, the motion of the key is stopped when the bottom of the head of the key meets the front rail, which is appropriately padded. Key dip is regulated at this juncture, with more padding giving a shallower dip (Figure 1-6). In a rack stop, as found on Flemish instruments, the top of the rear end of the key is stopped with a padded touchrail fastened to the top of the guide rack. Key dip is regulated either by the amount of padding sewn to the touchrail, or by adjusting the height of the touchrail (Figure 1-7). Finally, the action may be stopped when the tops of the jacks contact the padded inner surface of the jackrail. This is the manner in which the manuals of a French harpsichord are stopped, and dip is regulated by the amount of padding on the jackrail or by adjustment of the rail's height.

The upper keyboards of two-

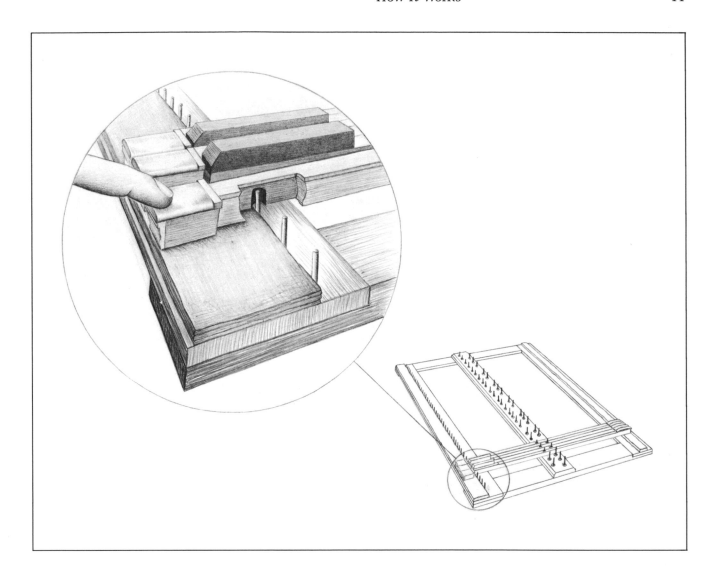

manual harpsichords differ little from the lower, except that the key levers are shorter and the keyframe often does not have a front rail. French double-manual harpsichords have a coupling mechanism, in which either the top manual slides in or the bottom manual pulls out. This brings some dogs, which are wood posts mounted at the ends of the lower manual keys, in contact with the bottoms of the rears of the upper manual keys, thus pushing up those keys and their jacks when the lower manual is played. This allows the front 8′ to be added to the sound of the back 8′; uncoupled, only the back 8′ (considering the two 8′s only) is available from the lower manual. Figure 1-8 should make this description clear. English, and most of the classical Flemish double-manual harpsichords do not couple; instead they use a dogleg action (not to be confused with coupler dogs). It is given this strange name because the front 8′ jack (which, with a determined effort, could be imagined to look like a dog's leg) has a step cut into it so that it can be lifted at one of two

FIGURE 1-2.
Keys guided by pins under the key head.

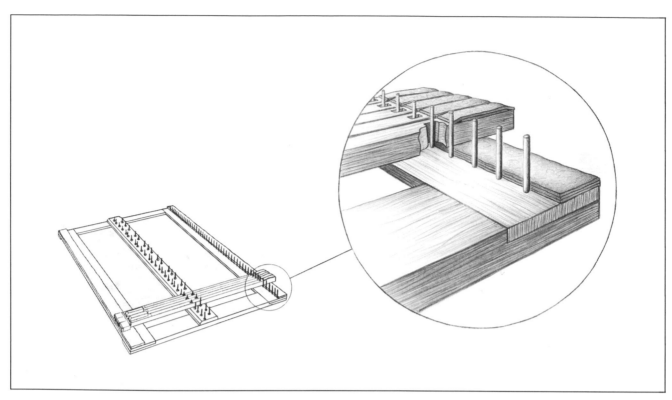

FIGURE I-3.
Keys guided by pins through the backs of the key levers.

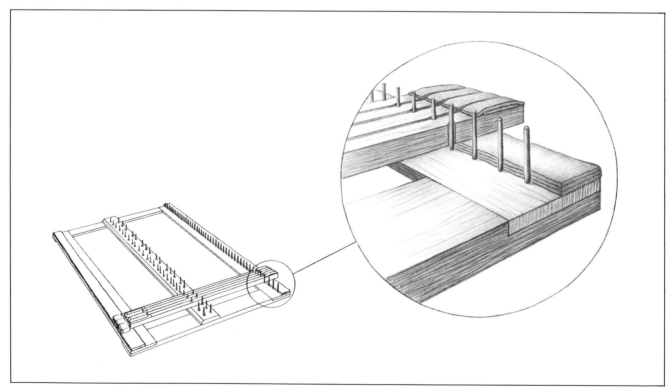

FIGURE I-4.
Keys guided by pins between the backs of the key levers.

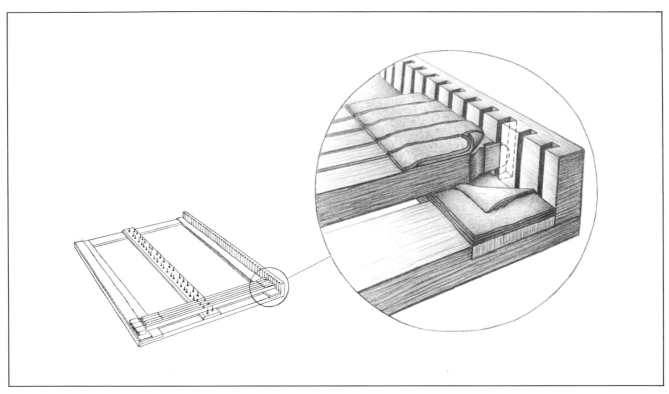

FIGURE 1-5.
Keys guided by slips in a rack.

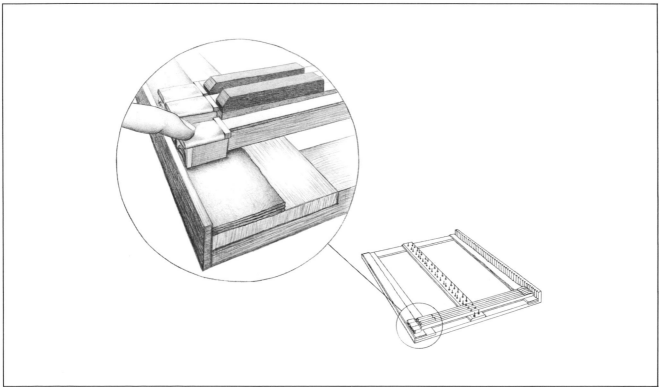

FIGURE 1-6.
A head stop.

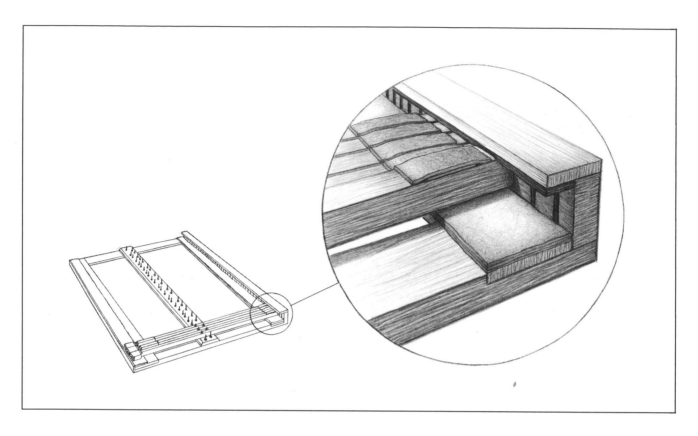

FIGURE I-7.
A touchrail stop.

points; thus, dogleg jacks can be operated from either the upper or the lower manual, and both 8's are available on the lower manual. The front 8' can be shut off by moving its register, but then it cannot be played from either manual (Figure I-9).

A light, responsive action is desirable in almost all harpsichords. For this reason, builders usually attempt to keep the mass of the keys as low as possible commensurate with the touch desired. Keys are often balanced by carving wood out of the front as well as by adding weight to the rear (Figure I-10). The position of the balance points is also important, since it affects not only the balance of the keys, but also the effort needed to depress the keys, the extent of the dip, and the velocity with which the plectra pluck the strings.

The tops of the key fronts are covered with a variety of materials. Italian harpsichords normally have boxwood naturals, but sometimes ivory or bone. Sharps are made of fruitwood, often stained and covered with slips of ebony. Flemish instruments usually have bone naturals, with oak or fruitwood for the sharps. French keyboards use ebony naturals and sharps, but the sharps are covered with slips of bone. English harpsichords cover the naturals with ivory, and their sharps are stained black. These are, of course, generalizations, and exceptions abound.

JACKS

While appearing to be rather simple objects, jacks, like keyboards, are fabricated with a high degree

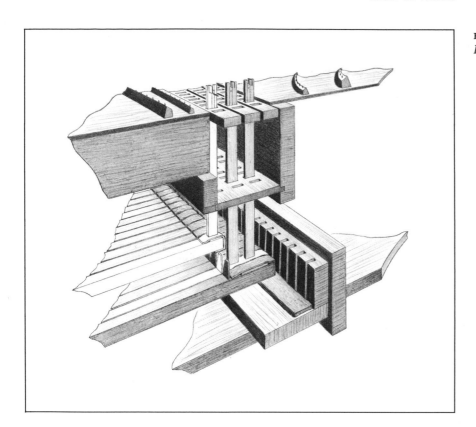

FIGURE 1-8.
French coupler action.

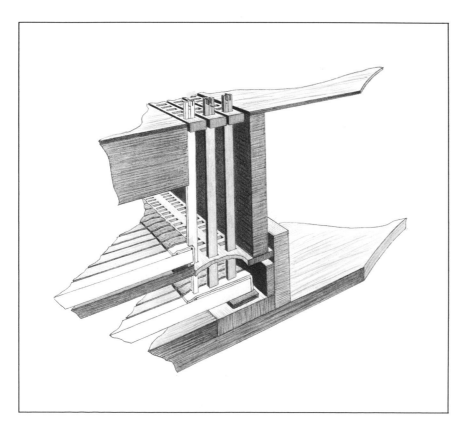

FIGURE 1-9.
English dogleg action.

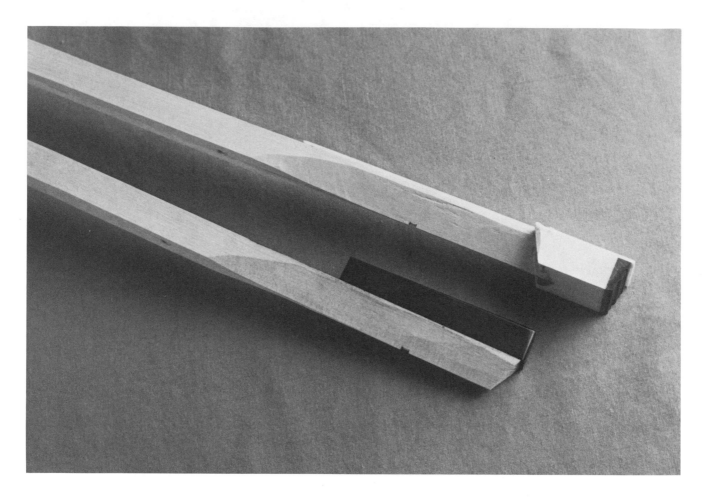

FIGURE I-IO.
Keys balanced by carving wood out of the front.

of sophistication. They could be thought of as the heart of the harpsichord's mechanical system, since it is the jacks that translate the motion of the fingers on the keys into the pluck of the strings.

Jacks are supported in guides, or registers, which are thin, narrow lengths of wood, approximately ⅜" thick and ¾" wide, that are found in the gap between the wrestplank and the bellyrail. The registers are slotted to admit the jacks (the French practice was to make the slots oversize and to cover the register with leather, which was then slotted to the size of the jacks). Terminology is somewhat imprecise here. The words "guide" and "register" are often used inter-

changeably, even though the word "register" also refers to the sound and/or the mechanism of a choir of strings, as in "the back 8' register has a mellow sound." Furthermore, the word "slide" is sometimes used to distinguish a movable upper guide from a fixed lower. A separate guide is required for each row of jacks. Italian harpsichords and bentside spinets have registers called box guides—bars of wood some two inches deep through which slots are cut. Box guides combine the functions of upper and lower guides (Figure I-II).

On harpsichords with more than one set of strings, some of the registers are made so that they can be turned on or off. This is done by making the upper

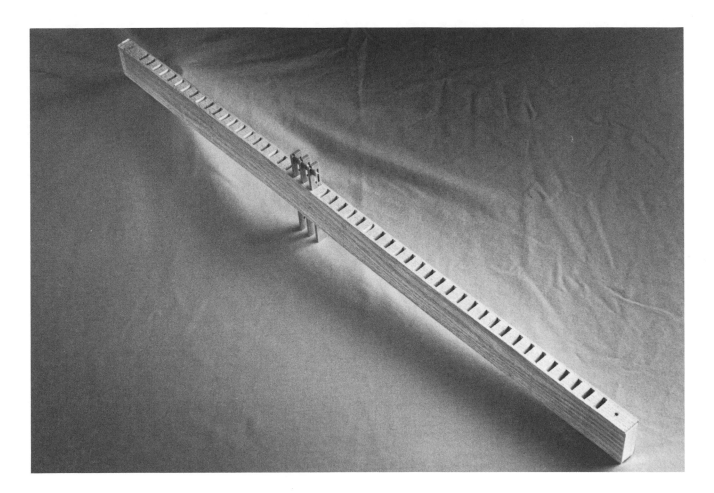

guide movable end to end, with just enough motion so that the plectrum either misses the string (register off) or plucks it (register on) when a key is depressed and its jack is raised. The guides are moved either by levers found on the wrestplank (as on many German harpsichords), or by levers that come through the name board (as on later French harpsichords); otherwise, the ends of the guides themselves project through the cheek of the case (as on earlier Flemish harpsichords and $1 \times 8'$, $1 \times 4'$ Italians). Non-movable guides are found only when there is one set of jacks on a manual, as on the upper manual of a French harpsichord, or on a single-strung instrument like a virginal.

Northern harpsichords have separate upper and lower guides: the lower, just over the keys, is fixed, and the upper, at the level of the soundboard, is normally capable of on-off motion. Separate upper guides are necessary so that individual registers can be turned on or off independently, but the lower, fixed guide can be one piece, combining all the slots of the two or three upper guides into one member (Figure 1-12).

Modern jacks are made of either wood or plastic. Although a number of woods are suitable, European varieties of pear and apple proved themselves centuries ago as excellent materials for jacks. They are of medium density, easy to work, and have

FIGURE 1-11.
A box guide.

FIGURE I-I2.
*Upper (movable) and
lower (fixed) guides.*

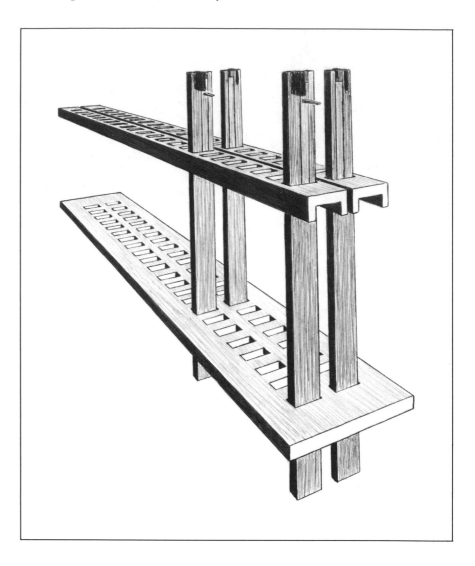

smooth, close grains. Most wooden jacks are still made from them. A jack has a wide slot cut through it at the top, into which is set the tongue, usually made of holly. The jack also has another, narrower slot in which the damper cloth is wedged. A mortise is cut through the top of the tongue to receive the quill. At appropriate points a hole is drilled through the jack, and a slightly larger one through the tongue. An axle, usually made from a pin, is driven through the assembly, and the tongue is now free to swivel in the slot. Another two holes are drilled in the jack, beneath the tongue, and a spring of boar bristle, plastic, or wire is inserted here (the Italians often used a thin, flat brass spring instead of a boar bristle). Riding in a groove cut into the tongue, the spring insures that the tongue, displaced by the act of plucking the string, will return to its resting place.[1]

The plectrum is a part of the harpsichord that has engendered many complaints over the centuries. Bird quill was used in the harpsichords of old, and experience proved that only quills made from the primary feathers of crows (sometimes ravens) were suitable. Bird quill was used for hundreds of years, but when the harpsichord was revived at the beginning of this century, hard leather was almost universally employed. Since the early 1960s a plastic called Delrin has become the preferred quilling material, and it is used by most builders.

It was said that Bach spent fifteen minutes tuning and maintaining his harpsichord every time he sat down to play; undoubtedly some of that time was spent replacing the quills, since crow quill wears out and, being organic, reacts to changes in temperature and humidity. Leather also wears out, reacts to climatic changes, is even more finicky in its adjustment, and has an additional disadvantage in that there is little historical justification for its use (aside from its specialized application in the *peau de buffle*). Delrin has proved to be a satisfactory substitute for quill, although there is no historical justification for it at all. Delrin work-hardens, but it has an extremely long life; if cut properly, the quills can last anywhere from several years to a decade or more. Nevertheless, cutting Delrin quills properly is a skilled procedure, and improperly cut quills can lead to many annoying problems of regulation.

There are those who insist that Delrin, properly voiced, is indistinguishable in sound and feel from crow quill, while others assert that crow quill provides an ultimate tonal flexibility that Delrin does not quite achieve. For this reason a number of builders are returning to crow quill, and others will at least supply it for customers who are willing to put up with its idiosyncrasies in return for the "ultimate experience." But crow quill, to some extent at the mercy of the weather, and with its high breakage rate, also requires a great deal of patience.

Plastic jacks look very much like wooden jacks. Some makers give the tongue a top screw which can be used to adjust the distance by which the quill underlaps the string; some jacks have adjustable end pins; some do not have axles passing through jack and tongue, but instead have little nibs projecting from the sides of the tongue, which snap into corresponding depressions in the jack; some have springs attached to the tongue rather than the jack. Axleless jacks have an assembly that combines the function of tongue and spring. French and Flemish jacks taper in width and breadth; they are designed to fit snugly in their register slots only when the jacks are at rest. Italian jacks are usually shorter than northern jacks, and are therefore made thicker to give them a little more weight. Sometimes they are even leaded. But regardless of type, material, or accoutrements, every jack will have a tongue, spring, quill, and damper.

Let us try to visualize the events that take place when a string is plucked. As the key is depressed the jack begins to rise, and the damper, rising with it, leaves its contact with the string. After the jack has traveled about $3/32''$, the plectrum contacts the string, exciting it like a clavichord tangent. The resulting sound is quite faint, but quite reproducible (particularly on bass notes) by anyone who wants to explore the effect for himself. This "clavichord effect" becomes part of the sound of the harpsichord—the initial part of the tone, called the transient.[2] As the pressure of the plectrum against the string increases, the plectrum begins to bend, taking a roughly parabolic shape, and the string is raised. The pressure of the string against the plectrum thus begins to contain a lateral component, tending to force the jack to one side while the string slides down the parabolic curve. Finally, the string slips off the end of the plectrum and begins to vibrate.

Momentum carries the key to the bottom of its dip, and the jack to its maximum height, where its top is stopped by the jackrail. When the key is released, the jack is lowered until the bottom of the plectrum contacts the string. In the absence of prior knowledge one would expect that this would stop the jack from descending all the way, but the plectrum is angled, and its tip is cut in such a way as to cause the tongue to swivel back, thus allowing the plectrum to go around the string. Having done its job, the tongue is returned to its resting point by the force of the spring. The jack then comes to a halt, stopped by the padding on the end of the key. At the same time the damper contacts the string, causing it to stop vibrating. The contact of the plectrum and the damper with the string both produce another sound, which is simply recognized as part of harpsichord tone. Of course, all this takes place in far less time than it takes to read about it.

STRINGS

It has been known since at least the sixteenth century that a string sounds best when it is stretched to a tension near to its breaking point. That tension is not as high for metal string as it is for gut (tuning instructions in seventeenth-century lute and gamba tutors often began by advising the player to tune the top string as high as it would go without breaking). For the sake of convenience (that is, the convenience of not having to replace broken strings on a daily basis), it is usually assumed that from a half to a whole step below the breaking point is as high as one can practically go with metal strings, and usually one goes lower than that.

Things such as the angle of side bearing, down bearing, and back pinning can also affect the breaking point. Otherwise, at what point a string breaks depends on its composition: brass, for example, breaks before iron; iron breaks before steel. The problem for the harpsichord builder, therefore, is to choose strings that can be stretched to the "proper" point, whatever that might be. Thus, knowledge about the breaking points of various kinds of wire is important. Such knowledge can also provide information about the pitch levels to which the old instruments were tuned. For these reasons some research has been done on the metallurgy of harpsichord wire, although a great deal more is needed.[3] It is generally agreed that the kinds of wire being produced today for pianos and other purposes, called "music wire" in the trade, are unsuitable for harpsichord use.

Consideration must be given to the spacing of the strings. This is not much of a problem on a single-strung instrument, but the difficulty increases greatly as more strings are added. With two sets of 8' strings, or $1 \times 8'$, $1 \times 4'$, each jack fits between a wide pair of strings. This does not sound too daunting, but it must be remembered that enough room is needed to turn off either register, without having the back of either jack hit the adjacent string. The problem is magnified when the spacing between strings is decreased by yet another set of strings. These are not insurmountable problems, but they are mentioned simply to point out that the spacing of the strings and the register slots must be carefully done if problems are to be avoided.

Let us return to our description of the way the jack set the string into vibration, to the instant just before the string slid off the plectrum. At that point we followed the movement of the jack, but now we need to examine the motion of the string. Stretched to its maximum, the string, which has been lifted by the plectrum, resembles a line rising rapidly from the nut to the apex of the lift and descending slowly from apex to bridge. That apex forms a sort of "kink" in the string (Figure 1-13). When the string rolls off the plectrum it immediately attempts to reestablish its equilibrium; the kink created by the lifting action of the plectrum moves down the string until it contacts the bridge pin.

Transferring some of its energy to the bridge, the kink is reflected back toward the nut. It transfers some of its energy to the nut as well, but not nearly as much as it does to the bridge, since on most harpsichords (virginals are an obvious exception) the nut is set on the relatively massive and stable wrestplank rather than on the thin and flexible soundboard. The kink is reflected back and forth from nut to bridge, each time transferring energy to the bridge, until finally the string comes to rest.

The speed at which the kink travels is dependent on three factors: the mass, the length, and the tension of the string. These are the very factors that define speed of vibration, and, in fact, the speed at which the kink travels *is* the speed of vibration. Thus a kink that makes 440 round trips each second (formerly called cycles per second, or cps, but now known as hertz, or Hz) defines the standard pitch of a'— the "a' = 440" that every musician knows.

What has just been described is known as simple fundamental motion, but the string is vibrating in a much more complex manner than that. Anything that vibrates is capable of doing so in a variety of ways, simultaneously. One has only to think of the loudspeaker, which is capable of vibrating at so many different frequencies at once that it can reproduce the assorted vibrations of an entire symphony orchestra. But while loudspeakers want to vibrate over an entire range of frequencies, strings want to vibrate only in whole-number multiples of the fundamental. Thus our string just described,

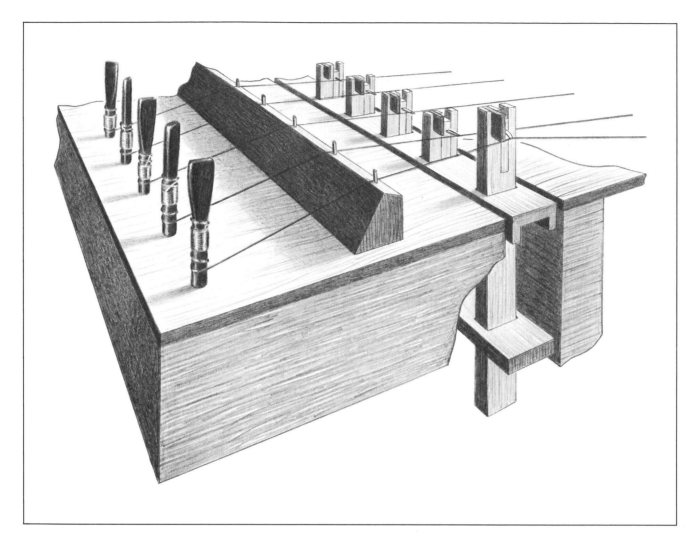

vibrating at 440 Hz, also wants to vibrate at 880 Hz, 1320 Hz, 1760 Hz, and so on, all at the same time. These various modes of vibration are known as partials, sometimes imprecisely called overtones.

If the partials indeed vibrated at exactly these whole-number ratios, they would be called harmonic partials, or harmonics. Actually, they do not occur in *precisely* those simple one-to-one ratios, although they come very close to it. The reason that they do not is because strings have thickness as well as length. A *very* thick string would not be a string at all, but a bar, and bars do not vibrate in whole-number ratios at all; thus all strings have some element of this inharmonicity, or inability to vibrate harmonically. Inharmonicity is very much a part of harpsichord tone quality, and without it we would probably describe the sound as rather bland.

The makeup of the partials in a given string's vibrating pattern varies with its material, thickness, length, and tension—the same elements that affect its pitch. Any attempt to describe the factors that produce one set of vibrational patterns over an-

FIGURE I-13.
A harpsichord string just prior to its release from the plectrum.

other would involve us in complexities far beyond the purpose of this book. Nevertheless, it is worth mentioning that high-pitched strings vibrate with practically nothing but fundamental. The fundamental of a bass string, on the other hand, is not very strong (if it was it would be slapping against the soundboard and the other strings) and generates little sound pressure. Bass strings, are, however, rich in their partial structure. This statement of physical fact tends to confuse people. A strong, distinctive bass is one of the marks of a good harpsichord, and builders have been known to make statements about the attention they pay to getting a "strong fundamental" in the bass of their instruments (Figure 1-14).

One might well ask how those bass notes can sound so good if they are, in fact, weak in the most important element of their tone. The answer is found in a psycho-physiological phenomenon called heterodyning, which will be explained shortly. In the meantime, it is sufficient to know that harpsichord strings vibrate in a pattern in which the bass strings have fundamentals that produce little sound pressure, but have many prominent partials; in the middle range, the fundamental becomes progressively stronger and the partials weaker; and in the upper range, the fundamental is very strong and the partials even weaker or almost nonexistent.

Some consideration must be given to the point at which the plectrum will pluck the string. The closer to the nut the string is plucked, the less the fundamental will be present, and the

more the higher partials will be excited. This results in what is commonly described as a nasal tone. But the closer the string is plucked to its center, the more the fundamental and the odd partials will tend to be emphasized, and the less the upper partials. The result is a plainer tone quality. Although it does not seem as if there is much latitude for their placement on a harpsichord, merely separating the plucking points of the two 8' strings by the width of the 4' register is sufficient to produce a noticeable distinction in tone color. Later we will see that some South German harpsichords spread the plucking points of the two 8' strings in the bass in an effort to make their tone colors more distinguishable. And in many Italian harpsichords the gap is slanted away from the keyboard, thereby providing deeper plucking points for the bass strings. Plucking points on virginals are more variable, and their position actually forms the basis on which one distinguishes between the Flemish virginal and muselar.

SOUNDBOARD

If the jack is the heart of the harpsichord's mechanical system, then the soundboard occupies a similar position in relation to its acoustical system. It is also one of the most mysterious elements of the harpsichord, since its efficiency depends on the interrelationship between its thickness, mass, and grain pattern, as well as the location, mass, and cross section of the bridges glued to its top, and the various ribs, the

cutoff bar, and the *boudin* (4' hitchpin rail) glued to the undersurface of the board (Figure 1-15).[4] Northern soundboards were almost always tapered, or thinned at selective points, to make the board more compliant at certain frequencies; Italian boards usually were not thinned, and the compliance was controlled by other means.

The soundboard is glued firmly to the case, to liners that encircle the spine, tail, bentside, and cheek. The front of the soundboard is glued to the top of the bellyrail, a member that extends from spine to cheek, and comprises the far wall of the gap. Bellyrails sometimes extend down to the bottom boards of the harpsichord, particularly in Southern instruments; on Northern instruments they are usually in two parts, separated and offset (Figure 1-16). We need mention only one more case part, the bottom, to fully describe the enclosed box that makes up the body of the harpsichord. And we need to mention it because that box encloses a volume of air, and air, like everything else, vibrates.

Now we must return to our vibrating string, this time fastening our attention on the behavior of the soundboard as the kink travels down the string. The kink, as stated earlier, transfers a certain amount of its energy to the bridge, impacting the pin 440 times per second for the a' above middle c'. In turn, the bridge transfers this energy to the soundboard. In fact, it transfers not only the energy of the fundamental but of the partials as well. The bridge, however, tends to be selective: it may reduce the energy content of some of the

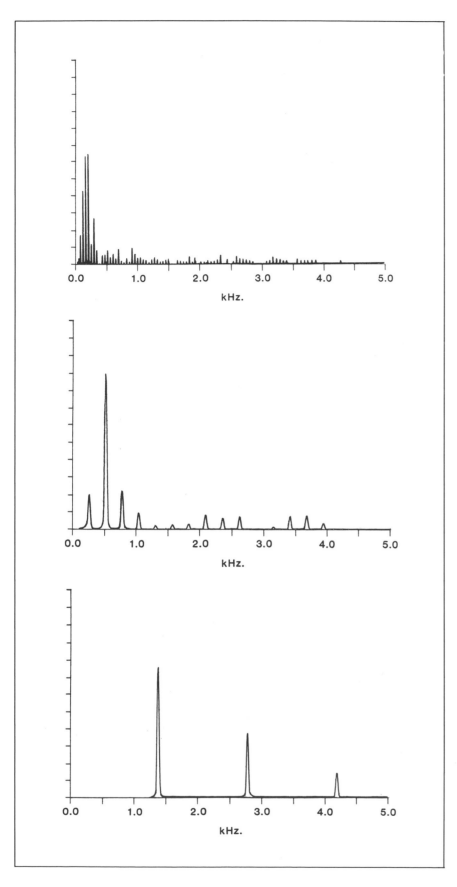

FIGURE I-14.
Three typical harpsichord spectra, each taken approximately one second after the pluck. Frequency is read horizontally, on a logarithmic scale. The height of the peaks, given in arbitrary linear units, represents the amount of energy in each partial. (Spectra courtesy of Thomas Parsons)
(a) The spectrum of c (an octave below middle c'), showing well over 40 partials.
(b) The spectrum of c' (middle c'), showing 14 partials.
(c) The spectrum of f"(an octave and a half above middle c'), showing only 3 partials.

FIGURE I-15.
(a) A typical heavier Northern soundboard barring.
(b) A typical lighter Southern soundboard barring.

partials, it may deny others any access to the soundboard at all, and it may allow full flow to some partials that it particularly favors. In this sense the bridge acts as a selective filter, allowing some partials through, denying others, and enhancing yet others.

The bridge is also an important factor in controlling the impedance match between the strings and the soundboard, since it is necessary to meter the rate at which the energy of the string is transferred to the soundboard

(the term *impedance*, borrowed from electrical engineering, refers to a measure of resistance). A perfect impedance match, with no obstruction or reflection from the bridge, would allow all the energy to be transferred at once. The result would be a loud and not too musical "bang." A really poor match would have just the opposite effect—it would take forever for the energy of the vibrating string to dissipate, but little sound would be heard.

Like a loudspeaker, the

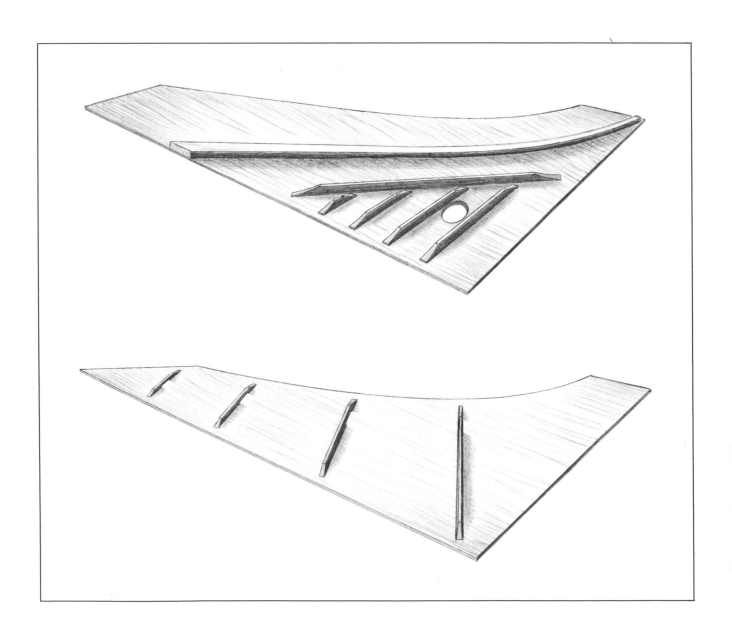

FIGURE I-16.
(a) A one-piece bellyrail.
(b) A two-piece bellyrail.

soundboard itself would like to vibrate at all significant frequencies; it does do that, but it also has favored frequencies. These are its normal modes, frequencies at which it wants to vibrate at much greater amplitude than usual. Thus the soundboard imposes *its* characteristics on the energy imparted to it by the vibrating string.[5] Finally, the air in the body of the harpsichord

88- 1715

LIBRARY
ATLANTIC CHRISTIAN COLLEGE
WILSON N. C.

also vibrates, and it has *its* favored modes. The interaction between air and wood vibration is a complex one, about which little is known, but, since both air and soundboard are capable of vibrating at favored frequencies, one may also drive the other. Most often they couple, to vibrate together at a frequency other than ones that they favor independently (Figure 1-17).

What has just been said about the vibratory properties of harpsichord soundboards literally applies doubly to virginals and muselars. The soundboard of these instruments is divided by the register, so that they actually have two soundboards, each with its own bridge. Each soundboard has its own normal modes, and while there is much overlap throughout most of the instrument's range, the left soundboard tends to favor the bass frequen-

cies, and the right soundboard the treble.

ROOM

We talk about instruments as if they exist independently of any sort of environment, but except for those designed for the outdoors—the bagpipes, perhaps—the room in which an instrument is played must be considered an important part of its tone. Any acoustical environment (other than the middle of a meadow or an anechoic chamber) has its own characteristics, its own way of coloring the sound. This is no secret to us as performers; we are very much concerned with the effect a given hall has on the way we play, the way we hear others around us play, and the way our instrument sounds to our listeners. Like most musicians, we

FIGURE 1-17.
The response curve of a 1640 Ruckers harpsichord. Frequency is read horizontally, on a logarithmic scale. Arbitrary linear units of energy are read vertically.

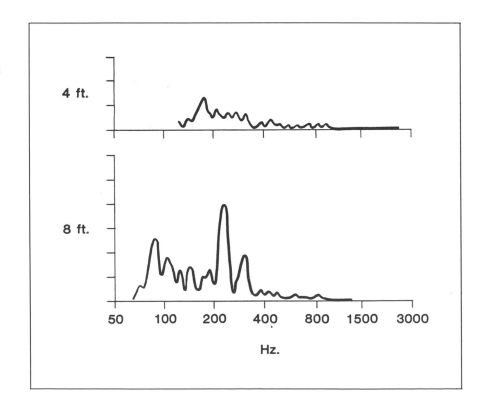

have a good seat-of-the-pants knowledge of room acoustics; we know that a room with carpets and draperies sounds less live than one with a wooden floor and paneled walls, and that a small hall provides a more intimate sound than a large one. These distinctions are caused primarily by the ways in which the room reflects and absorbs sound waves, and the presence of standing waves—frequencies at which the room (like a soundboard) wants to respond with a greater than usual amount of energy.

To summarize what has been said so far about the production of harpsichord sound, the initial energy is provided by the player, who sets the string into a complex pattern of vibration. The bridge acts as a selective filter, allowing some frequencies of the vibrating string through, but not others. The soundboard imposes its own characteristics on the frequencies it receives, suppressing some and enhancing others.

The vibratory motion of the string is a physical one, creating areas of pressure and rarefaction in the air around it. The string, however, is so thin that it moves relatively few molecules of air— certainly not enough to create pressure waves of a magnitude that will be picked up by the human ear. Therefore, almost none of the sound we hear from the harpsichord comes *directly* from the vibrating strings. Both the soundboard and the air inside the harpsichord, however, move with far greater amplitude, and they create pressure waves that are capable of putting the room's air into vigorous motion. If the air in the room is now vibrating, which it is, then we now are

faced with yet another volume of air with *its* normal modes. But this is simply another way of describing the acoustics of the room—another way of saying what was stated just a few paragraphs ago: the room is going to color the harpsichord sound.

LISTENER

Finally, we come to the last and most important link in the chain. To paraphrase the schoolboy's question, "If a harpsichord creates pressure waves (in this instance, presumably by itself) and there is no one around to hear it, does it make a sound?" There are, of course, two answers to that question: yes, it makes a sound, if sound is defined in the physical terms of string, wood, and air vibrations; but it does not make a sound if the word is defined as part of the process of hearing.

Air is the medium through which we normally hear. The pressure waves with which we are now familiar impinge on the ear, and through complex mechanical and electrical mechanisms are translated into the psycho-physiological phenomenon that we call sound. By now it will come as no surprise that the ear, like every other element of this chain, also colors what is being perceived as harpsichord sound.

We know that the ear combines the various frequencies impinging on it, hearing them not as separate entities, but as a single entity, a gestalt, identified as pitch. Thus, when we talk about a note whose frequency is 440 Hz, and identify it as the a'

above middle c', we really mean that the *fundamental* frequency of that pitch is 440 Hz; we also recognize that it contains partial components near 880 Hz, 1320 Hz, 1760 Hz and so on. One might suppose that the absence of one of those partials would confuse the ear, but it really does not present a problem. The ear tends to supply partials that are sums, differences, and multiples of the frequencies that make up the pitch in question. The ear will strengthen weak frequencies and even supply those that are missing.

This is the process of heterodyning (another useful term taken from electrical engineering), referred to earlier when we discused the vibrating properties of strings. It is the same process by which we recognize Uncle John when he talks to us on the telephone, even though the speaker of that device is much too small to vibrate at the lowest frequencies of his voice. Hence a bass note, which will be deficient in its fundamental, will have that frequency strengthened, and it will be supplied if it is missing altogether. Let us take as an example the lowest GG on the harpsichord, a note that has a frequency of about 50 Hz. We know that a string that long, that thin, at that relatively low tension, plucked near its nut, will not generate much sound pressure in its fundamental mode. Thus, the fundamental, although physically present in the vibrating string, is going to be a weak component of the collection of frequencies that reaches the ear, and it may even be absent altogether. The ear, however, recognizes that the partials near 100 Hz, 150 Hz, 200

Hz, 250 Hz, and so on, belong to the compact collection of closely related frequencies that make up the pitch GG, and it has no trouble supplying a 50 Hz frequency of its own.

The other sort of coloring the ear provides is more physical. The auditory mechanism "hears" the high pitches of instruments such as the harpsichord very well, but in bass frequencies it is quite inefficient. To compensate, the world of musical instruments has arranged itself so that those instruments that generate low-pitched sounds do so with comparatively more strength, while sounds in the upper registers are rather weak by comparison. It boggles the mind to realize that the bass area of the harpsichord, where the ear simply does not make good use of the sound energy it receives, is producing a tremendous amount of power, while the treble end of the instrument, where the ear hears very efficiently, is emitting far less energy (see Figure 1-17 again). The net result is an incredibly even perception of sound level over the entire range of the instrument! If I may be permitted to quote myself, "One cannot help but view with wonderment the exquisite balance between string, wood, air, room, ear and brain that we call the 'sound' of a harpsichord."[6]

Chapter 2

A Short History of the Harpsichord[1]

We do not really know where the harpsichord was invented. The first clear reference to its construction and action is found in a Burgundian manuscript of ca. 1450.[2] There is iconographical evidence showing that it was known through most of Europe by that time, and that there seemed to be considerable building activity going on in Germany.[3] However, it was the Italians who perfected the instrument and who, for the next three hundred years, exported it all over Europe. Throughout most of the sixteenth century, Italy seemed able to satisfy the harpsichord needs of western Europe, with little or no competition from Germany, England, France, Flanders, or anyplace else. But toward the end of the century some makers from Antwerp—primarily those of the Ruckers dynasty—also entered the export market.

For almost a hundred years the two styles competed with each other, until the intense Flemish activity came to an end in the last quarter of the seventeenth century. The Italians, however, continued to build with undiminished vigor. Their instruments were simple, cheap and reliable, and they were ideal for playing continuo and for accompanying. Italian harpsichords were found in opera pits, theaters, churches, teaching studios, and conservatories, as well as in courts, drawing rooms, and bedchambers. They were the workhorses of European music—a fact worth remembering as we discuss the various national schools of harpsichord building, for despite the assumed suitability of this or that harpsichord for a particular repertoire, more often than not it was an Italian instrument on which the music was played.

ITALY

There are obvious and important distinctions between Italian and Northern European harpsichords. Perhaps the best way to comprehend them is to first understand the significance of what is traditionally called *the scale*: the length of the string that sounds c″ (the c above middle c). Italian builders used a relatively short scale, somewhere in the neighborhood of 10 inches to 11 inches. They more or less doubled the length of the string for each descending octave, down to about the c below middle c′ and even lower, and halved it for the upper octave. This layout of the string band, called a just curve, resulted in the deep curve of the bridge and bentside so typical of Italian harpsichords (Figure 2-1). These instruments were undoubtedly meant to be strung in brass, since brass strings of these lengths are nearer their breaking points when tuned up to pitch.

FIGURE 2-1.
Plan view of an Italian harpsichord.

However, the situation is not quite so simple, because there were also Italian harpsichords with scales around 14 inches, implying either iron stringing or transposition (the breaking points of iron and brass are about a fourth apart).[4]

The harpsichord cases the Italians built in the sixteenth century were surprisingly thin—about ³⁄₁₆″ thick or less, usually made of cypress. They were braced internally with some stiffeners glued to the ½″ bottom, with a series of "knees" whose purpose was to keep the case sides at right angles to the bottom, and with some flying buttresses, or struts, that took the thrust from the bentside and transferred it to the bottom (Figure 2-2). The soundboards were made either of the same cypress wood as the case, or of European spruce. In the gap, the harpsichord was provided with a box slide for each set of jacks. The keyboard projected from the case

(Figure 2-3). Such a case is extremely light; the greatest weight of the instrument comes from the wrestplank and the keyboard. But it is also very strong.

To protect the thin edges of the case, and to give it something of a more elegant look, the builders ran molding around the inner and outer sides of the tops of the case members and glued another piece of molding (the cap molding) on top of the resulting sandwich. Molding also ran all around the bottom of the instrument on the outside of the case, and smaller moldings lined the juncture of soundboard and case walls. Bridges and nuts were also given a molded section. With all this molding, and with their projecting keyboards, these harpsichords had a very elegant look indeed.

These light, thin-case harpsichords were then provided with a sturdy outer case (perhaps made by someone other than the builder), to which was attached a

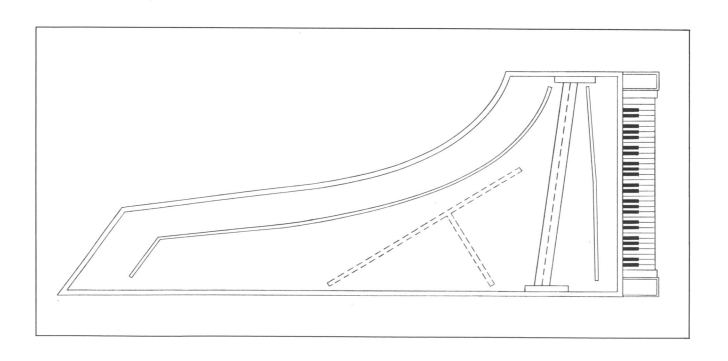

lid. The cheeks of the outer case were square, extending past the projecting keyboard, forming a keywell (Figure 2-4). This type of harpsichord is often known as an "inner-outer." Later the Italians built thick-walled instruments as well, but by the use of molding and cypress veneer made them *appear* to be inner-outers. We distinguish between these two types of harpsichords by calling the first "true inner-outers," and the second "false inner-outers." By the eighteenth century, Italian builders had abandoned the inner-outer convention almost entirely.

The outer case was usually painted or covered with leather or some other material; in any event it was the outer case, rather than the inner, that received any painted decoration. The form of the inner instrument, with its projecting keyboard and the architectural embellishment of its molding, usually was considered sufficiently satisfying in itself. If it was to be decorated at all, it would be with carvings, sculpture, mother-of-pearl inlays, and

(a favorite) ivory buttons. This philosophy of decoration, along with the deep, justly curved bentside, gave these harpsichords a strikingly different look from the Flemish-style instruments.

Almost all the extant Italian harpsichords from before 1600 now have dispositions of $2 \times 8'$. Although some originally were disposed in this way, most of them were built with either a single 8', or $1 \times 8'$, $1 \times 4'$, and altered later on. The compasses of these instruments is a matter of dispute, calling in matters of brass vs. iron wire, pitch ranges, and scale lengths, but the tentative conclusion seems to be that smaller instruments had a range of four octaves, C/E–c‴, and larger instruments had a wider range, from C/E–f‴.[5] The difference in range may imply transposing the music to a higher pitch level, since there is no known sixteenth-century harpsichord music that ascends to f‴.

The symbol C/E refers to short octave tuning, both a process and a physical element of keyboard instruments used well into the eighteenth century. The bottom

FIGURE 2-2.
Typical internal bracing of an Italian harpsichord.

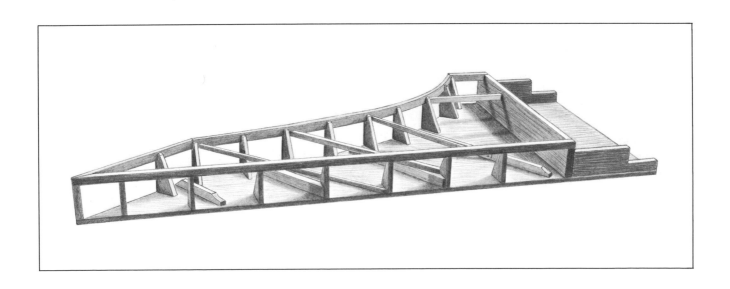

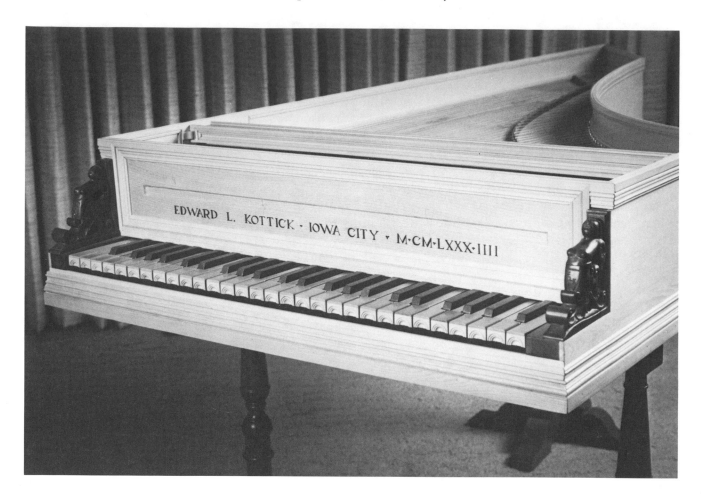

FIGURE 2-3.
Italian keyboard, projecting from the case.

note of the keyboard *looks* like E, but is intended to be tuned to C. The accidental that looks like F-sharp is tuned to D, and what looks like G-sharp is tuned to either E-flat or E, depending on the musical requirements. Thus, the keyboard's bottom octave sounds, from the lowest key up, C, D, E-flat or E, then F, G, A, B-flat and B. From this point on the keyboard is chromatic.

The short octave seems unwieldy, and it is difficult for us to understand why it persisted for so long. To our way of thinking, it certainly would not have *hurt* to have supplied those accidentals, which would then be there when needed. But our forebears were much more practical than

we are. Since nobody wrote music that required those notes, why go to the expense of putting them in? And what composer would bother to write them if few keyboard instruments had them? Even in the seventeenth century, and well into the eighteenth, when instruments were given chromatic keyboards as a matter of course, the lowest accidental was often omitted on the grounds that it was so seldom required. And, after all, if you just *had* to have that note, some other note that you were not using in that piece could always be tuned to it.

Nevertheless, some Italian harpsichords (and other instruments as well) were given split-

sharp short octaves: the bottom two sharps were separated front and back, and each pair was actually two keys. The front of each sharp played the note assigned to it by short-octave tuning, and the back of the sharp played the proper accidental. Thus the front half of the F-sharp key played D, but the back half played F-sharp. To complicate the situation a little more, some instruments had split sharps on other notes as well, but these had nothing to do with the short octave; instead, they were intended to provide extra accidentals for mean-tone tuning, in which the accidentals are not enharmonic. Thus the back half of a split g'-sharp would be a'-flat.

The distinctive "speaking" quality of the Italian harpsichord has been described many times. Its pluck has an explosive energy, its sound is clear, penetrating, and resonant, and its tone is relatively short-lived. While this description is not inaccurate, the tone of properly restored antiques sounds neither as explosive nor as short-lived as previously thought. Nevertheless, all Italian harpsichords seem to have at least some of this "speaking" quality. This characteristic, although in large part a result of the thin-walled, resonant case construction, was something obviously desired by the Italian builders (and presumably by their customers), since later on, when

FIGURE 2-4.
The Italian harpsichord in Figure 2-3 in its outer case.

the Italians started building the heavier, Northern-style cases, they still built instruments whose sounds conformed to this ideal.[6]

Many have admired the balance of form, structure, and function found in sixteenth-century Italian harpsichords. The cases were light, but strong, built on engineering principles more elegant than those found in Flemish instruments. The short scales and light stringing made no excessive demands on the strength of the case. The deeply curved bentside provided a grace of its own, and the architectural quality of the molded surfaces fulfilled the purpose of embellishing as well as protecting the thin case sides.

Thick-walled false inner-outers became common in the seventeenth century and were built for some time. The 2 × 8' disposition became the norm. Surprisingly, the C/E–c''' range became more common than the wider C/E–f''' compass, thus lending some credence to the supposition that these two sizes were more concerned with matters of transposition than of suitability to a repertoire. The compass did expand in the eighteenth century, however, to five octaves or something close to it. Nevertheless, the Italian harpsichord displayed an almost cavalier disregard for the "advances" found in the French and English instruments. Despite many outstanding exceptions, it continued to retain the characteristic crispness of tone, the simplicity of disposition, and the elegance of the just curve established centuries earlier, although as more notes were added in the bass the tails got longer and the curve became more elongated. If it can be said that the Italian harpsichord "evolved" very little, it can also be said that there seemed to be little need for it to do so.

The Italians also built virginals (they called them *spinettos*), mostly at 8' pitch, but also at 4' pitch (*ottavinos*); in fact, some 4' instruments in harpsichord shape were made as well. Like the harpsichords, virginals were first built as thin-walled true inner-outers, later as false inner-outers. The thin-walled instruments were usually polygonal, a shape roughly dictated by the string-band, which, on a virginal, runs at right angles to the keys. The outer case, however, was almost always oblong (usually called "square," in the arcane jargon of the keyboard world), sometimes surrounding the projecting keyboard to form a keywell, sometimes not. The false inner-outers were oblong (Figure 2-5).

The geometry of these virginals was arranged so that the keyboard was about in the middle of the case; thus the jacks plucked the bass strings at a point around a fourth or fifth of their length, far deeper than was found on harpsichords. These deep plucking points, and the fact that the virginal normally had both bridge and nut on free soundboard, gave these instruments a distinctive sound, with a clear, sparkling treble, an incisive tenor, and a particularly round, contrasting bass.

Virginals normally had a single set of 8' strings. It was difficult if not impossible to have more strings or jacks than this because the jacks, set into a box guide, were arranged in pairs. Each pair sat between a wide-spaced pair of strings; each jack pointed in the opposite direction from the other, and each plucked the nearest string (Figure 2-6). Ranges varied, as in the harpsichords, from C/E–c''' to C/E–f'''. Virginals were considered to be domestic harpsichords, that is, keyboard instruments suitable for an amateur. Nevertheless, they seem to have been built with the same care as the harpsichords, and because they were intended for display at home, often received more elaborate decoration.

Another home instrument the Italians made was the bentside spinet. It may have been invented by an Italian builder early in the seventeenth century, although it never achieved much importance in Italy. Examples were made in other countries as well, but it was in England that the bentside spinet found its greatest development.

Clavicytheria, or upright harpsichords, were also made in Italy. Although they probably were built almost everywhere, the evidence of the extant instruments indicates that they were more common here than elsewhere.[7] Playing a clavicytherium is a sensual experience: the soundboard is directly in front and the sound is projected right at the player.

FLANDERS

Somewhere past the middle of the sixteenth century some Flemish builders started making harpsichord cases out of thick, soft wood (about ½" European poplar or lime), using both case sides and bracing for strength.

The case supports consisted of some bottom braces (wide boards set on edge, running from bentside to spine across the bottom) and some top braces (boards about the same size as the bottom braces, running across the case in the same direction, but under the liners, with the wide face horizontal).

Although these cases were no less strong than those being built in Italy, the Flemish accomplished with muscle what the Italians achieved with more graceful engineering (Figure 2-7). The scale, around 14 inches, made it impossible to double the string length every octave; instead, each string was foreshort-ened slightly from the mathematical ideal favored by the Italians, and the proper tension was achieved by progressively increasing the diameter of the strings as they descended. It is mainly for this reason that the shapes of Italian and Flemish cases differed so dramatically: instead of the robust, just curve of the Italian, the curve of the Flemish bentside increased moderately from tail to cheek—a gentle section of a parabolic arc (Figure 2-8). It should also be noted that the cheeks of the Flemish cases were square, with the keyboard inset into the keywell, like an Italian in an outer case or like a false inner-outer (Figure 2-9).

FIGURE 2-5.
False inner-outer Italian virginal.

Rather than glue molding to the case walls, the Flemish cut a molding into the inside of the top of the case. This molding was left varnished, while the rest of the case was painted and covered with paper. The Flemish builders also used a different system of supporting the jacks: rather than the box slide favored by the Italians, they used fixed lower guides, and movable upper guides whose ends protruded through the cheek of the case (Figure 2-10).

Flemish harpsichords were decorated inside and out.[8] The soundboard was painted with birds, insects, flowers, fruit, and sometimes people, animals, and angels. The inside of the case and lid were covered with papers, and mottoes were painted on the inside of the lid.[9] A marbled finish was generally painted on the outside of the case and lid, although

FIGURE 2-6.
Jack-string placement on a virginal. Note how each jack of a pair faces in the opposite direction.

FIGURE 2-7.
Typical internal bracing of a Flemish harpsichord.

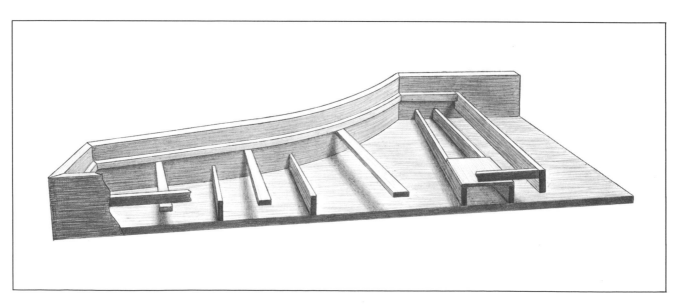

an alternate and doubtless more expensive scheme was a painted representation of black iron strapwork, with cartouches and jewels, on a red ground. In marked contrast to the architecturally oriented Italian philosophy of harpsichord decoration, the Flemish covered almost every square inch of the harpsichord with paint or paper.

Flemish harpsichord building was centered in Antwerp and was dominated by the members of the Ruckers family (succeeded by the Couchet family in the seventeenth century). The Ruckers built many different types of instruments, in a variety of sizes.[10] Their single-manual harpsichords, which were probably their stock in trade, were disposed 1 × 8', 1 × 4' with a buff stop, and with a range of C/E–c'''. However, this little instrument was built in several sizes (and

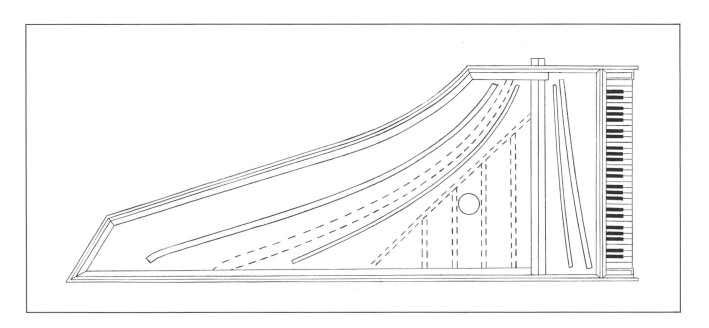

FIGURE 2-8.
Plan view of a Flemish harpsichord.

FIGURE 2-9.
Keywell of a Flemish harpsichord.

FIGURE 2-10.
Flemish-style movable upper guides.

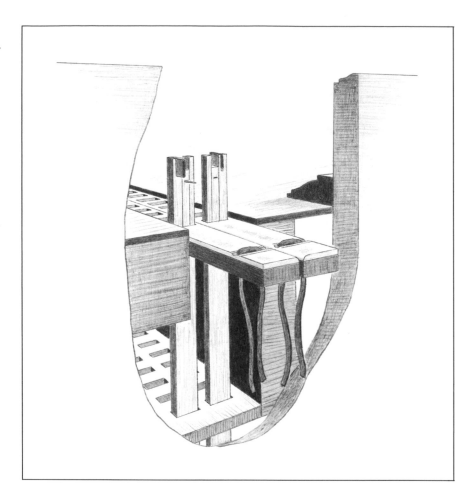

thus several pitch ranges). It may well be that harpsichords were purchased by the foot, perhaps to fit a specific space.[11] The tone of these instruments had a more sustaining quality than their Italian counterparts, and the pluck was less obvious. The sound was darker and more nasal, but like the Italians, and, for that matter, all the national styles, there was the separation of treble, tenor, and bass registers that is so much a part of harpsichord sound. The 4′ register on these instruments was probably fairly strong, adding brilliance and power when coupled to the 8′.

The Flemish also made double-manual harpsichords on which the keyboards did not line up: the lower keyboard sounded a fourth lower than the upper.[12] These were also disposed 1 × 8′, 1 × 4′, so that even though there were four registers and four sets of jacks, only one keyboard could be used at a time. Thus the harpsichord was really two instruments of different pitch ranges. Although it has been customary to describe the unaligned double as a transposing harpsichord, a recent view holds that it was a timbral change, rather than a transposition, that was desired.[13] Whatever the reason, it should serve to remind us that our understanding of what these Flemish builders were trying to accomplish four hundred years ago may be very dim indeed.

As with Italian harpsichords, ranges became extended in the later seventeenth century, and older instruments were enlarged to bring them up to date. Other dispositions, such as 2 × 8′ and 2 × 8′, 1 × 4′ became more common, and double-manual harpsichords with aligned keyboards were built.

This flourishing harpsichord trade declined before the end of the third decade of the seventeenth century, which was long after Antwerp had lost its formerly powerful role in world trade. Nevertheless, harpsichord makers continued to build in Antwerp, and eighteenth-century Flemish instruments came from the shops of Dulcken, Bull, Delin, and others.

Few extant Ruckers harpsichords have escaped the rebuilding process that seemed to go on constantly, so it is not easy to speak with surety about the Ruckers sound; nevertheless, the Flemish builders established a harpsichord aesthetic quite different from the Italians. It was a more singing tone—more sustained, less highly colored, and capable of greater brilliance. While it did not strive for the clarity of the Italians, it achieved a suaveness of tone that most Italians lacked.

Flemish builders seem to have made even a greater variety of virginals than they did harpsichords. Whereas the Italians usually more or less centered the keyboard on their virginal cases, the Flemish put the keyboard in one of three specific locations: on the left side of the case, in the center, or on the right (Figure 2-11). Those instruments with keyboard center plucked the strings at points similar to the Italian virginals; those with keyboard left plucked the bass closer to the bridge, more like the plucking points of the harpsichord; and those with keyboard right plucked the strings further from the bridge, almost in the center. The hollow, flutey sound of this last type was so distinctive that the instrument had a name of its own: the *muselar*.

Like the harpsichords, Flemish virginals were built in a variety of sizes, from 8′ instruments all the way up to 4′, although the physical layout of the smaller models required that the keyboard be closer to center. Virginals and muselars were also built in such a way that they could combine the 8′ and 4′ instruments—a double virginal, or *mother and child*, as they were called. The mother had a large opening in the front of the case—on the right side if it was a virginal, on the left if it was a muselar—into which was slid an octave virginal. The main instrument could be used as a normal virginal or muselar; but, if desired, the octave child could be slid part way out of the main instrument, thus exposing its keyboard. Then one could play either the 8′ or the 4′ instrument, or they could be played together, for duets perhaps, or for lessons. Finally, the octave virginal could be completely removed from its recess and set on top of the 8′ instrument, whose jackrail previously had been removed. Through slots cut into the bottom of the child under the backs of its keys, the 8′ jacks pushed up the 4′ keys, which in turn played the 4′ strings, thus turning the mother and child into a 1 × 8′, 1 × 4′ virginal![14]

The Flemish made yet another type of combined instrument. Looking like an enormous oblong box, this was a harpsichord of one or two manuals, with a virginal built into what would normally be the bentside, and with an oblong lid over the whole thing. As with the unaligned double-manual harpsichords, it is difficult for us to understand the rationale for such an instrument, unless it was simply a desire to use what would otherwise be the "wasted space" of the bentside. Certainly one could only play either the harpsichord or the virginal at one time, although the combination could be used for duets. At any rate, these are imposing-looking machines, and, along with unaligned doubles and double virginals, they indicate that the Flemish builders were delightfully inventive in the ways in which they combined the kinds and sizes of harpsichords. But for all that, once they had established their basic models they became as conservative as the Italians.

FRANCE

France, England, and Germany had harpsichord builders working during the seventeenth century, and all their surviving instruments show varying degrees of Italian and Northern influences. French instruments in particular seemed to partake of the characteristics of both Flemish and Ital-

FIGURE 2-11.
Three styles of Flemish virginals:
(a) keyboard to the left, (b) keyboard
centered, (c) keyboard to the right
(muselar).

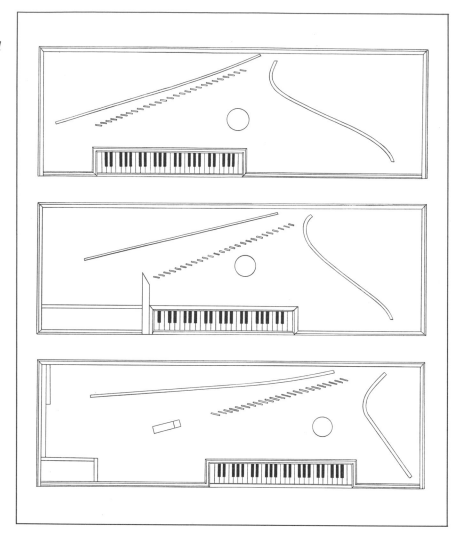

ian models. Although they appeared Northern in shape and had painted soundboards, they exhibited Southern characteristics such as thinner walls and shorter scales (although neither as thin nor as short as the Italian models), and their rosettes were Italianate in style. They were generally made of unpainted walnut but sometimes decorated with elaborate marquetry. They were mainly two-manual instruments, with aligned keyboards, and usually had a range of GG/BB–c‴ (GG/BB refers to a short octave arrangement in which the lowest note looks like BB but sounds GG).[15] Nevertheless, regardless of the reportedly excellent quality of these harpsichords, the Flemish instruments, particularly those of the Ruckers family, had developed such a strong reputation that the products of the late seventeenth-century builders who worked in the Northern tradition soon overwhelmed the "antiquated" Italianisms of the local craftsmen.

Ruckers instruments, rather than being discarded, were rebuilt and enlarged to keep them musically useful, and redecorated to keep them current with fashion. The rebuilding process, which in France was known as *ravalement*, was of two major types. In the first (Dowd's *Class II ravalement*[16]), a few more keys were squeezed into the case, usually in the bass, to fill out the short octave chromatically, along with the necessary strings, jacks, and extensions to the bridges and nuts. Sometimes an instrument with only one set of 8' strings was given a second set. Particularly in Italy, but also elsewhere, a 4' set of strings, along with its nut and bridge, was often removed and replaced with a second 8'. A Ruckers nonaligned double could be made into a French harpsichord by adding a second set of 8' strings, eliminating one of the 4' registers with its jacks, providing new, aligned keyboards, and giving it a new range of G/B–c'''. Other changes could be made as well, as long as they did not involve any substantial alterations to the case.

The second type of *ravalement* (Dowd's *Class III*[17]) involved a significant enlargement of the compass—something that could not be carried out without rebuilding the case. In a typical *ravalement* the rebuilder might graft new wood onto the spine, bentside, cheek, nameboard, soundboard, bridges, and nuts; and he would replace the old wrestplank, keyboard, registers, and jacks with new ones. Then he would redecorate the whole instrument in contemporary style or match the decoration of the new portions to the old. Earlier *ravalements* of this type expanded the range to four-and-a-half octaves; the later rebuilds went to the full five octaves.

Although they certainly made instruments under their own names, eighteenth-century French builders made a specialty of rebuilding Ruckers harpsichords: all in all, they went to what seems like an inordinate amount of trouble just to keep a soundboard and a little second-hand lumber. Obviously, however, they considered it worthwhile, *particularly* in the case of the Ruckers harpsichords. These instruments had a reputation similar to that which today accrues to Stradivarius violins. Just as those violins were rebuilt to suit changes in musical taste, so were the Ruckers harpsichords. Ruckers soundboard wood in particular was highly prized, and virginals and muselars often were cannibalized for their soundboards and roses. As might be expected, a healthy trade in counterfeit roses sprang up, and more than one newly-built harpsichord was made to look as if it had "extra" wood grafted to it—in essence, a phony *ravalement*. Such an instrument might command twice the price of a "new" harpsichord.[18]

A number of harpsichords underwent the *ravalement* process several times. The Couchet double in the Boston Museum of Fine Arts, for example, was built as a single in 1680, had its range expanded in 1758 by Blanchet, and was completely rebuilt and enlarged by Taskin in 1781. This instrument is thus known as the 1680/1758/1781 Couchet/Blanchet/Taskin. And the rebuilding process was by no means limited to Flemish harpsichords: one could cite by way of example the Paris Conservatoire's 1697 Dumont, which was *ravaléd* al-

most a century later (1789) by Taskin, and which is therefore known as the 1697/1789 Dumont/Taskin.

Just as Flemish harpsichord building a century earlier had been centered in Antwerp and dominated by the Ruckers-Couchet dynasty, the most important builders in eighteenth-century France were in Paris, and were members of the Blanchet family (succeeded by Pascal Taskin, who married the widow of the last Blanchet, in 1766).[19] The harpsichords built by the Blanchets were quite similar to the Ruckers instruments that continually passed through their shop for *ravalement*, although the framing was heavier, and the French builders introduced many refinements into their construction.

Early in the eighteenth century the French harpsichord had almost achieved the form by which we know it today: a large, two-manual instrument, with $2 \times 8'$, $1 \times 4'$ (but usually without a buff stop, which did not appear with regularity until the second half of the century), with its stop levers protruding through the nameboard. The range was close to five octaves, from FF/GG–e'''. Later, the FF–f''' range became standard. By the middle of the century these were elegant instruments, often built with sophisticated techniques of joinery. Keyboards were made with great care, to ensure a light and reliable action. Upper and lower guides were covered with leather, with slots pierced for the jacks, which were slightly tapered both in width and thickness. The bentside usually differed from the Flemish models in that from a half to a third of the tail was straight, with the curve concentrated in the treble section.

The instrument was set up so that the closest set of jacks (the front 8′) was operated from the upper manual, and plucked one of the 8′ choirs of strings. The farthest set of jacks, on the lower manual, plucked the other set of 8′ strings (the back 8′). In between, the middle set of jacks, also on the lower manual, plucked the 4′ strings. Thus, the instrument had the following tonal resources: on the upper manual the close-plucking, more nasal 8′; on the lower manual the plainer 8′ alone, the 4′ alone, or 8′ and 4′ together. The buffed 8′ was also available on the lower manual, although on some harpsichords it was the front 8′ that was buffed (and on some others, a choice of either 8′). In addition, the performer could play from both keyboards simultaneously. The keyboards could also be coupled by pushing in the upper manual, making the front 8′ available on the lower manual as well as on the upper. Then the front 8′ could add its sound to the back 8′, or all choirs could combine for the full $2 \times 8′$, $1 \times 4′$. And the front 8′ could still be played from the upper manual (see Figure 1-8). Such a harpsichord was capable of a great deal of tonal variety, from the pizzicato-like buff stop, through the contrasting timbres of the two 8′s, through the more powerful sound of the combined 8′s, or the increased brilliance of an 8′ and a 4′, to the majestic sonorities of the full instrument.

The eighteenth-century French harpsichord had a complex, singing tone, with a quality that has been described as a "bloom," or a tonal development that takes place after the pluck. Although it achieved neither the presence of the Flemish instruments nor the immediacy of the Italians, it had a singing, sensuous sonority, and a resonant, booming bass, which seemed to surround the listener in a cloud of sound uniquely suited to the French literature. This sound lends itself so well to the application of *agréments* that it could almost be said to invite them. While on a Flemish or Italian instrument ornaments sometimes tend to sound like accented intrusions, on a French harpsichord they lend to the music a sense of rise and fall, of purpose and direction. It is no wonder that ornaments often seem to be something applied to Italian music, while they are an integral part of the French style.

In the typical decorative scheme, the outside of the case and lid were painted one color, and the interior surfaces another. Greenish black and pale vermilion were the most common combinations. Bands of gold leaf in rectangles were laid on the outside of the case, on the cheek, bentside, tail, and the inside of the lid and flap. The moldings were also gilded. The soundboard was decorated with flowers and fruit, very much as the Flemish had done it, but in a much more painterly style. Almost always, a scene just behind the gap, facing the player, showed a bird perched on a tree stump. Although the tree was presumably dead, a faint red glow often emanated from within it, and a live branch or two grew from the trunk. The theme is one of resurrection, and the idea of the harpsichord as a secular symbol of life through death was a powerful and pervasive one, since a tree must first be killed in order to bring a harpsichord to life.[20]

The stand on which the instrument sat was probably built by a cabinet-making shop (probably one specializing in tables and chairs), and could be as simple or elaborate as the customer wanted. Similarly, if he wanted a fancier decoration, there were *ateliers* that specialized in more complex case paintings, such as the chinoiserie seen on some of these harpsichords. Also, a lid painting could be supplied if desired. In fact, the entire instrument could have figures and scenes painted on it, if that was the customer's taste, and if he could afford it.[21]

The painted French double-manual harpsichord, with its gold bands and moldings, its decorated soundboard, and other details of its tasteful ornamentation, set on a Louis XV stand with its elaborate apron and gently curving cabriole legs, or on a more restrained Louis XVI stand with its fluted legs, presented an appearance of refined decoration combined with elegance of design. It was a countenance that paralleled the elegance of expression, the restraint, the power, and the nobility of its sound.

After 1750, steps were undertaken to expand the harpsichord's expressive possibilities. Taskin began rebuilding old unaligned two-manual Ruckers with a new kind of register, the *peau de buffle*, and soon new instruments were made with this feature. It will be remembered that the unaligned Flemish doubles had four registers—1 × 8', 1 × 4' for each manual. In earlier *ravalements* three new registers were supplied, occupying the space of the original four; but Taskin kept the four-register scheme, using the rear-most one for a set of jacks "quilled" with soft leather. When properly regulated, the leathered register allowed a dynamic control achieved by touch, very much like on the new pianos. Evidently it was extremely difficult to keep the *peau de buffle* in proper regulation; nevertheless, the desire to achieve dynamic control through touch was so strong that even some instruments without a fourth register had one of their 8's supplied with leather.

Another of Taskin's inventions was a system of five or six knee levers with which to change stops. The player could not only make register changes while playing, but one of the levers, called the machine stop, could take the registers off one at a time, thus giving a decrescendo from full harpsichord down to *peau de buffle*. The effect could be reversed for crescendo.

Cultural historians often apply the term Rococo to the years that ended the French Baroque, and it is sometimes used in a pejorative sense to refer to over-emphasis on ornamentation without corresponding emphasis on formal structure. As the term applies to architecture, art, and musical composition, it also applies to musical instruments. France never really embraced the clarity and balance of the large baroque forms such as the Italian concerto grosso, or the elaborately fugal style of German music. Instead, they were more concerned

with elegance of line, with appropriateness of harmonic language, with melodic decoration, and with color. Just as these musical values became inflated after 1750, so did the corresponding characteristics of the harpsichord. Soundboard painting tended to become even more painterly, the flowers blowsy and almost impressionistic in effect. The blue borders, often so classically reposeful in the earlier French harpsichords, now sometimes danced around the bridges, never allowing the eye to rest. These decorative aspects are the visual analogs of the search for unusual tonal effects and the exploitation of new resonances. Nevertheless, these late French instruments, the ones built after 1750, were magnificent harpsichords. Their sound, more complex than ever, has often and aptly been described as majestic. But, all in all, the accretions found on them, while ingenious, had little to do with traditional harpsichord literature.

French builders also made octave spinets, virginals and bentside spinets, and these were sometimes elaborately decorated; as might be expected, such instruments were of negligible importance to the mainstream of French harpsichord building.

ENGLAND

As mentioned earlier, seventeenth-century English harpsichord makers built instruments that had many Southern and/or Italianate features, and there is evidence of the influence of other traditions as well. Judging from the few surviving examples, they

were also quite individual, suggesting a proclivity for tonal variety. Interestingly, almost all the remaining examples have a *lute stop*, which is a set of jacks that pluck a choir of strings close to the nut, producing a nasal sound. This feature became almost standard on later English harpsichords. Other than that, these instruments show a range and variety of constructional conventions and decorative schemes. Some were undecorated, with thin-walled cases of oak and shorter scales; others had the more general appearance of harpsichords of the Northern schools.[22]

The eighteenth-century English harpsichord is said to have been established with the work of Hermann Tabel, an Antwerp builder who evidently had been trained in the Couchet shop, and who immigrated to London around 1700.[23] In turn, he trained the builders Shudi and Kirckman, also immigrants (Shudi was originally a joiner in Switzerland, and Kirckman had been a German cabinetmaker). They and their families, in turn, dominated the English harpsichord market for the rest of the century.

These builders made their cases of oak, strongly braced, with relatively thick sides. Their cabinet work, as might be expected from their early training in woodworking, was excellent. The bentsides were straight for most of their length, with a tight curve at the cheek. The cases were beautifully veneered in natural wood, usually mahogany, but sometimes walnut or elm, with inlay stringing and cross banding. The bentside was divided into two or three panels. Cross banding and inlays of contrasting woods were employed inside the case as well, and sometimes this portion of the harpsichord was decorated with spectacular marquetry. Like the Italian builders who relied on the intrinsic beauty of the material for its visual effect, and like some of their seventeenth-century predecessors, they normally did not decorate their soundboards.

The range of these harpsichords was five octaves, from FF–f‴, but without the low FF#. They were disposed 2 × 8′, 1 × 4′, and were built both as single and double manual instruments. Unlike the French builders, who separated the two 8′ registers with the 4′ jacks, the English put the two 8′s together and the 4′ last. And instead of the shove coupler used by the French, they used a dogleg action without a coupler (see Figure 1-9). Since their jacks were next to each other, and therefore plucked their strings at similar distances from the nut, there was little tonal distinction between the two 8′s. This made little difference, however, since the two 8′s could only be heard together or one at a time. They could not be played one from each keyboard, in the manner of a French double. On the other hand, the tonal similarity assured an excellent blend when the two 8′s played together. Tonal variety between the two 8′ choirs was provided instead by a lute stop.

The lute stop on these harpsichords consisted of an extra row of jacks that was placed in a slot cut into the wrestplank, close to the 8′ nut (Figure 2-12). Riding in upper and lower guides, they

plucked the same set of 8′ strings as the front 8′ jacks, but because they were so much closer to the 8′ nut, they produced a much more nasal sound. The instruments also had a buff stop. Thus the player could command a single 8′ or the lute on the upper keyboard. Either a single 8′ or both 8′s together could be available on the lower manual, and the 4′ could be added to these for the full harpsichord. Usually one of the 8′s could be buffed, and the softer, nasal lute stop was available on the upper manual for a strong contrast between manuals, or between forte and piano.

Like the French, the English makers began to experiment with register-changing and crescendo-diminuendo devices soon after the middle of the century. At this time harpsichords were fitted with machine stops, whose function was very much like that of the device that Taskin was putting on his instruments. The English machine stop was operated by a pedal (rather than a knee lever), and it took the registers off one at a time, until only the pungent lute register was left. Another device that became quite common was the Venetian swell. This was a separate lid, inside the normal lid, consisting of louvers (as in a Venetian blind) that could be opened or closed by another pedal. When the swell lid was down and the louvers were closed, the tone of the instrument would be muffled; gradually opening the louvers produced the effect of a crescendo. A cheaper sort of swell, called a nags-head swell, was also used; in this type, part of the lid itself could be opened or closed,

producing the same crescendo-diminuendo effect as the louvers, but in a less sophisticated fashion. Combining either of these swells with the machine stop, however, could produce convincing dynamic changes.

Some experimentation also went on in increasing the range of the harpsichord; Shudi made a number of very large instruments that descended to contra CC.

These eighteenth-century English instruments were powerful harpsichords, with penetrating trebles, strong tenors, and booming, drumlike basses. They became even more powerful toward the end of the century. Although they imposed their strong character on any music played on them, the result was by no means unattractive, and they could make a commanding, magisterial sound that few non-English instruments could match. Ultimately, it becomes difficult to relate the powerful tone and the dynamic devices of these instruments to the conventional harpsichord literature.

In appearance, though, they were stunning, quite in contrast to the French instruments which, while certainly magnificent in their own way, nevertheless depended on the artifice of paint and gold for their effect. The English instruments were imposing in the restrained classicism of their "natural" wood finishes and in the magnificence of their cabinet work. All in all, eighteenth-century English harpsichords could well be considered the most attractive harpsichords ever made.

Some clavicytheria were made in England and in Ireland late in the eighteenth century, and were,

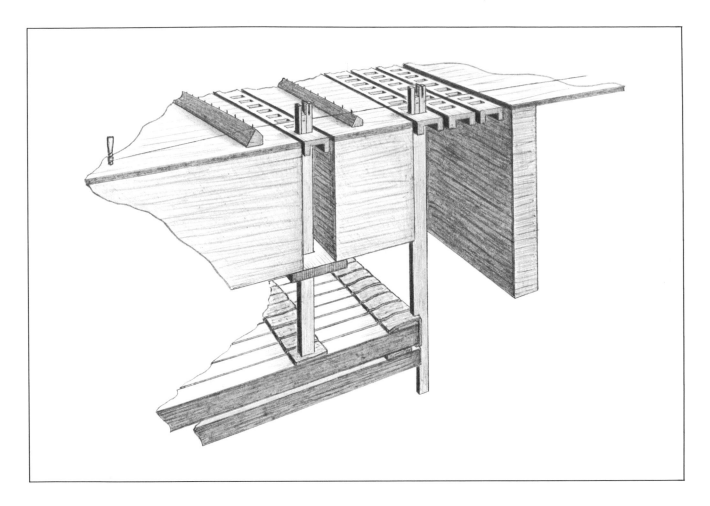

as might be expected, handsome instruments.

Although we know of only a few English harpsichords built during the seventeenth century, there are a number of surviving virginals and almost countless bentside spinets. The English virginal, at least in outward appearance, was quite similar to the large Flemish left-plucking virginal, although the scale was shorter, and the case was made of oak rather than poplar.[24] As with the Flemish models, the soundboard was painted with flowers, fruit, and birds, and paper and paint were used on the case. A peculiarity of the English virginal was its vaulted or coffered lid; when closed, with the fallboard up, the virginal, which was about six feet long and two feet wide, looked suspiciously like a darkly-colored coffin. When opened, however, one was greeted by a colorfully painted soundboard and embossed gilt decorations. The inside of the lid and the fallboard were almost always painted with a "park" scene, often involving musical and/or mythological subjects in a nature setting. Although these scenes all differed from each other, they were nevertheless known collectively as "St. James Park" scenes.

The way in which the production of English virginals appeared and disappeared is something of a mystery; the first one we know of was built in 1641, the last one

FIGURE 2-12.
An English lute register.

in 1679. As Hubbard puts it, "Like a marching platoon of soldiers they burst into view in 1641. . . . There are no stragglers, no prototypes, and few variants."[25] The earlier instruments had ranges from about C–d‴ or e‴, the later from GG (usually short octave). They were similar in sound to the Flemish virginals, although the harder oak and the shorter scale of the English models produced a tone that was a little more penetrating and not quite so round.

Bentside spinets appeared in England around the middle of the seventeenth century, and continued to be built for about as long as harpsichords were made in England. In fact, building bentside spinets seemed to be the activity to which most eighteenth-century harpsichord makers were confined, leaving the production of harpsichords proper to the Shudis, the Kirckmans, and a few others. Many examples—fine ones at that—were also made in the United States. For a while, both bentside spinets and virginals were produced at the same time. Curiously, neither seems to have influenced the other. The spinet was finished in natural wood, with little ornamentation, no rosette, and an undecorated soundboard, while the virginal was fully papered and painted.

The English version of the bentside spinet was quite Italianate. It had the short scale and thin case that we have come to expect by now, but it also had a characteristically Italian projecting keyboard, and it even had a box register. Although the case grew heavier and the scale longer in the course of the eighteenth century, it never lost these last two characteristics. The range commonly found on the earlier examples was GG/BB–d‴, but this increased to GG–g‴ by early in the eighteenth century.

The appeal of the bentside spinet lay in its shape, which was the most space-saving of all the ways in which one could arrange case, string band, and keyboard. It was never the serious musical instrument that the harpsichord and the virginal were; its shape did not prove to be as efficient as a sound generator. Nevertheless, it was much prized as a more-than-adequate home instrument.

GERMANY

There is only one German harpsichord that has survived from the sixteenth century,[26] and only a few have survived from the seventeenth; not many remain from the eighteenth century either, so we do not know nearly as much about German harpsichords as we do about the instruments of other schools. Germany did not have the large numbers of builders making harpsichords as in the other countries we have looked at. In fact, it appears that German builders were more interested in making fine organs and clavichords than they were in making harpsichords, despite the fact that they had some outstanding composers writing for that instrument.

It is possible to identify three schools of German harpsichord building in the eighteenth century: the Northern school, which included Hamburg and Berlin; the Central, or Saxon school; and the Southern school. But "school" may be too precise a word to describe the activities of the builders in these regions. There were some famous builders in Hamburg: Hass (father Hieronymus and son Johann), Fleischer, and Zell for example; nevertheless, Boalch lists only fourteen makers of harpsichords, clavichords, and pianos who built in Hamburg during the eighteenth century, and fourteen in Berlin (including Charlottenburg, the suburb where Mietke worked). As for the Saxon school, Boalch lists eighteen builders in Dresden, where the Gräbners worked, and only two in Freiburg (Saxony), where Gottfried Silbermann was located. If we compare these figures to the ninety builders working in London during the eighteenth century, and the ninety-three in Paris, we can begin to see the difference between a school and an activity that may have been carried out by organ and clavichord builders on a more-or-less casual basis.[27]

The unusual and spectacular instruments of the Hasses are the ones that most often come to mind when German harpsichords are mentioned. Three of the handful that survive have 16′ choirs, two of those have 2′ stops as well, and one has three keyboards. These seem to be experimental instruments, probably representing the application of an organ builder's ideas to the harpsichord. They are large and quite impressive visually, if not always aurally. They were carefully made, with a great deal of attention given to details of sound as well as decoration. Like other Hamburg builders, the Hasses normally decorated their soundboards. Usually the keyboards and the keywells were beautifully, though somewhat eclectically, decorated with ebony and other woods, tortoise shell, mother of pearl, and ivory.

There has been a recent surge of interest in the harpsichords of Michael Mietke, and for good reason. First, Bach is known to have purchased one in 1719, while he was Music Director at Cöthen, and one can safely presume that he played it with some regularity. Second, it has been established recently that two harpsichords now in Charlottenburg may well have been made by Mietke. Third, it seems distinctly possible that Bach played one of them. Finally, it is at least possible that Mietke built some instruments (although not the two in question) with 16' registers.[28]

Many agree that one of the best extant Hamburg instruments is the two-manual harpsichord made by Christian Zell in 1728 (now in the Museum für Kunst und Gewerbe, in Hamburg). Its scale is Northern, and its case is of the softer wood preferred by the Flemish and the French. The bracing is a mixture of Northern and Southern practices. Zell used large knees, while other Hamburg builders used deep bottom braces (which, however, were sloped down from the sides of the case so that they were, in effect, knees joined along the bottom). The bridges and nuts show the molded section characteristic of Italian harpsichords, and it has other Italianate and Southern features as well. The Zell has the rounded tail normally seen on Hamburg instruments (although the double bentside was common in England

and France in the seventeenth century, and in late Flemish instruments). The instrument is disposed $2 \times 8'$, $1 \times 4'$, with a dog-leg action.

The Zell, the 1764 Hass (Edinburgh), the 1750 Hass (Yale[29]), and the 1716 Fleischer (Hamburg, Museum für Hamburgische Geschichte) all sound convincingly Northern, something akin to a French harpsichord; but they seem to do it with a Southern accent in that they speak more cleanly than a French instrument, with more hardness, clarity, and brilliance. It is this characteristic more than any other that seems to distinguish the best of the Hamburg instruments from the other national schools.

The Saxon school, which included a handful of builders living in Dresden and Freiberg (Saxony), seem to have had even less unity of practice. One can only say that the instruments are more simply decorated, more individual, and they do not seem to be as carefully built. The case work is reminiscent of English harpsichords, and a strong French influence can be seen in the keyboards, actions, and dispositions.

The Southern German instruments (mostly seventeenth-century examples) also show Italianate features, but they were highly decorated, inside and out. One interesting feature of these harpsichords is that the builders made the sounds of the two 8' registers more distinct from each other in the bass by increasing the distance between the two sets of 8' jacks as they approached the spine. Thus, the jackrails on these instruments are about twice as wide in the bass as they are in the treble.

The Germans built many bent-side spinets—evidently far more of these than harpsichords (although not nearly as many as the English). These vary from small to large, from plain to handsome, from nondescript-sounding to tonally superior. They built some clavicytheria too, and some of these are complex, quite ornate, and well made.

It is not surprising that German harpsichord building never coalesced around a national school, since Germany itself was not a unified nation in the seventeenth and eighteenth centuries. Furthermore, the primary activities of so many of those builders involved the organ and the clavichord; harpsichord building seemed almost to be a sideline, albeit in many cases an important one. Nevertheless, the best examples of German building combined Northern and Southern tonal characteristics in a uniquely satisfying manner. These instruments seem to lend themselves to almost any music played on them, and for this quality alone must be considered significant. The large harpsichords of the Hasses, on the other hand, are important in that they recorded some interesting efforts to marry organ sound with harpsichord technology. Unfortunately, their importance (and the importance of the 16') was greatly exaggerated early in the twentieth century, when harpsichord building was once more resumed.

There were other harpsichord builders in Europe aside from those found in Italy, Flanders, France, England, and Germany, but in almost every case their instruments related to one or another of the regional styles described herein. However, it should not be assumed that every French builder, to take an example, built instruments like the ones being made in Paris; instead, builders tended to produce the instruments that were like the ones they commonly saw and heard. Thus, Spanish and Portuguese harpsichords were similar to those made in Italy. Similarly, Scandinavian builders were influenced by the instruments of the Hamburg school and are sometimes considered to be part of it.

Chapter 3

The Harpsichord in the Twentieth Century

The last historical harpsichord, a Kirckman, was built in 1809, according to that company's records. By that time every other harpsichord maker we know of either was making pianos or had gone out of business. No one ever dreamed that eighty years later, in 1889, the production of harpsichords would resume—but then, no one would have predicted the early music movement.

THE REVIVAL HARPSICHORD

The pioneers of the harpsichord revival were not really interested in reviving what we now call early music; most of the early keyboard composers we take for granted today—Sweelinck, Frescobaldi, Scarlatti, Buxtehude, Handel, Couperin, Rameau, Byrd, Purcell—were unknown or represented by one or two encore pieces. (Bach, of course, was played regularly, but according to conventional wisdom, had he only known of it, Bach certainly would have preferred the grand piano, with its massive metal frame, overwound strings, bland tone, and even scale, to the puny harpsichord.) Instead, the revival of the harpsichord was more the result of two independent but related tendencies of the late nineteenth century. On one hand, there was the Romantic desire for objects of antiquity. The harp-sichord, with its quaint paint and gold leaf, its flowered sound-boards and its silvery sound (when it could be gotten to sound at all), was certainly that.[1] In fact harpsichord recitals, given as sort of musical antique shows, did occur from time to time during the nineteenth century.

On the other hand, there was the search by contemporary artists—painters, sculptors, and writers, as well as composers—for new effects, new sounds. It was no accident that Pleyel and Erard, the two firms that first began producing revival harpsichords, built their first instruments (both loosely modelled after the 1769 Taskin now in Edinburgh) for the Paris Exposition of 1889. It was at this great fair that Western sculptors and painters found inspiration in African art; it was here that composers heard the sounds of the Javanese Gamelan (an Indonesian percussion orchestra) for the first time. And it was here also that musicians heard the tinkly sounds of the harpsichord. Its appeal, therefore, was twofold: something old, yet something brand new.

The point is an important one. It was not the intention of the revival builders to recreate the historical harpsichord; instead, they hoped to make a new (yet old) sound available by building a twentieth-century version of the instrument. To these builders, most of whom were steeped in a now century-old tradition of advancements in piano building, the harpsichord seemed like a hopelessly outmoded, fragile device.

If harpsichords were to be built, they reasoned, at least let them be built like real keyboard instruments, which is to say, like pianos. Let them have strong framing members, or even metal frames; then the bottom could be dispensed with. Give them long piano scales, using modern music wire at high tension; then give them a soundboard as thick as a piano's, so that it would not be pulled out of shape and warped by the tension of the strings. Use hard leather for the plectrum material, since the effort it took to pluck the strings would defeat something as fragile as bird quill; and leather, if still organic, at least was easily available and capable of commercial production. Give them all the resources of which the harpsichord was capable, including 16' stops, lute stops and half-hitches (a device that moves a register of jacks slightly, but not completely, away from the strings, so that the strings are plucked by only the tips of the plectra, thus producing a softer sound); then supply the instruments with pedals, so that the variety of colors and dynamics thought necessary for a harpsichord could be under constant control, without the need for the player to remove his hands from the keyboard.

The harpsichord was provided with a keyboard that, except for range, was similar in appearance and touch to the piano. By this time the piano keyboard had evolved into a massive mechanism, designed to deliver a powerful blow to stiff, taut strings and to absorb a considerable amount of punishment from the player. The balance points were lined with felt, so that all that mass and energy could be made to operate quietly. The keys were weighted with lead, so that there would be no question of their working effectively in their felt bushings. Similarly, the harpsichord was given heavy, weighted keys of piano dimensions, with bushings and felt everywhere. As in the piano, the action had a deep key dip, and it was stopped at the heads of the keys. Such a keyboard worked beautifully for the piano, and it seemed to work for the harpsichord as well. Of course, it was recognized that the energy required to pluck a thin harpsichord string was far less than that required to hammer a heavier piano string into vibration; but the revivalists, with their genuine belief in progress, saw no reason why the harpsichord should not emulate the piano as much as possible.

Furthermore, many of the larger instruments were given the so-called Bach disposition, a registration taken straight from the organ, which put one 8' and the 16' on the bottom manual and the other 8' and the 4' on the upper manual. There was much arguing back and forth between those who considered this arrangement authentic and those who saw that the disposition of the single instrument from which it was taken (an anonymous harpsichord in Berlin) was not original. Needless to say, the "Bach disposition" was laid to rest decades ago, along with pedals and half-hitches.

Here we have the picture of the revival harpsichord, with its piano keyboard, its many registers, its constantly shifting colors, its quest after piano-like dynamic possibilities, and its case of natural wood whose grain often ran perpendicularly, rather than horizontally as on the antiques. Most of these instruments made only a dull, thin, soupy sound: with all the mass and tension built into them, they could scarcely do anything else, although the best of them could be said to have had a character of their own. At any rate, they were the means by which the twentieth-century world was reintroduced to the sound of the harpsichord. As their popularity increased, it became something of a fad to own one. To satisfy the home and school market, the large German manufacturing firms made small (one might even call them tiny) versions of harpsichords, with open bottoms, heavy framing, and with even less sound than the big dreadnoughts. When played, they went tinkle-tinkle. The larger of these little machines were often burdened with a set of overwound 16' strings, almost always with the unlikely disposition of $1 \times 16'$, $1 \times 8'$, $1 \times 4'$.

These instruments were accepted without question, because few people had ever heard an old harpsichord, and if they had, it had probably been in poor condition. Also, the reintroduction of the harpsichord was helped by the growing popularity of the phonograph. Through the recordings of Wanda Landowska and a few others, hundreds of thousands of people came to know what was thought of as the sound of the harpsichord. The invention of the long-playing record after World War II, which started the search by record companies for new repertoire to record, speeded the process along immeasurably.

It is easy to vilify these revival instruments, and perhaps understandable. Nevertheless, they appear to have been a crucial link in the chain of events that led to the introduction of the modern harpsichord. If pianists had not played them, no one would have built them; if no one had built them, there would have been no demand, finally, for the historical harpsichord. And pianists played them *because* they felt like pianos. Had they been presented with a modern harpsichord, with a $2 \times 8'$, $1 \times 4'$ disposition, an historically light action, and limited means of changing registration, only a handful of dilettantes would have played them, and the demand would never have been created.

We owe homage to the great pioneers like Arnold Dolmetsch, who built not only harpsichords (he made his first one in 1896), but many other baroque and renaissance instruments as well. Dolmetsch's personality was so strong that one suspects he would have created the whole early music trend singlehandedly, had it had not been underway already. Wanda Landowska, the first modern virtuoso of the harpsichord, was another one of these trailblazers. The amazing thing about Landowska was not so much that she abandoned a career as a pianist for one as a harpsichordist—a move that must have been considered singularly foolhardy—but that she was able to play so brilliantly

on those Pleyel revival instruments.

Revival harpsichords, whether by builders like Dolmetsch, whose inspiration was drawn from the English craft movement, or by German harpsichord factories like Sperrhake, must now be seen to comprise a legitimate class of instruments. They were built for a period of almost seventy-five years, and there is a sizeable literature of twentieth-century music written expressly for them. Museums are collecting them as prized objects (or at least with the expectation that they will become so), and (dare I say it?) the day may yet come when builders will make copies of them.

The harpsichord world did not reject the revival instruments out of hand when builders started making modern, classically oriented harpsichords. Many people had grown so accustomed to them that anything else sounded wrong. Also, it was hard to kill the myth that the historically oriented harpsichords were fragile, delicate instruments, inherently unstable in regulation and tuning. In fact, it was the opposite that was true—the revival instruments, with all their heavy framing, thick soundboards, high string tension, half hitches, and complex dispositions, were forever out of adjustment and could hardly be made to stay in tune for any reasonable length of time. Years ago I had under my care (for only a year, I'm happy to say) an enormous metal-framed Pleyel, with 16' stop, overhead piano-style dampers, and—believe it or not—*two* tuning pins per string: one for coarse and one for fine adjustment. I knew

enough about harpsichord regulation to realize that I could spend all my time just maintaining the instrument, so I decided to keep only a single 8' tuned and in adjustment. As it was, I had to spend at least a half hour with it each time it got its twice-weekly workout.

Finally, it should be noted that although it has become virtually impossible to buy a new revival harpsichord in North America, there are still parts of the world in which they are alive and well, and there are still people who prefer their sound and touch to anything else.

THE MODERN HARPSICHORD

The evolution of the modern harpsichord seems to have occurred in two stages. In the first, people like Frank Hubbard, William Dowd, and Hugh Gough came to realize the inherent superiority of the historical models over the revival instruments, and in the 1950s began to develop instruments inspired by them.[2] These harpsichords, built on classical lines, with historical scales and case dimensions, light stringing, proper framing members with bottoms, and $2 \times 8'$, $1 \times 4'$ dispositions, had a lively and silvery sound. For the first time in this century, new harpsichords were approaching the sounds of the antique instruments. The discovery was made that the builders of yore, rather than operating in some sort of pre-industrial dark ages, were knowledgeable, sophisticated craftsmen. Now, rather than trying to improve on Taskin, builders tried only to equal him.[3] Nevertheless, these instruments still lacked some of the qualities that we now expect in a classically inspired harpsichord.

The stability of the harpsichord was of great concern at that time, since one of the axioms of the revival instruments was that the harpsichord needed its massive framing members and metal frames to give it a piano-like ability to maintain tuning and regulation at all times. While eschewing the structural abuses of the revivalists, the first-generation modern builders used plywood cases, Plexiglas lower guides, and metal registers, all designed to overcome the harpsichord's natural tendency to expand and contract with changes in temperature and humidity. Actually, rather than control this movement, these building practices exacerbated it. To compensate, the builders retained the adjustment screws that had been put on the revival harpsichords: screws to regulate coupler play, register placement, jack length, damper height, and tongue placement, to mention the most common ones. Keyboards were generally more massive than found on historical models, and were still bushed with felt, as on piano keyboards.

The invention of Delrin, which replaced leather as a plectrum material in the 1960s, may have been one of the major factors that led to the next phase of the modern harpsichord.[4] Like crow quill, Delrin allowed for a certain amount of give and take impossible with leather plectra. It thus became possible to build lighter cases using plank wood and classical framing, wooden registers,

light actions, and unbushed keyboards. Taken together, these things helped regain the sound and the touch of the harpsichord as it had been heard for hundreds of years prior to the nineteenth century. In the process it was discovered that these instruments, built on less compromised classical lines, were more stable than those of the previous generation. The "progress" made by the better harpsichord builders at this time now seems so inexorable that, Delrin or no, this next step probably would have been taken anyway, even if it meant going back to crow quill. In any event, by the end of the 1960s a few builders such as William Hyman and Martin Skowroneck, to name two, took the plunge and were among the first to use wooden registers, plank-wood cases, light actions, and unbushed keyboards.

In the pantheon of the modern harpsichord, places of honor must be reserved for Wolfgang Zuckermann, Frank Hubbard, and David Way for their role in its development. Zuckermann was responsible for the very concept of the harpsichord kit, back in the early 1960s. His kit instrument was only five feet long, with a straight rather than a bent side, with heavy framing and a piano-style keyboard; but it had some classical elements too, such as a thin soundboard with historical bracing. This little instrument (which the Zuckermann people now affectionately refer to as the "Five-foot Z-Box") was not up to the level of the good modern harpsichords, a fact which Zuckermann himself readily acknowledged, both in his construction manual and in *The*

Modern Harpsichord. Nevertheless, inadequate as it may seem now, it was more satisfactory than almost any of the revival harpsichords then so common. Zuckermann's greatest contribution seems to have been the introduction of the two corollaries of kit building: first, with only normal woodworking experience but with a great deal of determination it was possible for the average person to build a harpsichord; and second, if the finished product could be only as good as the kit, it also could be only as good as the builder.

Shortly thereafter, Frank Hubbard produced a kit of his own, a first-generation modern harpsichord, which could be built in either a single- or a double-manual version. Hubbard's kit was of a different class. It was far more complex and difficult to build, but in the hands of a talented craftsman it was capable of being turned into an instrument that could compare with Hubbard's own instruments.

David Way became president of Zuckermann Harpsichords in the 1970s, and was soon producing kits that, properly built, resulted in excellent musical instruments. Way gained a great deal from his association with William Hyman, who, before his untimely death in 1974, helped him design some of the instruments in his catalog. Hubbard also died an untimely death, in 1976. Since then his shop has been run by Diane Hubbard. Both Way and Hubbard have continued to improve the quality of their kit instruments, and many of today's fine builders owe their start to the construction of a Zuckermann or a Hubbard kit. Other people have entered the kit market from time to time, with varying degrees of success, but their influence has been negligible.

Only a few more words remain to be written in this chapter, and they concern the modern eclectic harpsichord. By their nature these instruments are not easy to define. One could describe them in a backhanded fashion, as modern harpsichords that bear looser relationships to the historical schools than the instruments we have been describing, and in some cases little relationship at all. From the very beginning of the era of the modern harpsichord there have been builders who believe that recapturing the classical instrument, no matter how successfully, is essentially sterile in nature. These builders feel that the harpsichord had undergone a constant evolution prior to the nineteenth century—which, of course, it had—and that if it is to remain a viable contemporary instrument, modern builders must continue to experiment with its elements.

Such a builder might approach the design of a harpsichord by saying, "I would like to see what happens if I combine a case constructed in the French manner with an Italianate soundboard"; or, "I would like to build a harpsichord that combines the clarity of an Italian with the singing quality of a French"; or, "Here is my guess as to what a mid-seventeenth-century South-German harpsichord sounds like." These eclectic builders have produced many interesting and provocative instruments, and in so doing have contributed to our knowledge of how the harpsichord works. What relationship these instruments have to the classical harpsichord literature is a judgment that history will have to make.

Chapter 4   Buying a Harpsichord

Having fought for years to get the money, to convince your business office to allow you to hold over funds from your yearly budgets, you have submitted a winning proposal to your administration and they have decided to give you the rest of the needed funds. Finally, you have the money, and your institution is going to buy a harpsichord. Or perhaps you have saved your own money, given piano and organ lessons, and gone without desserts. Suddenly, Aunt Hester dies and you get a bequest from her estate. Now you have the money to buy a harpsichord, and you want to get the instrument of your dreams. Or it may be that you have recently become interested in the harpsichord and have decided that owning one would enrich your musical life. Money is not a real objection, but you want to get the *right* instrument.

Whatever your reasons for buying that harpsichord, there are questions you should consider first. What *kind* of harpsichord should you buy? Should it be modelled after a French, Flemish, Italian, English, German, or some other type? If you decide on a French instrument, should it be seventeenth- or eighteenth-century French? If a Flemish, early or late? A Flemish as it was built originally, or as it was rebuilt in the seventeenth and eighteenth centuries? Or should you not consider a "pure" harpsichord at all, but instead elect to purchase an eclectic instrument?

How large a keyboard do you need? Should you buy an instrument with a short octave? Should you consider getting a used instrument? Should you buy a kit and build the harpsichord yourself? Should you have someone else build the kit for you? Should you buy from a local or nearby builder or from a famous maker who lives half a continent away?

These are the questions to be explored in this chapter (if you have not already done so, read chapters 1 and 2 first), and for some people, an exploration it will be. If you are new to the harpsichord, you will be led through territory that may appear forbidding at first; but knowledge is power! Although the chapter will supply few clear-cut answers, at the very least it will arm you, the prospective buyer, with information you need to make a more informed purchase.[1]

WHAT KIND OF HARPSICHORD SHOULD YOU BUY?

It was much simpler to buy a harpsichord twenty-five years ago, when revival instruments were almost the only ones available.[2] Since there were fewer builders than there are today, there was less to choose from.

The instruments were all generic (that is, they did not refer to any particular regional style), and harpsichords were bought more or less by the pound: two manuals cost more than one, five octaves more than four, seven pedals more than five, three registers more than two. In a sense this is still true, because larger instruments are more expensive than smaller ones. Today, however, in addition to matters of range, registration, and number of keyboards, we must also deal with the bewildering array of national or regional styles. Thus we find ourselves asking if a two-manual Flemish with a four-and-a-half octave range is "better" than a single-manual Italian with five octaves, or if a two-manual Flemish is "better" than a two-manual French, or if a five-octave German is "better" than a five-octave English.

Even before you can answer the question, What kind of harpsichord should you buy?, you have to ask another: What are you going to use it for? Buying a harpsichord is something like buying an automobile. To get around town you might choose something small and maneuverable, but you would probably like something larger and more comfortable for highway driving. If you transport a lot of equipment a station wagon might be best, but you would probably prefer a van if you also enjoy camping.

So it goes with harpsichords: just as there is no automobile that will serve all needs equally well, there is no harpsichord that can do it all equally well. A harpsichord can be used in a number of different ways: to play continuo with one or more solo instruments and with chamber groups and orchestras of various sizes; for continuo and solo work, as in a collegium situation; for concertos with orchestra; for professional-level recital work; and as the source of solace, comfort, and satisfaction for amateur harpsichordists of all levels of accomplishment. All these requirements might be filled by a large two-manual instrument, but that would be like buying a station wagon or a van just to drive around town: it will do the job, but not nearly as efficiently as something more specialized.

Many types of historical harpsichords were discussed in chapter 2, but only a few of them are made with any regularity today. Take Italian harpsichords, for example. Although the $2 \times 8'$ disposition was always common, the early ones were frequently built with a single $8'$; an additional $8'$ often was added to an existing instrument, but sometimes not until a hundred years later. Another normal disposition for the early Italians was $1 \times 8'$, $1 \times 4'$. Later, to meet changing musical needs, the $4'$ was removed and another $8'$ installed. Some late Italians were built $2 \times 8'$, $1 \times 4'$, perhaps in an attempt to imitate some of the flexibility of Northern instruments. There were even some two-manual Italian harpsichords built, although most of the two-manual Italians in museums are not authentic.[3]

These various types of harpsichords all "speak" Italian, but they speak different dialects. I recently built a small Italian, modeled after an anonymous instrument made in Venice around 1575 and rebuilt twice in the seventeenth century. Although its sound is unmistakably Italian, it is quite different from the long-tailed eighteenth-century Italians to which we have become accustomed. It has the typical crispness of attack, but it sustains more than some of the later Italians. If it can be said that the later Italians are bass-dominated in tone quality, then this earlier instrument is treble-dominated. But the treble dominates in tone quality, not in balance; indeed, its four distinct registers blend beautifully, reminding one of a consort of renaissance recorders. This is not to say that all sixteenth-century Italians have that quality, but it is an indication that there is no single Italian sound. Yet few of today's builders are making anything other than the late $2 \times 8'$ models.

Other examples abound. At present no one seems to be making small Flemish harpsichords pitched a fifth higher than normal, or Flemish virginals in anything but $8'$ size. I know of only one modern Flemish unaligned double (although undoubtedly there are others), and have never seen a modern example of the harpsichord with the virginal in the bentside (although by now someone has probably built one). The clavicytherium does not seem to have caught on much at all, and modern copies of English virginals, though popular in England, are rare in this country. Almost every builder makes late eighteenth-century French harpsichords, but few equip them with knee levers and machine stops. The *peau de buffle* was not uncommon a few years ago, but seems to be out of favor now.

Except for instruments considered more specialized, such as virginals and muselars, few harpsichords are built with a mere four-octave range.

Nevertheless, new and different harpsichords are exhibited at almost every trade show, and something considered esoteric only a few years ago—a muselar, or a mother and child virginal, is now seen with regularity. There are two things of which you can be certain: first, builders build what people want to buy; and second, if there is something you want, you will find more than one builder who will be glad to make it for you.

With the understanding that modern versions of the antique instruments will probably differ at least in some respects from their models, let us discuss the national schools once more. This time, however, we will consider these harpsichords from the viewpoint of the modern builder and from the requirements of the modern player.

Italian harpsichords, as we know, are instruments whose "speaking" character makes them ideal continuo instruments, where they supply the strong rhythmic drive needed to accompany instruments and voices. Modern Italians are relatively inexpensive, but, like their prototypes, relatively inflexible. Both true inner-outer and false inner-outer Italian harpsichords can be found. Almost invariably disposed $2 \times 8'$, they have one keyboard and a range of from four-and-a-half to five octaves. Although the antique prototypes were usually intended to be played $2 \times 8'$, almost all contemporary builders supply register levers so that either 8' alone can be used. (The two 8' jacks pluck right next to each other, so the distinction in tone color between registers is usually minimal; more useful is the option of playing on one or both sets of strings.)

An Italian harpsichord such as the one just described suits the music of the English virginalists (the English used the word virginal, or pair of virginals, to refer to any instrument in the harpsichord family), and, depending on the range, Italian composers from Frescobaldi through Scarlatti. Other styles of music are more or less enhanced by the crisp Italianate sound; seventeenth- and early eighteenth-century German music sounds good on it, but it is not at its best with French music. On the other hand, in our search for the best all-around instrument we should remember that it was the Italian harpsichord that came closest to filling this role in the seventeenth and eighteenth centuries.

Flemish harpsichords built today range from small four-octave singles, through medium-size four-and-a-half-octave single- or double-manual instruments, to large five-octave double-manual versions. Like modern harpsichords of almost every national style, they are all intended to sound at 8' pitch, either at $a' = 440$ Hz, or at the commonly accepted low baroque pitch of $a' = 415$ Hz. At any rate, most builders offer them with transposing keyboards, so that without retuning the pitch level, and with a minimum of bother, the instruments can be used at either pitch. The small ones, built after the early Flemish prototypes, are seen infrequently, since their restricted range limits their use in later music. A medium Flemish single is a useful and versatile instrument, and there are more of them in service today than almost anything else. With a $1 \times 8'$, $1 \times 4'$ disposition (sometimes $2 \times 8'$, $1 \times 4'$, sometimes $2 \times 8'$) and a buff stop, it is more flexible in its tonal capabilities than most Italians. Its sound is not nearly as dry and percussive as an Italian. Although it neither sustains nor blooms like a French harpsichord, it allows the voices in contrapuntal music to be heard with clarity. Although not as rhythmic as an Italian, it can provide a satisfactory continuo. It serves the virginal literature very well. Thus, unless your needs are more specialized, you can scarcely go wrong with a medium Flemish single.

A larger Flemish, with a second choir of 8' strings and another manual, provides still more versatility. Bigger cases and wider compasses move these instruments closer to the French sound, and they have greater solo capabilities.

No historical harpsichords underwent more continual and extensive rebuilding than the Flemish instruments. Few exist in their original dispositions and compasses. Few builders make them that way, and probably even fewer people want them with what is considered to be a limiting compass. Thus, it is worth noting that a "Flemish harpsichord" probably represents a model of an instrument that had been rebuilt several times, and that may be speaking with at least a little bit of a French accent.

The French double, by which we mean the late eighteenth-century French harpsichord, is often called the queen of harpsichords. On its five-octave FF–f‴ range and its two keyboards, and with its $2 \times 8'$, $1 \times 4'$ plus buff disposition, one can play anything written for the harpsichord (except for the Scarlatti and early Haydn pieces that go up to g‴). It is, as we have noted, a singing instrument, with a complex, blooming sound that wraps the music in a golden haze. It is considered to be the ideal instrument for the important eighteenth-century French harpsichord literature. Nevertheless, a singing sound and a golden haze are not what is wanted for continuo work or for the Fitzwilliam virginal book, and the sound of an Italian, a Flemish, or a German instrument is probably more suitable for Bach.

To those whose knowledge of harpsichords is limited it would appear that something like the French double is the instrument of choice for continuo with an orchestra. After all, it has two keyboards and all those choirs of strings, and, being so big and imposing, it *must* make a louder sound than one of those puny-looking Italians. But, although larger instruments have more complex sounds, it is the smaller ones that tend to sound the loudest. The presence of the Italian tone enables it to cut through the orchestral sound, while the complex bloom of a French gets swallowed up by the orchestra. For the same reason, the French double is probably not the most appropriate instrument for concertos with orchestra.

Since only a handful of seven-teenth-century French harpsichords are extant, making it difficult for us to judge their sound, it is understandable that these prototypes have been neglected by modern builders.[4] Nevertheless, a number of makers have produced copies recently.

Some years back, a few builders experimented by grafting Italian-style barring, hollow wrestplanks (a feature of some Italian harpsichords), and other elements of Southern instruments onto essentially eighteenth-century French practice. It was claimed that this marriage of Northern and Southern practices must indeed represent the seventeenth-century French sound, but little evidence was offered to support the thesis. Other builders have attempted to combine various elements of the national schools in new ways. Some of the results of this eclecticism are interesting and worthy of consideration, although it must be remembered that these builders are trying to expand our concept of harpsichord sound rather than recapture the sound of the historical instrument.

In this, they are following in the footsteps of many of the great builders of the past, people whose inventive minds prevented them from turning out a product identical to those constructed by their predecessors. Harpsichord building has always been a process of creating "variations on a theme," with the builders tinkering with the parameters of construction, mechanics, and acoustics. This is what these modern builders are attempting to do. Although my personal bias is toward the historical sound (more about this at the end of this section), I affirm and appreciate the value of this sort of experimentation. Some sort of eclectic harpsichord could well suit your requirements, as long as it is recognized that there may be many things about it at variance with the sounds the historical composers had in mind when they wrote for the harpsichord.

Eighteenth-century English harpsichords are popular in England, where one finds many of the antiques in playing condition as well. Although they are being built in this country, for some reason (perhaps having to do with the cost-effectiveness of veneering) they do not seem to have caught on with either builders or players. This is a little difficult to understand, since the English built powerful harpsichords, and if Venetian swells seem a little gauche for modern taste, lute stops, pedals, and machine stops should accord perfectly with our twentieth-century love for gadgetry. In the eighteenth century these instruments were often made with single manuals, but most of the modern versions seem to have two. An English has a strong sound, one that seems to come into its own with a texture that is essentially homophonic, such as one finds in much of Handel's music, rather than the coloristic sounds of French music or the contrapuntal textures of Bach. But as stated earlier, these are magnificent instruments, and the imposing character of their sound does not really seem to interfere with almost any sort of music played on them.

The English, it will be remembered, also had an earlier indigenous practice. Like the early French harpsichords, these instruments have been little explored by contemporary builders, or at least not by those in North America. English bentside spinets, on the other hand, have been popular for years—probably because a full five octaves can be gotten into a very small space.

Ten years ago, the French harpsichord was considered to be the best all-round instrument. Five years ago, the larger two-manual Flemish harpsichord was given that place of honor. Now, some think that instruments modelled after the Northern German school best fill that role. It is not unlikely that English harpsichords will be the next instrument of choice.

Modern versions of German harpsichords have been produced for some time now, and some builders make a specialty of them. It is somewhat difficult to pin down the sound of the German instruments. As we have seen, constructional practices could vary widely between the Southern, Northern, and Central parts of Germany. Nevertheless, historical German harpsichords I have heard (excluding the unique Hass instruments with 16'), have a somewhat cleaner sound than their French counterparts, and this characteristic is combined with some of the tone quality associated with the shorter scales of Southern instruments. These German instruments seem to suit a variety of repertoires.

The big Hasses remind one of the organ, and that does not seem to be what the modern performer wants, although a number of modern versions have been made.

Finally, there are the late Flemish harpsichords (frequently represented by modern copies of the Smithsonian's 1745 Dulcken), the late harpsichords of the Scandinavian countries, and the Italianate instruments of Portugal and Spain. These have not been extensively explored by modern builders, but given recent history it seems likely that their time will come. None of these instruments is the "perfect" harpsichord. Each has its own set of characteristics, more desirable in some circumstances, less so in others.

There is another way of viewing this cornucopia of national schools and styles, and that is to more or less ignore them, and instead look at the time frames involved. It might be useful to consider the presumption that *any* harpsichord—French, Italian, or whatever—modelled after an instrument of, say, 1720, is more appropriate for the music of Bach, Rameau, or Scarlatti than any harpsichord based on an instrument dating from one hundred to one hundred fifty years earlier, or even fifty years later. To me, my little ca. 1575 Venetian copy seems appropriate for anything written around the beginning of the seventeenth century. Its bright treble, clearly defined alto and tenor, and dark bass seem to suit Froberger, Frescobaldi, and the English virginalists better than the sound of a long-tailed eighteenth-century Italian, with its flutey treble and booming bass. On the other hand, fluty trebles and booming basses enhance much eighteenth-century music, no matter what the country of origin.

The weight of the evidence supports this more pragmatic view. When Rameau played Handel—if he played him at all—he played him on his French harpsichord. When Handel was in his early thirties he played Scarlatti on an Italian harpsichord, but that was because he was in Italy; if he played Scarlatti's music after he got to England, it was on his enlarged Ruckers, or on an English harpsichord. Our eighteenth-century ancestors approached music making from a practical stance foreign to our performance-practice orientation. If Rameau wanted to play Handel, he certainly would not have sought out an English harpsichord on which to play him. The idea would have been ludicrous to him, and in any case he would have felt uneasy with the touch and the sound of an English harpsichord, just as the English traveler Charles Burney casually dismissed the touch and sound of the instruments in France.[5] No—Handel's music would stand or fall on Rameau's French double, and the latter would have considered the statement that "you can't play English music on a French harpsichord" to be nonsensical. One must also take into consideration the fact that Italian harpsichords, as pointed out earlier, were more widespread throughout Europe than anything else.

Finally, there is the complication of the specific model, copy, or school you may favor. Suppose you settle on a French harpsichord (as so many have) as best fulfilling your needs or those of your institution. Should you buy a copy of the Edinburgh 1764 Taskin? Or the Paris 1697 Dumont, as enlarged by Taskin in 1789? Or the Boston 1756 Hemsch? Or an instrument that is only loosely based on a particular historical model? Or an instrument that makes no reference to a particular historical model, but instead is designed in the *school* of Taskin or Hemsch or someone else?

Enough questions! Now let us try to put together some answers. We are, after all, trying to decide what kind of instrument to buy. Let us not get like the centipede who, when asked how he could possibly walk on all those legs, found that when he actually stopped to think about it, it was impossible for him to walk at all. Read the information given here, discuss it with other people, visit trade shows, and carefully observe what works and what does not work for others. Without question, you should play as many different harpsichords as possible, and try to listen with both your ears and your fingers. Then you have to make up your own mind. And having done that, try not to agonize over it. If it is *really* the sound of a German harpsichord that you like, go ahead and buy one. You will be playing it, listening to it, and living with it for a long time. If it is not the ideal instrument for all of the harpsichord music you play, neither is anything else— and at least it is better than playing it on the piano.

Now for some more of my personal biases: take them or leave them as you see fit.

Given the choice between a one- or a two-manual harpsichord, a serious harpsichordist will probably opt for the two (provided, as always, that the money is available), with the classical $2 \times 8', 1 \times 4'$ disposition. The upper manual will not be used *that* much, but when it *is* needed—as in, say, Bach's *Italian Concerto*, or the *Goldberg Variations*, or in the *pièces croisées* of Louis Couperin, it is there. Furthermore, tonal and dynamic changes are made far more easily and naturally on the two-manual instrument. Of course, you will have little need for that upper manual if you are a relative beginner (although some say the opposite, since the second manual provides the neophyte with the means of varying his otherwise dull playing), and in this case you may be better off getting a single-manual harpsichord with either $2 \times 8'$ or $1 \times 8'$, $1 \times 4'$. If nothing else, there will be less tuning and maintenance to do.

Later, after you have developed the proficiency to play the more advanced literature, you may want to trade it in for a larger harpsichord. If you do decide to follow this course, it will be wise for you to purchase a good instrument to begin with. First of all, it will be much more difficult, if not impossible, to learn proper touch on a poor harpsichord; second, even if you can learn on it, it will be frustrating; and third, it may be impossible to trade it in when a larger (or better) instrument is desired.

If you think there is any chance that you will want to trade your instrument for another some day, discuss the possibility with your builder before you buy. Some will take back their own instruments on a trade, and this could influence your decision to buy from a particular maker. Few will accept someone else's instrument in trade—normally, the owner has the burden of finding a buyer. In some sections of the country this may not be easy.

Unless your instrument is going to be used strictly for continuo and/or earlier music, you should get a harpsichord whose range is at least four-and-a-half octaves, usually GG–d‴. There does not seem to be much point in buying an Italian so authentic that it virtually drips tomato paste (like my little ca. 1575 Venetian copy), but that cannot play Bach, Handel and Scarlatti because it lacks the range (even GG–d‴ will not play *all* of Handel or Scarlatti); or a little Flemish whose sound transports you back to sixteenth-century Antwerp, but on which nothing later than Sweelinck can be played. For the same reasons, and with the same caveat, it is best to avoid an instrument with short-octave tuning if it is to be your one-and-only all-round harpsichord. You will not miss those notes when you play John Bull, but you will certainly miss them when you try to play Bach. Much the same holds true for Italian, Flemish, and English virginals and bentside spinets. They are great to have as second instruments, and far more versatile than one might expect. But as your one-and-only all-round harpsichord a virginal or a spinet, with its one set of strings, is limited.

All this cautionary language assumes that you are not looking for precisely that type of specialized instrument (as I was when I built that Venetian). If you are, you are way ahead of the point I am trying to make here. Either you are purchasing a second or third instrument, or you have your own, presumably good, reasons.

For a beginner or a more casual player, some of the advice just given may not apply. A virginal or a spinet may be all the harpsichord you need, and can cost considerably less than a larger instrument. A virginal with short-octave tuning down to GG may be thought of as lacking notes, but really, just the opposite is true. Originally, most of those instruments went down to C; by adding the short octave, the modern builder is giving you more notes. If you are a serious harpsichordist, and it is to be your only instrument, avoid the short octave. But if you already have your one-and-only all-round harpsichord, a virginal or spinet can add an exciting dimension to your music making.

Finally, having decided on a school or style, should you buy a copy of a particular historical instrument, or should you look for an instrument based loosely on a historical model or on a school? I have heard many copies of the Edinburgh 1769 Taskin, but I have heard the original too, and I have never heard a copy that sounded like the harpsichord that Taskin made. I have heard many copies of the Smithsonian Dulcken, but none of them sounds like the original. Not only that, most of the copies do not even sound like one another. Not that they all sound bad—not by any means! Some of the close "copies" of the 1769 Taskin I have heard were really good. But I have heard some equally fine modern instruments based on the general practices of the Blanchet-Taskin school, rather than on a particular instrument. And I have heard some indifferent instruments built to the same set of plans or to the same school, and lots of instruments in between.

There is a lot more to harpsichord building than copying the dimensions of the parts and duplicating them. Wood is an organic material, and no two pieces, not even out of the same tree—not even out of the same log or billet—have the same mass, elasticity, and grain pattern. A builder has to know how to manipulate the materials he has at hand, and he cannot do it by slavishly copying a 200-year old instrument.[6] The lesson should be clear to anyone: worry more about the quality of the instrument than whether the builder is following a particular historical model or a particular school, as long as he is working in one of the historical traditions that produced the sort of harpsichord in which you are interested.

NEW OR USED?

A few years ago I received a call from the head of the music department of a small college in Iowa, seeking my advice. They had a moderate sum of money set aside for a harpsichord and someone had offered them, at what seemed to be a ridiculously low price, an enormous twenty-five year old German-built revival instrument with $2 \times 8'$, $1 \times 4'$, $1 \times 16'$, pedals, knobs, buttons, whistles, bells, and vertical case-wood grain. I tried to dissuade my colleague. I told him that the instrument represented an attempt to marry piano technology to harpsichord building, the result of which, while sometimes impressive, was a breed of instrument that bore only a superficial resemblance to the historical harpsichord. For the same amount of money I offered him a medium Flemish instrument that would do everything his institution demanded from a harpsichord, which was mostly continuo, accompanying, and some solo and collegium work. In any case, I advised him not to buy the white elephant. Unfortunately, I was not persuasive enough; his school purchased the monster, thereby getting an instrument that (1) in its disposition was far more complex than they needed; (2) was entirely unsatisfactory for what they did need, or for any other purpose; and (3) would require constant, painstaking, expert maintenance because of its complexity.

Obviously, that is *not* the kind of used harpsichord to buy. There are a lot of those revival instruments out there, and their owners are just waiting for the unwary to come by. The price is always right—in fact, it almost seems like a giveaway, which it is: they are giving away a box of troubles and you are giving away good money for it. But with increasing frequency it is possible to find an instrument made by a reputable builder, owned by someone who is trading up (say, from a four-and-a-half octave Flemish single to a five-octave French double), and who is selling it because he needs the money to help pay for his new instrument. Less often, fine instruments come on the market because people tire of them, or because for some unfortunate reason they need the money worse than they need the harpsichord. Harpsichords may also be found at estate sales. At the present writing there is at least one enterprising business, The Harpsichord Clearing House, offering a listing service for used instruments. Anyone hoping to buy or sell such an instrument would benefit by subscribing to such a service. If nothing else, it will provide useful information on the condition of the used harpsichord market.

A used instrument can represent a good buy, but get the advice of a harpsichord technician (this does not mean your cousin, who has built one kit instrument) to help you decide if your purchase is a wise one, or go to one of the people just mentioned who specialize in dealing with such instruments. In general, good harpsichords, like good wine, improve with age: poorer ones develop all sorts of maintenance problems and are more likely to sound like vinegar. Although not universally true, the finest harpsichords appreciate in price as well as in quality, and you could pay more for a prized older instrument (the word "used" has little meaning in this context) than you would for a merely "good" new one.

Unless you are a knowledgeable harpsichord technician, it is probably best to avoid considering a used harpsichord that has some sort of problem, simple as the solution may appear. You may be told that, "all it needs is a good voicing;" or, "it just needs restringing;" or, "just patch those soundboard cracks and it will be fine;" or "you can fix that sinking soundboard with a happiness bar." Maybe so, maybe not. Let the seller fix it up first, then you decide if you want to buy it. It goes without saying that harpsichords with cocked cheeks, rotated wrestplanks, jammed gaps, or any other kind of structural damage should not be considered. Minor cracks in the soundboard at the cheek can be ignored, provided that the treble part of the soundboard is not creeping into the gap.

SHOULD YOU BUY A KIT INSTRUMENT? SHOULD YOU BUILD IT YOURSELF OR HAVE SOMEONE ELSE BUILD IT?

Do not turn up your nose at kit instruments. Both Zuckermann Harpsichords and Hubbard Harpsichords, the two companies responsible for the harpsichord kit phenomenon, have remained successful at it for over twenty-five years, and continue to produce sets of parts from which the amateur can construct his own harpsichord. The kits are well designed and the materials are first rate. They should be—they are the same designs and the same parts that go into the justly famed custom instruments made by these two firms. Potentially, these parts can be made into instruments as good as those that can be scratch-built by a professional builder. For those purists who feel that a good harpsichord can only be built by a craftsman working alone, using nothing but hand tools, hewing out his instruments one at a time, sinking his artistic soul into each one, let it be known that harpsichords were never built in this way; in fact (with the exception of non-standard instruments built to special order), harpsichords were *always* built from kits. All the producing harpsichord shops of the past and present cut out sets of parts for batches of instruments at one time. The worker in the Dowd shop or the Hubbard shop who goes to the bins and pulls out a bentside, a spine, a wrestplank, and so on, to build a case, is doing nothing more or less than you do when you build a kit (one often hears of people "putting together" kits; one "puts together" erector sets— one *builds* harpsichords).

There are three elements that go into the making of a first-rate harpsichord: the excellence of the design, the quality of the materials, and the skill and experience of the builder. The kits supply the first two; you must supply the third, along with a great deal of patience. Although many people think that building the case is the most difficult challenge, this is really a relatively simple and straightforward part of the job and can be completed by almost anyone who has done some basic woodworking. Skill and experience become important in building the soundboard, in establishing the geometry of the instrument, and in voicing and regulating. Here the amateur builder (or the poor builder) is at a distinct disadvantage.

Realizing this, both companies try to support their builders as best they can. Zuckermann Harpsichords has a network of agents who can help the kit builder at crucial moments. Unfortunately, agents are not to be found everywhere, although the builder can usually pick up the telephone and talk to an agent or to the shop. Hubbard Harpsichords prefers to deal with builders directly, on the telephone, sometimes referring the builder to a near-by successful former kit builder. A prospective kit builder would do well to check the proximity of a Zuckermann agent or a well-thought-of Hubbard customer before undertaking to build his own instrument, although these days practically no one is very far from *someone* knowledgeable, and almost all of them are willing to help (although one should expect some charge from a professional who has no particular ties to your kit company). Although I am a Zuckermann agent I have assisted many Hubbard builders with their instruments, and I doubt that I am unique in that way. Other companies are producing harpsichord kits, but they are more intended for the "craft" market—for the people who think it would be neat to own a harpsichord, or who, having built grandfather clocks for all twelve of their grandchildren, are now looking for another long-term project.

If you are building the instrument for yourself, all you have to do now is place your order and wait for the call from the shipper. But if it is your institution that is ordering the kit, there are several ways in which you can proceed. One popular way is to give one or several students academic credit to build the instrument. Although it seems like a good idea, this method is almost inevitably doomed to failure. Leaving

aside the ethics of the exploitation of students and the granting of academic credit for a non-academic project, the instrument usually is poorly built. The students no doubt have the interest and the desire, but they lack the experience, and furthermore are faced with the deadline of semester's end. And when they leave they take with them any knowledge about the instrument's maintenance they may have garnered. I have visited many colleges that have a useless instrument (which nevertheless may be potentially good) sitting in the corner of a storeroom, built from a kit by a student now gone. No one now knows how to repair it or take care of it. Few things have done more to give the kits an undeservedly bad reputation than this practice.

An institution purchasing a kit instrument should consider having it built by the company, by a local builder, or by a local agent if there is one. Not only is the builder or the agent committed to supplying a first-rate instrument, but he will usually maintain and adjust it, at little or no cost for the first year or so. He can teach those who use it the simple maintenance required, and he is available in case problems arise. If the institution is really in a financial bind, needs the instrument, but cannot afford to pay for a completed harpsichord, it might consider having someone on its staff build it, in consultation with the agent or the company. Although I am sure there are exceptions, turning the construction over to students does not seem to work well and frankly, as an educator, I cannot

condone the practice. On the other hand, it is not unlikely that a properly motivated professor, piano technician, or local craftsman—someone with talent and experience in woodworking—can, with the agent's help, turn out a good instrument.

In fact, whether to buy a kit instrument or not turns out not to be the question at all. In terms of the quality, it makes little difference whether the instrument is made by a good builder from a fine kit (by now it must be obvious that the word "kit" is a misnomer when applied to harpsichords) or by a good builder from scratch. Without meaning to take anything away from scratch builders, given excellence of design and materials, the question of who cuts out the parts is not very important.

There is, however, one final but important consideration: are you *capable* of building your own harpsichord? Have you had any experience at all working with your hands? Do you have the patience needed to spend weeks working on a keyboard, performing each of a seemingly endless number of tasks fifty-four times, or sixty-one times, or whatever the number of keys on your instrument? My practice has been to rely on my customer's judgment of himself. I give him a realistic estimate of the tasks involved. If he thinks he can do it and would *enjoy* doing it, I am justified in feeling fairly certain that he will do a creditable job. But if he lacks basic hand skills, has little patience for "quiet" work, and intends getting through the building task as quickly as possible so that he can start playing, I urge him to try to find some way to earn the money to pay me or someone else to build the harpsichord for him.

SHOULD YOU BUY FROM FAMOUS MAKERS, EVEN THOUGH THEY MAY BE HALF A CONTINENT AWAY, OR SHOULD YOU BUY FROM A LOCAL BUILDER?

The build-your-own harpsichord movement was a product of the 1960s and 1970s, when North Americans were discovering the joys of working with their own hands. The kits were of a much simpler order then, and only cost several hundred dollars. People, it seems, built their own (or dreamed of doing it someday), and there are, without doubt, more kit-built harpsichords in existence than anything else. Today the kits are complex, sophisticated, and expensive, but considering the potential result, still well worth the price. Nevertheless, fewer people are willing to risk the substantial investment required to build their own instrument. Instead, they are turning to professional builders. Some of these professionals are "one-off" builders, people who enjoy making many different sorts of harpsichords. By necessity, they are forced to create a design, a drawing, and a complete set of parts for each individual instrument they make. Others are production builders, who offer a limited number of instruments. These people reserve a certain amount of shop time for cutting out multiple sets of parts (kits, one might even be

tempted to exclaim) for production runs of the same model.

The distinction between these types of builders is not intended to be judgmental. One-off builders, production builders, or kit builders—any one of them may or may not turn out excellent harpsichords. However, be warned about the kind of builder that David Way calls the *autodidact*. This person values only knowledge gained through his own experience. The study, research, techniques, successes, and failures of others are of little interest to him—he is too busy reinventing the harpsichord to notice them. The autodidact rarely exhibits at trade shows, where builders have a chance to see what others in the field are doing; in fact, he rarely goes to trade shows. His prices are very low, since the only way he can sell instruments is to practically give them away. Like harpsichord builders of all kinds, the autodidact is probably a nice person, interesting to talk to, and full of theories about harpsichord building. But his instruments are probably best avoided.

The autodidact should not be confused with the kind of maker whose attitude toward harpsichord building is hopelessly romantic. If someone insists on working in a shed in the country, with no electricity, using only hand tools, that is fine—judge only the worth of his final product.

Where does all this leave the potential buyer? Can you rely on a famous name, or on that strong recommendation from a professional performer, or on the chance that a builder will make

an instrument for you "just like you made for Susie Brown"? Let us return to our original question for some guidance: should you buy from that famous maker, or should you trust the local builder?

But first—what is a famous maker? People like William Dowd, Eric Herz, Diane Hubbard, John Phillips, and David Way are famous makers because they have been around for a long time, because during that time they have turned out consistently fine products, and because they show every promise of continuing to do so. A famous maker should be distinguished from one who might appear to be famous because his name is currently in vogue. Such builders seem to slip in and out of favor, particularly on a regional basis. They may be producing excellent harpsichords—they probably wouldn't be *à la mode* if they were not at least decent, but they are not *famous* makers until they have the track record of someone like Dowd or Herz.

You are probably the person who is going to have to play that instrument, teach on it, tune it, maintain it, and take the credit or the blame for the way it plays and sounds. If you live in Iowa and are convinced that the best harpsichords are made by Dowd in Boston, or by Phillips in Berkeley, and if you or your institution can afford one of these instruments, by all means buy it. Dowd and Phillips deserve their reputations: many people have purchased their instruments, and they are famous precisely because they deliver a consistently good product. You will get a fine instrument, and with it comes a maker's name that you can mention with pride.

But there is also this to consider: Dowd or Phillips is probably going to be half a continent away when your harpsichord has problems. You should also realize that neither Dowd nor Phillips, nor any other builder, can afford to keep your finished instrument around for the better part of a year while it gets thoroughly played in and regulated. Although the better builders will not let the harpsichord leave until they are satisfied that it has undergone at least its initial breaking in, sound business practice dictates that the instrument leave the shop as soon as possible, since final payment will not be forthcoming until it is delivered. Thus, some of the tonal finishing of the instrument is inevitably left to you. This will not be a problem if you are capable of doing it yourself (as many harpsichordists are), or if you have access to a qualified harpsichord technician; but it can be a serious drawback for some.

The better builders try to avoid leaving the buyer in the lurch. A purchaser should expect the maker to support that new instrument in some way, either by visiting it himself or by making some deputy available to you. A few harpsichord makers send a detailed maintenance manual along with the instrument. No instrument comes with a lifetime guarantee of service, nor should it; but it should be looked at professionally, at least during the first few years it is in the owner's hands. If it seems that the builder has no interest in

what happens to his instrument after it leaves his shop, you might consider going to someone else.

There were only a handful of really good makers around a decade ago, but the level of the quality of harpsichord building has risen dramatically since then. Almost anyone should be able to find a good maker within a few hundred miles. Names like Anderson Dupree, Robert Greenberg, Willard Martin, Lynette Tsiang, and Allan Winkler are well known to people in the harpsichord world, and they are representative of the many fine builders that can be found almost anywhere in North America. Today, it is a fallacy to think that there are only a few great harpsichord builders in the world—that someone has secrets unknown to anyone else. Dowd and Phillips may be better builders than your local builder, but not because they know something no one else knows. And your builder, or the Zuckermann agent, can give your instrument the support it needs in that difficult first year and thereafter. Your local builder may be pretty darned good, too, and your Zuckermann agent *should* be capable of doing work as fine as David Way's custom shop. I am not suggesting that one alternative is better than the other, but all should be weighed carefully.

How, then, can you judge the product of your local builder? Again, there are questions that you need to ask. I realize that the list that follows is daunting, but it is necessary. Under many circumstances some of the questions may be difficult

or impossible to answer, but together, the answers define a good instrument.

Does he do a workmanlike job on his keyboards, or do they show uneven spacing, skewing, gaps, and varying dips? Do they have the proper weight and balance, or are they over-weighted so that the keyboard will feel more natural for pianists? Are his jacks reliable, or do they stick with regularity, develop jittery tongues, and include lead weights to assist the job that gravity is supposed to do? (But note that Italian harpsichords and virginals often have heavier jacks than Northern instruments.) Are his instruments properly regulated, or does the 8′ whisper and the 4′ shriek? Do his instruments feel good under the fingers, or does it take a lot of effort to make music with them? Is his stringing trustworthy, or does he string too heavily or too lightly? Is his voicing long-lasting and dependable, or do his plectra break frequently?

Do his instruments make the sort of sound and volume you want? Do they whisper when you want a roar, or are they crude when you want a refined sound? Do his instruments tend to self-destruct? Is the soundboard coming apart before the instrument is even sold? Do his harpsichords improve with age, or do they get harsher and less musical? Are the resonances in his instruments in the right places, or has he put them in unusual registers of the harpsichord? Are his instruments cleanly and appropriately decorated, or are they sloppily and hastily finished? Does he charge a competitive price for his instruments? A harpsichord whose price is substantially lower than the going rate may be a good buy; on the other hand, you may be paying for the builder's education and getting an instrument of lesser quality.

There are a number of steps you can take to get some indication of a builder's competence. You can ask people who own his instruments, although that may be a worthless exercise. No matter what its faults, an owner tends to speak of his instrument in glowing terms. To do otherwise would be to admit that poor judgment prevailed and good money was spent for a less-than-ideal harpsichord. Few owners will do that. I have had people complain bitterly to me about some feature or other of their instrument (and sometimes these were serious flaws), then turn around and recommend the builder to someone else, extolling his work.

A prospective buyer should make it a point to visit meetings of early keyboard societies, such as the Midwestern Historical Keyboard Society or the Southeastern Historical Keyboard Society, and events such as the Boston Early Music Festival, where the better builders exhibit their instruments, and where one has opportunities for comparison. Experiences such as these, however, can be mind-bending, sending the brain into harpsichord overload. I will never forget the 1980 Bruges Festival, in Belgium, when I entered a hall that seemed the size of two football fields. The floor was completely covered with harpsichords. Seated at each instrument was a possible buyer, fingers moving busily over the keys, trying mightily to hear that instrument above the general din. Hovering over the harpsichord was the builder, explaining his philosophy of instrument building, anxious to make a sale and/or promote his reputation. It took several days before I was capable of making any sort of rational judgment about the instruments. But it was an invaluable experience, one I have put to good use many times.

We tend to fall in love with an instrument because its touch suits us, because it makes a particular sound that we like, because it looks particularly beautiful, or because its builder has some special mystique about him. European builders sometimes have that mystique for us North Americans. As hard as I find it to believe that one must go halfway across the continent to get a really good harpsichord, I find it even harder to believe that one must go across the Atlantic. Certainly, excellent instruments are being built in Europe—one could mention builders such as Andrea Goble and Milan Misina in England, Reinhardt Von Nagle (who for years ran the Paris Dowd shop), and Marc Ducornet (who runs the Paris Zuckermann shop) in France, and Reiner Schuetze and Hans-Dieter Neupert in West Germany—but instruments of equal merit are being built here. A colleague of mine recently bought a harpsichord from a builder in Holland. It is a nice instrument, but not any nicer than many that could have been purchased for the same or less money in this country. Unfortunately for my colleague, the instrument began to develop problems as soon as it got here (the Europeans build for their own climate, and their instruments often do not fare well in the extreme climatic contrasts found over so much of North America). At the moment it is unplayable; it can be fixed, of course, but I do not think it is necessary to put yourself in that sort of position in the first place.

You should also play as many harpsichords as you possibly can. This is the only way you will come to know your own preferences for sound and touch. Beginners are often too embarrassed to play in front of more advanced performers, but I can assure you, no one really cares about the level of your playing ability; on the contrary, most harpsichord builders and players are delighted to see an expression of interest in the instrument on any level. Furthermore, the best way to get over this sort of stage-fright is to do it. Finally, whatever momentary embarrassment is incurred by playing in front of others is not half as bad as trying to live for the rest of your life with an expensive instrument that simply is not right for you.

The buyer has to be very careful of what he is hearing when he sits down to play a harpsichord. As keyboard players, we tend to hear with our fingers, and if an instrument *feels* good we are likely to think it *sounds* good as well, even though a well-regulated harpsichord is not necessarily a good harpsichord. We can be dazzled by spectacular decoration, often done by someone other than the builder. We can become enamored with a colorful sound, even though a "beautiful" sound can become wearing when it is heard on a daily basis. The harpsichord is, after all, an "instrument" in the widest sense of the word: a tool, a means by which one makes music. If the tool imposes an unnecessary character—a "beauty" of its own—on the music, it is going to limit the performer. The best harpsichords I have heard are neutral in this sense (a neutral instrument does not mean one that is bland or gutless, or one that lacks the distinctive elements of its national style), capable of shaping the sound to the character of the music.

It is important that you play the instrument yourself, but also that you get someone else to play it as well. And get it into a quiet room. Listen critically. Just for a moment try to forget the sound of the tool, and concentrate instead on what it is doing to the music. The individual voices must be heard clearly. The soprano, tenor, and bass registers of the instrument should be distinct from one another, yet not so different that they seem to belong to different harpsichords. The bass should have enough character so that it is not swallowed up by the rest of the instrument. The tenor must have the strength of tone to make itself heard. The treble may be beautiful, but it should not tend to dominate the instrument. When appropriate, the 8' registers should have enough distinction between them so that they provide different colors, yet they should blend well when they are played together.

Do not forget about the regulation! The instrument should play easily, with an even and responsive touch. The keyboards should have the proper dip (see chapter 8), and the stagger should be adjusted so that one can play all choirs of strings together without undue stiffness of pluck (see chapter 9).

Let us suppose that you find an instrument that you think fits all your qualifications—one that almost plays itself, that seems to adapt to any sort of music you play on it; one that has life and presence, that is a pleasure to play and to listen to; one that fits your personal or institutional needs; one whose price is within reach of your budget, is attractively and appropriately decorated, and which meets all the other qualifications discussed in this chapter. I have seen a number of instruments like that at meetings and trade shows—instruments I would be proud to have built or proud to own. If it is for sale—buy it, and seek no further! But suppose it is not for sale, and you are going to have to commission the builder to make one "just like this one" for you. Now you may have a problem.

Excellent harpsichords like this one usually are built by makers who consistently turn out a high-quality product. But sometimes they are built by makers who do not seem to know the difference between good and bad, much less good and not so good. I am dumbfounded by builders who exhibit, in the same room, a fine instrument and a mediocre one. I am forced to assume that they really do not know the difference and

that their excellent work is more or less accidental. Anyone can produce an instrument that does not measure up to his best—there is no shame in that! But it seems to me that it would be better for the builder to leave that instrument back in his shop, rather than exhibit it in front of scores of other builders and hundreds, if not thousands, of players. The distressing fact is that some builders just do not know any better. You should be very careful in dealing with this sort of builder. It would be best to have him sign an agreement giving you the right to reject the instrument, for whatever reason, for a full refund, if there is dissatisfaction with it when completed. In fact, such a contract will be agreed to by any competent maker—some will insist on it themselves, and it should be part of the purchase agreement.

Some builders ask for a small, refundable deposit when an instrument is ordered. When the instrument is playing, but not yet decorated, the customer gets the chance to accept or reject the instrument. If he accepts, he pays the builder an amount equal to the worth of the undecorated harpsichord, and pays the balance on receipt of the decorated instrument. But if he is unhappy with the undecorated harpsichord, he may refuse the instrument and is refunded his deposit. If the builder is any good he should have no trouble offering the instrument to someone else. This is a good way to do business, and no builder should balk at this or a similar arrangement. The last thing in the world a builder needs is an unhappy owner, and for his own sake he should *insist* that a customer have refusal rights; to do otherwise is simply poor practice.

Let us try to sum this all up and look at the pros and cons of all these possibilities.

If you decide to buy a kit, or an instrument made from kit parts, consider the kind of support you may need, and what is available to you in your section of the country. If you order the kit to be built by the company's custom shop, you are now dealing with a "famous maker." You will get an excellent instrument, and you may also have the additional advantage of some sort of local support from the company. A possible disadvantage of one of these harpsichords is that it will bear the name, "Hubbard and Broekman," or "D. Jacques Way," and some may not like the idea of owning an instrument that is associated in any way with amateurism or the do-it-yourself harpsichord. This is really an unfair criticism—a good instrument is, after all, a good instrument—but to some, the name will be a criterion of overwhelming importance (although many top professionals play instruments with those names on them).

A similar sort of problem may exist if you have an agent or some lesser-known professional builder make the instrument for you. The name on the name batten is one of the most ephemeral elements of harpsichord building. Put A's name on it and ninety-nine out of a hundred harpsichordists will love it; but B's name could be all it takes to convince the same crowd that it is an inferior instrument.

People buy harpsichords from me because I build good, reliable instruments and I support them. My reputation also includes the fact that I am a university professor, and that I do research in the acoustics of the harpsichord—things that really have little bearing on my ability as a builder of harpsichords. But all of this, in the eyes of my customers, makes me a "professional"—a "name," albeit a local one; and so they are willing to pay me going rates for my product. In other words, my instruments are sold as much for who I am as they are for the company whose parts I use. For this reason, a builder who has no "name" cannot command the going rate or anything close to it. Therefore you must think seriously about who will build that kit for you. It may be possible to save some money now, by paying your brother-in-law to build it for you, but you may lose it if and when you try to sell the instrument.

You can, of course, build the harpsichord yourself, as thousands have done before you. There are important advantages to this choice: first, and not least, you have the *enormous* satisfaction of having created your own instrument! Second, in the process you will have learned a great deal about how the harpsichord works, and how to voice it, regulate it, and maintain it. But building it yourself has disadvantages: if you mess things up, you may have an expensive wooden box full of problems. As I have stressed earlier, this can be avoided by staying in close contact with the agent or the company, or by taking advantage of

any other support system available. As an agent, I have helped many people build good harpsichords, and not one of them has failed. On the other hand, I remember the instrument—a medium Flemish $1 \times 8'$, $1 \times 4'$ single—brought to me by someone who had *not* worked with me (he had not discovered my existence until well after he had finished the instrument). His harpsichord was a box of horrors, but fortunately he had not done anything wrong structurally. By prying up and reglueing the nuts, which he had positioned in the wrong place, and by completely redoing the musical parts of the instrument, I was able to turn a sow's ear into a fair silk purse. But I also had to charge him a hefty fee, which he could have avoided in the first place by letting me do my job as an agent.

There is one other disadvantage to building your own harpsichord. You may find it so satisfying that you will want to build another . . . and another . . . and another. . . .

I would be unhappy if anything said here has led you to believe that one-off builders are better than production builders or vice versa. One-off builders may be more restless, inquiring, and intellectual, but these are not necessarily qualities that produce good harpsichords. Production builders may be more orderly and organized, with clear goals and something of a business sense, but these also are not necessarily the qualities that produce good harpsichords. Furthermore, many production builders do a certain amount of one-off building, and most one-off builders have a production model or two that keep their shops going.

I would be equally unhappy if I biased you toward buying your instrument from a famous maker rather than a local builder, or vice versa. The famous name may carry somewhat more assurance for the quality of the instrument, but the local builder may be able to support his harpsichord in a way that the famous name cannot. And the local builder may be just as good as the famous maker. Many are.

In short: first, determine as clearly as possible what you need in a harpsichord. Second, buy the harpsichord whose national style, range, number of keyboards, number of registers, and other features best suit those needs. Third, consider *all* possibilities when purchasing an instrument: one-off, production harpsichord, famous maker, local builder, or kit-built. None of these options guarantees a fine instrument, none precludes one. Fourth, you would do well to stay away from the autodidact. Fifth, unless you are a competent harpsichord technician yourself, try to assure that your instrument is supported in some way during its first year or so. Sixth, educate yourself as much as possible about the look, sound, and feel of good harpsichords. This you cannot do merely by reading this book. Seventh, do *not* buy a harpsichord on impulse.

Finally, I trust you realize that these are only my ideas of how to go about buying a harpsichord, and there are probably as many ideas on the subject as there are harpsichordists. When you go shopping for a harpsichord, the watchword is the same as it has been for the last seventy-five years: caveat emptor! Let the buyer beware!

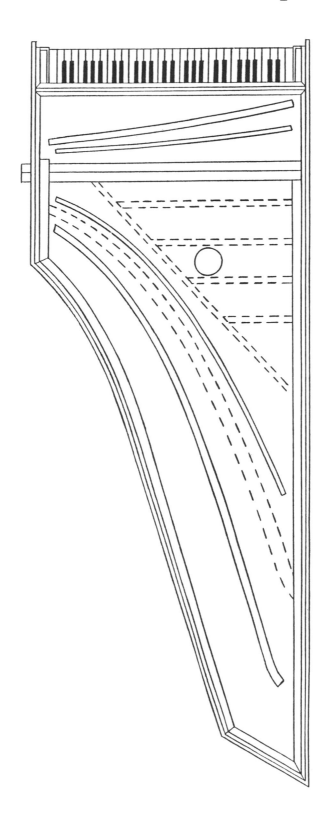

Chapter 5 The Tool Kit

The way in which the harpsichord works may be a good deal more complex than most people suppose, but it is neither difficult nor time-consuming to keep one in good condition. Some knowledge (which, it is hoped, will be gained from this book) and the proper tools (which you will supply) are really all that are required. By spending a few minutes with your instrument from time to time, you can avoid real problems. Proper maintenance also assures you that your instrument responds to your playing with maximum efficiency, as it was designed and built to do. There is no better reason for a harpsichord owner to keep his instrument in top shape.

Some of you reading this book will have to bear with the basic information to be presented in this and in some of the subsequent chapters. I keep thinking of that friend of mine and her first attempt to voice a new plectrum by putting the jack on her breadboard and trying to make it look like the one next to it. Many of you reading this book are in that class, and you are reading this book because I have promised to tell you *exactly* what to do. I am told that there was once an automobile owner's manual whose instructions on starting the car began with, "First take a position behind the wheel." *That* is starting with first things first, and it is the way I intend to proceed here. So before we even begin with a list of the tools and supplies necessary for normal harpsichord maintenance, let us talk about what we mean by a tool.

I have seen owners of expensive harpsichords attempt to work on their instruments with 29-cent drugstore screwdrivers, cheap pliers, and dull hobby knives. Your instrument deserves better than that, and top-quality tools are not much more expensive than the junk. They can save hours of frustration, they work better, they do not chew up your instrument, and they are more fun to use. With the exception of the specialized tools such as the tuning fork and the tuning hammer, almost all the tools listed in this chapter can be found in any decent hardware store. If you have trouble finding what you want, consult one of the many hobbyist tool catalogs.

TOOLS

Tuning fork. Many people do not have them—they just run over to the piano and "take an a," then run back to the harpsichord while they try to remember it. That may be all right if you *never* play with other instruments, but there are advantages, relating to the stability of the instrument, to using the same reference pitch each time. Having spent all that money for a harpsichord, splurge a few dollars on a tuning fork.

Even if you do have a fork, is it loud enough? Some people spend minutes—sometimes quite a few—whacking a toy-like fork on their knee and trying to get it to their ear, teeth, the soundboard, a molding, to anything resonant to which it can transfer the energy of its puny little sound before it disappears altogether. If your hearing is so acute that you can get along with one of those toys, fine. If not, do yourself a favor and get a good, solid, *loud* fork. You will spend less time getting your reference pitch, and the pitch you get will be much easier to match.

Get the fork that gives you the reference pitch you need. If you require an a′ or a c″ at 415 Hz pitch, or 409 Hz, then get one. They are available, and your builder, technician, or agent should be able to help you. Your local music store probably does not stock them but can order one for you.

An a′ from an electronic tuning aid is a luxury I enjoy whenever I can, but I do not own such an aid. You may find it worth your while to do so, particularly if you have trouble setting a temperament (see chapter 13).

Tuning hammer. You got one with your instrument, and it probably works just fine. But sometimes the ends of those things get chewed up. I have seen them break—I broke one myself some years ago. Perhaps you lost the hook that came on the end, and can no longer make string loops with it. If it is hard to use, or if it creates more problems than it solves every time you put the hammer on a pin, then it is time to replace it.

Wire cutter. You are replacing a broken string. You reel the proper length off a coil of wire and— then what? A wire cutter works a lot better than your teeth. A small one is all you need; a large one will only get in your way, and you do not have to cut heavy cable.

Hammer. A common, ordinary light-duty hardware-store hammer will serve the purpose. You will not be building harpsichords with it, but you will find it handy for driving in tuning pins when you replace broken strings. You may also need it for less usual maintenance tasks such as straightening and leveling keys.

Hook or nail. These tools are used for making the string loop. You will use one or the other, depending on which loop-making method you choose.

Voicing knife with spare blades. The voicing knife consists of a handle and replaceable blades. There are many hobby or office knives that fit this description, but the one most commonly used is the X-Acto knife with number 11 blades. Actually, it is not the knife that concerns us, but the blade attached thereto. You will recall Murphy's Law: whatever can go wrong, will. This must be a corollary of Murphy's Law: if there is a blade in the X-Acto knife, it will be dull. Not normally dull, or usually dull, but *always* dull. "But," you say, "I only used it once, last month, to cut a plectrum. How could it be dull?" It not only can be, it is. Perhaps your spouse used it to scrape the old parking sticker off the windshield of the car, or one of the kids used it to cut an article on space travel out of *Time* magazine, for a homework assignment. Even unused, the knife seems to get dull.

Obviously it is a good idea to keep a supply of sharp blades, but that is not always possible, because the people who make hobby knives do not seem to make *sharp* blades. I sharpen the blade before I use it. If you can do that, fine; but most people cannot, and I do not advise you to buy an expensive stone and try to learn a difficult sharpening technique just so that you can cut a plectrum. Nevertheless, you are going to have to do something about the edge on that blade before you start cutting with it. As it comes from the package it simply is not sharp enough to cut that tough Delrin plastic.

Those blades receive their final factory "sharpening" on some kind of emery cloth belt. The last side to pass over the emery turns up an almost invisible wire edge, or burr. This burr must be removed if the blade is to be expected to cut smoothly, and that can be done by *stropping* the blade on a piece of leather. Any kind of hard leather can be used. Some hobby shops sell a piece of stropping leather on a stick, but you can also use shoe leather, a leather belt, or a leather briefcase; use your imagination. To strop, put the blade in the handle. Lay the bevel of the blade *flat* on the leather and draw the blade toward you. (The bevels are the slanted surfaces on either side of the bottom of the blade. The cutting edge is at their junction.) Flip the knife over to the bevel on the other side and draw it away. Back and forth, just like spreading peanut butter (Figure 5-1). Note that the bevel must be flat on the leather; *if it is not you will be dulling the blade, rather than sharpening it.* For a practical demonstration, find an old-fashioned barber and watch him touch up the edge on his old-fashioned razor on his old-fashioned strop.

This does not mean that the blade will not be dull the next time you need it!

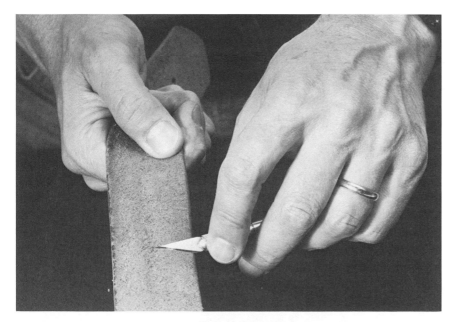

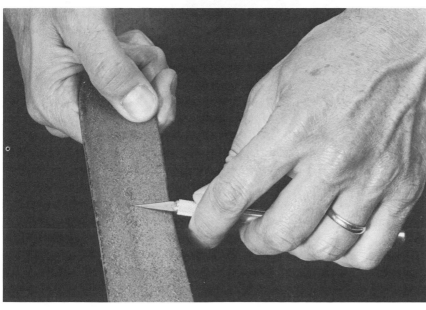

FIGURE 5-1.
Stropping the bevel of the knife on a belt.

Voicing block. This is the surface on which you cut and voice plectra. The block may be of any manageable size or shape, as long as it is made of some close-grained hard wood and the cutting is done on end grain. To allow cutting on both edges of the plectra I like the top of my block to be no more than ⅛ inch thick. If the block is thicker than this, you can taper the sides so that the cutting surface is of that dimension. A width of up to about ½ inch for the block itself works fine. Other than that, it makes little difference how long the block is, or even how thick, as long as the cutting surface is the correct thickness. Figure 5-2 shows two extremes in voicing blocks.

I do not want to be dogmatic about the voicing block. If you are using something different from what I have described, and are successful with it, I advise you to stick with it. In fact, some people do not even use a block, but voice on their thumbnails.

One builder I know voices the quills against his taped fingers. Neither of these methods is recommended to the neophyte voicer.

If you are cutting and voicing Delrin plectra, either use a black wood, such as ebony, or put some black ink from a felt-tip or marking pen on the cutting surface. The contrast between the white plastic and the dark wood gives a much clearer view of what is happening. Conversely, use a light wood block if you are working with black crow quill.

Small, long-nose pliers. Something about five or six inches long will be useful for removing broken plectra, and you will find other uses for it as well. It can be larger if you cannot find something that small, but the smaller the better. Try to find one with smooth rather than serrated jaws. If your hardware store does not carry them, try a hobby shop or an electronics supply store. If you can get one with a wire cut-

FIGURE 5-2.
Two voicing blocks.

ter built in, you will not need a separate tool for that purpose. Please—spend a few dollars and get *good* pliers. Unless the jaws are flat and close properly, this tool can do more harm than good.

Small scissors. For cutting overlong dampers and paper shims of various sorts. You may think that you can use the pair from the kitchen or the sewing box, but you will not be able to find them when you want them. Your tool kit needs its own pair.

Medium or large screwdrivers. You need as many screwdrivers as it takes to exactly fit the screw slots for which they are intended. These could include name-batten screws, keyboard screws, register-lever screws, and any other screws you might have to remove, replace, tighten, or loosen (aside from the small screws that will be handled by the jeweler's screwdrivers). The only way to be sure that you have the right sizes is to take the screws with you when you buy the screwdrivers. You may be lucky enough to find that one screwdriver fits several screw slots, but do not count on it.

Set of jeweler's screwdrivers. My set of six jeweler's screwdrivers is a handy regulating tool. The smallest size can be used as a miniature punch, and it's just right for pushing out tongues on axleless jacks. I use the next size to make a plectrum a little longer, by pushing it through from the back of the tongue. The third and fourth are ideal for seating a plectrum in a tongue, and the largest size is big enough

to use as a small-to-medium screwdriver when I need one. The three smaller sizes are also useful as miniature handles, to turn capstan screws. One of these screwdrivers will have the proper size blade to turn such things as end pins, voicing screws, damper screws, or any other adjustment screws. A set of screwdrivers like this is invaluable and also comes in handy when those little screws on your eyeglasses come loose.

Six- or eight-inch mill bastard file. That is what they are called in the hardware trade. This tool is used to remove that bulge on a plastic jack, and for shortening a jack that has no end pin. You will find other things that could use a swipe from a file from time to time. If your file comes in a protective plastic sleeve, keep it in there when it is not being used. Otherwise, wrap it in something. Files are dulled more from banging around than from use. Files and file handles are separate items, and your file should have a handle.

Six-inch steel rule. You are going to need this to check your key dip. You will find other things from time to time whose measurements you will want to check.

Small, sharp tweezers. This is a tool that you will use oftener than you think, and when you need it nothing else will do. It will pick up that damper that you dropped—the one that is about to fall through the keys. It will retrieve a paper shim that is no longer needed. It will pick up anything—dirt, paper, plectra,

tongues, pieces of wire, and hairs shed on the soundboard by the cat—that is lodged beyond the reach of your fingers. It can also be used to manipulate and massage plastic tongue springs.

Stand tool. The stands or tables that harpsichords sit on usually are built so that they can be partially disassembled for moving. Your builder should have given you the proper tool for this: some sort of wrench, nut driver or screwdriver. If not, get one.

SUPPLIES

You should have spare wire, and I know you do; but do you have enough of the sizes that tend to break most frequently, or is the bulk of your supply in the gauges that seem to last forever? Take the top brass string on your instrument as an example, because that is the string that breaks most frequently. Say it breaks on the average of once a year; if you have enough to replace it three times, you may think you have a three-year supply. But that is not the way I figure it; I figure that the string is going to break at just the wrong time, when I am rushed and rattled. Under these circumstances I may inadvertently kink the wire when I try to replace it. Then, when I get it up to tension—snap!

On the next try I make the loop too tight, compressing the metal (particularly easy to do with soft brass wire). I bring it up to tension, and—snap! Now I am really upset, but I realize that I am going to go through a lot of wire unless I start doing things right. The next one I do carefully.

The loop is beautiful, the wire unkinked. It comes up to pitch—no trouble. Two minutes later the string has stretched and the pitch has fallen, so I bring it up to pitch again—only I put the tuning hammer on the wrong pin. Snap! There goes the wire next to it, same gauge, and I'm out of string.

String is not very expensive, so get plenty in those needed gauges.

Not all harpsichord wire is the same. The trend has been toward the use of softer wire, similar to that used on the antiques. It is possible to buy wire—steel, brass, bronze—in the needed gauges from piano supply houses, and even from well-stocked hardware stores, but it is unlikely that it will be metallurgically proper. Order your replacement wire from your builder, and find out exactly what kind of wire he *is* using.

Extra plectra, tongues and damper felt are things that should have come with your instrument. If you have used them up or never got them, contact your builder. You should also have a few spare jacks and extra regulating screws and endpins, if your jacks are equipped with them.

There are some other supplies that you may never need, but I am including them for the sake of completeness: felt or flannel cloth for adjusting keyboard dip; balance paper punchings for leveling the keyboard; a 3×5 card to cut up and use for shims; a small roll of ½- or ¾-inch masking tape for padding; some pins for axles, if you have wooden jacks; a tool for easing keys, such as an awl; a box of round toothpicks to plug holes and to use as glue sticks; and a small bottle of white or yellow glue.

All these tools and supplies should be packed neatly in a small tool box, and should go with your harpsichord when it travels. It is when the perfectly regulated harpsichord gets into a new environment that all the corollaries of Murphy's Law take over: plectra never break, except before a concert; dampers never leak, except when the harpsichord is played by a world-famous performer, and so on. I am certain some of you have experienced all these and can supply the rest without my help.

Let me close with a story that will illustrate this last point. Some years ago, a small college not too far from Iowa City bought a French double from me. It was delivered early in the year, and spent spring and summer in the cool temperature and stable humidity of the music department, which was deep in a chapel basement. All summer long I was receiving ecstatic reports on how stable the instrument was, and how they had not even had to tune it since they got it.

Then they engaged a well-known harpsichordist to give an inaugural concert, and brought the instrument up from the basement to the stage just two days before the recital. I had agreed to tune the instrument, but I ended up regulating everything on it that could be regulated, while the instrument responded to the completely different, and constantly changing, temperature and humidity of the Iowa fall. Fortunately, I had my tool kit with me, complete with those extra supplies that are rarely used. I spent two solid days with that instrument, right up to concert time and including intermission. If they had brought the harpsichord up two weeks before the concert (as I had asked them to do), it would have had time to make its changes and settle down. Then it could have been thoroughly regulated and would have been fine.

Chapter 6

The Strings

Strings break for a variety of reasons. The house is closed up while you are away on vacation; the temperature and humidity rise and your instrument expands, pulling the pitch up a half step or more; you return home to three broken strings. If you suspect that this may happen to your instrument, or if it has happened before, tune it down a half step before you leave. Aside from broken strings, it is possible for the instrument itself to sustain damage by allowing it to rise a half step and remain there for a long period of time: the cheek-to-bentside joint can open up, the hitchpin rail can pull loose, and the soundboard can split from the shear force in the treble. And you will certainly be breaking strings.

Strings will also break if you insist on tuning a harpsichord back and forth between modern (440 Hz)and low (415 Hz) pitch. If you must have both pitch levels available, you should have a transposing keyboard. Your builder, or another, if the former is not available, can convert your existing keyboard to a transposer; it is not very difficult. Aside from saving you broken strings, your instrument will be more stable in tuning and regulation.

It is not uncommon, particularly among novice harpsichord tuners, to think that you are tuning one string, while the tuning hammer is really cranking up the string next to it. It is particularly easy to do with virginals and bentside spinets where there is no straight line from string to tuning pin to key, to provide a visual orientation. If you have ever done it, you know how easy it is to convince yourself that the string *not* being tuned is changing slightly in pitch. But then, just one more little turn, and—snap! Try to remember: if the pitch does not seem to want to change when you turn the pin, it is probably a good idea to stop turning that pin and take another look at what you are doing. It is always a good idea to play the note and simultaneously touch the string with the tip of the tuning hammer, just to be sure you have the right pin. When you have touched the proper string, follow it down to the pin.

Then there are the strings that get broken from improper or inadvertent contact: the cat walks on the string band, the neighbor's kid throws his toy dump truck into the instrument (or, maybe worse, pulls it out), or you set the end of the lid stick on a string, rather than in its proper niche in the corner of the case. Allowing the tuning hammer to slip off the tuning pin and hit the string is another good way to break one, and so is bringing a corner of the music rack down on a few strings. The jackrail can also be used to similar effect, as can eyeglasses, metronomes, pencils, music, and other musical instruments. Any one of these, and—snap! There goes another string—perhaps not right away, but sooner or later. A lot of this can be prevented by keeping the harpsichord closed when it is not being played, and keeping junk off it and reasonably far away from it. A small table should be kept next to the harpsichord, and anything other than the music rack and the music actually being played (such as pencils, eyeglasses, paper clips, metronome, etc.) should be kept on it, rather than on the harpsichord.

Even if you manage to avoid all of these pitfalls, strings will break because they exceed the limits of their elasticity. It will be recalled from chapter 1 that strings sound best when tuned up somewhere near their breaking points. A string stretches out over a long period of time. It can finally reach that neck-jerking moment when it goes—snap! This is particularly true of the soft brass wire. Some of this can be avoided. If one of the top brass strings on your instrument is constantly breaking, try replacing it with a length of the first iron string—in other words, bring the iron string down one note on the stringing schedule. You will not harm your instrument by doing this. Harpsichords are somewhat individual in this respect, and crossover points (where you go from one gauge or material to another) are determined in part by trial and error, balancing sound against tension.

Brass strings can become corroded (particularly from contact with woods that contain organic acids, such as walnut), and this can cause them to break. Bronze strings sometimes break when replaced, because the replacement string has become brittle from age. This can be dealt with by re-annealing the string: heat it in an oven for twenty minutes at 500 degrees, before you put it on the harpsichord. It will be hot when you pull it out, so use some tongs or a kitchen glove. But it will be cool enough to handle in less than a minute.

Strings can also break if their hitchpin loops have been wound too tightly, if they are kinked in some way, if they pass over sharp or abrasive pins, bridges, or nuts, or if they cross over themselves at the tuning pin. These are things to avoid when a string is changed.

CHANGING A STRING

Tools and supplies needed: stringing schedule, string, hammer, wire cutter, nail or hook, tuning hammer, string brake, or another pair of hands.

There are three tasks necessary to replace a string: making the string loop, winding the other end of the string onto the tuning pin, and adjusting the downbearing. There are numerous ways of doing the first two, but I will describe only several. To help keep them straight each method will be summarized after it is described.

First, remove the music rack and the music and put them elsewhere. Second, remove the jackrail and put it with the music rack. Third, remove the jack whose string you are replacing—

just grasp it by the top and lift straight up, and put it with the music rack and the jackrail. Fourth, put the hammer down next to the harpsichord. You should be able to work around the lid stick, but if it is possible to open the lid all the way and have it rest against the wall, do so and put the lid stick with the other things.

Remove the broken string and any bits of it that remain, such as the string loop. If the broken string is one that has just been replaced, examine it and establish the site at which it gave way. If it parted at the tuning pin, you may have crossed the wire over itself at that point; if it was at the hitchpin loop, you may have wound the loop too tightly; if it was at the bridge or the nut, check those sites for sharp or abrasive areas; if it was somewhere other than one of these points, you may have kinked it. Whatever the reason, try to identify it so that you can avoid breaking the replacement of the replacement. Having examined the string, throw it and all its bits away.

Extract the tuning pin. How you do this will depend on what type of tuning pins you have: threaded tuning pins, looking like smaller versions of the familiar piano tuning pin; or tapered, threadless pins. (The former always have a hole drilled in the top for the string; the latter only sometimes do. Winding the string around a pin without a hole will be described and is not difficult; however, you can drill your own hole if it becomes necessary. This also will be described.) Threaded pins are removed by literally unscrewing the pin out of the wrestplank, counterclockwise, with the tuning hammer. Keep the pin vertical so that it does not enlarge the hole as it is unscrewed. Take the pin all the way out, and remove any of the old string still attached to it. Set it loosely back in its hole, so you will know where it is when you need it.

Tapered pins are removed by twisting and turning the tuning hammer one way, then the other, at the same time pulling up to the extent to which this is possible. Use the other hand to help the pin up out of its hole. Dowd suggests using a pliers if you have trouble,[1] and you may need to do this if the pin is in an awkward location. He also warns against wiggling the pin.[2] This will probably free it, but only because you have enlarged the hole. Tapered pins usually come out very easily, and you should have no problem.

Find the proper material and gauge of replacement wire by consulting your stringing schedule. If you do not have this information you will have to measure the diameter of the broken wire with a string gauge or a micrometer. Uncoil an amount of wire that will equal the length of the broken wire plus a generous additional foot, perhaps even more. On shorter strings uncoil no less than six feet of wire. Simply doing this preliminary operation can be a frustrating experience. If your coil of wire is held together with a twist, a bit of wire, or a piece of tape, I suggest that you back the wire out, one coil at a time, until you have freed the proper length. A much quicker, though more adventuresome method, is to remove the twists,

grasp the free end of the outside of the coil (it is not always easy to determine which is the outside end), and holding the coil loosely in one hand (but not *too* loosely), pull out to arm's length with the other. Then replace the twists. With either method it is possible to get some tangling of the wire. Be patient. Do not kink the wire. If you do, cut the kinked part off with your wire cutter, throw it away, and uncoil some more.

MAKING A STRING LOOP

Nail method. There are two ways in which you can now proceed: the first can be messy, since you may step on the string or get it tangled around your legs; also, there is less chance of making a good-looking loop this way. Nevertheless, it may be the easier way for you to make a loop that will be sure to hold. Find a nail, or something similar, whose diameter is larger than that of the hitchpin. If you are working alone, you will have to hammer the nail into the top of a workbench, near the edge; or put it in a vise, or hammer it into a board and clamp the board to the edge of a table. If someone is helping you, they can hold the nail or whatever device you may have come up with (like one of your jeweler's screwdrivers).

Hold the end of the string in one hand. With the other hand bring it around the nail at a point six or seven inches from the end. The hands are now in front of the body, the nail pulling the string into an angle less than ninety degrees (Figure 6-1). The closer the angle is to ninety degrees, the

tighter the loop will be, so check some of the loops on your instrument and try to replicate them. Be warned that very tight loops tend to break easily. Now make a loop by pulling gently on the wire and crossing your arms one over the other so that the angle formed is the same as it was previously (Figure 6-2). Now switch hands, so that the hand that was holding the short end is now holding the long, and vice versa. Once again pull, cross arms, and reverse hands. You now have two winds. Keep doing this until you have a loop of the proper length.

Now for the part I have not told you about: the winds have to form a double helix, or else the loop will not hold when you try to bring the string up to pitch. If one wire merely winds around the other it will slip; they have to wind around *each other*. The double helix is not difficult to achieve, and even if *some* of the winds are not double helices, the loop will probably hold.

String loops usually end with a section of straight turns. This is made by pulling the long part of the string straight out and winding the short part around it with the other hand. Since the string will tend to resist this winding, it may be necessary to hold the string close to the loop and restrain each wind with the index finger of the holding hand, while the other hand lets go so that it can reach under and grab the short end for another turn. When you have finished, either cut the unwanted portion off the end of the string with the wire cutter, or simply break it off by wiggling it vigorously against the winding. A completed string loop can be seen in Figure 6-3.

FIGURE 6-1.
*Pull the string into an angle of
ninety degrees or less.*

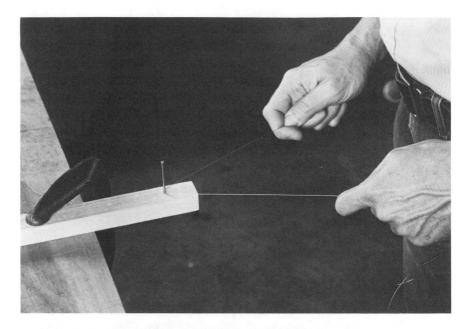

FIGURE 6-1.
*Pull the string into an angle of
ninety degrees or less.*

FIGURE 6-2.
Cross the arms, one over the other.

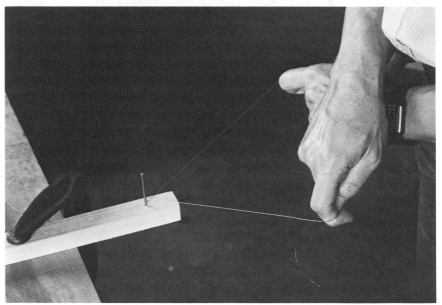

When the loop is finished, pull
it off the nail if it will fit easily
over the head; if not, free the
loop by pulling the nail out of
the bench.

To summarize:

1. Cut off an appropriate length
   of string.
2. Use a nail or something
   similar around which the
   loop will be made.
3. Hold the short end of the
   string in one hand, the other
   part in the other hand, and
   form an angle of less than
   ninety degrees around the
   nail.
4. Make the windings by passing one arm over the other,
   trading hands after each
   winding.
5. Finish off with straight
   turns.

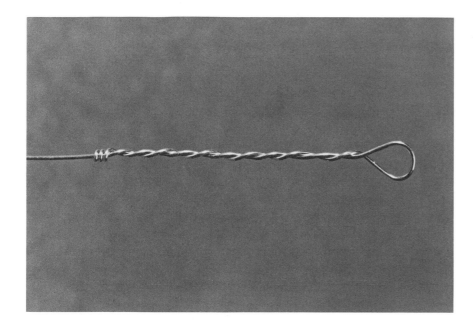

FIGURE 6-3.
A completed string loop.

Hook method. The second way of making a string loop is a lot faster, particularly if you are stringing up an entire instrument. It is also the more professional way. But neither of these attributes should concern you. Worry instead about coming up with a loop that will neither slip nor break. I am going to put this in italics because I want you to ponder it: *the professional builder makes thousands of string loops a year. You make one or two. There is little chance that your loops will look as good as his. Be happy if your loop holds.*

You will require a hook on a handle. If your instrument has threadless tuning pins, your tuning hammer probably has a hook on it; if not, get a cup hook and screw the end into a dowel about ⅜" in diameter and about four inches long.

Before you do anything else, put the hook and the wire cutter in your pocket. Then uncoil your string. Either give the coil itself to your helper to hold (Figure 6-4), or clamp the coil to the bench with a wire brake (felt under wood; Figure 6-5), or uncoil yet another foot of the string which your helper can wrap around his hand, or which you can tie to the bedpost. I have noticed that some harpsichord owners tend to treat string like a precious commodity, and try not to waste a single inch. String is relatively inexpensive. Keep a plentiful supply, and when you change one give yourself enough length to work with.

Walk away from the coil or the bedpost, end of the string in hand, being careful not to let the wire kink. When the string is extended to full length, take a couple of loops of the wire around the fingers of your left hand (left-handed people may want to reverse these directions). Or, if your hands are dry and your grip strong, you can simply hold the end in your fist. In your right hand you will have the hook (in your pocket, remember?), with which you will make the loop.

FIGURE 6-4.
The helper holds the coil.

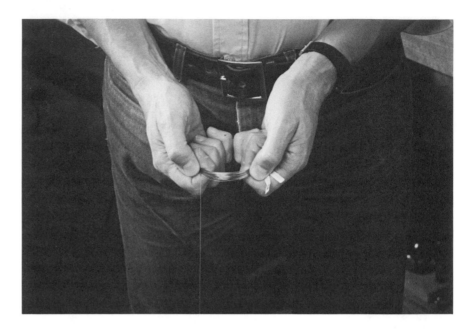

FIGURE 6-5.
A wire brake: a piece of felt under a block of wood.

Pull the wire taut, but not desperately so. Engage the wire with the hook about three inches from your left hand, and pull the wire into a less than ninety-degree bend (Figure 6-6). Remember, the closer the angle to ninety degrees, the tighter the loop will be, and a very tight loop will likely break. Keeping wire, short end, and hook all in the same plane, rotate the hook (which really means rotate the tuning hammer or the dowel), using the thumb and index finger. This is not easy to do with the heavier gauges of string, where you will have to press the shaft of the tuning hammer or the dowel against the heel of the palm of the hand with the other fingers, to hold it in place, while the thumb and index finger return to their initial position.

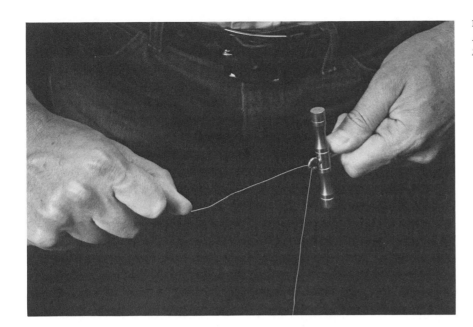

FIGURE 6-6.
Pull the string into an angle of ninety degrees or less.

The wire *must* form a double helix, just as in the nail method. The angle formed by the two parts of the wire must be bisected by the line of the shaft of the hook if a double helix is to result. This is controlled by the orientation of the hook, and the orientation of the hook is controlled by swinging the arm in or out from the body. Look at Figure 6-6 again.

Two other things have to be controlled at the same time. The first is the tension on both the long and short parts of the string; if they are very different it will be difficult, if not impossible, to make the double helix. The second is the angle that the two parts of the string form while the loop is being made. The more obtuse it is, the tighter the loop will be, particularly if string tension is high while the loop is formed. A loop that is too tight will compress the metal, and the loop may break when the string is pulled up to pitch.

Continue to rotate the hook until your loop is the desired size. The straight turns are simple. Release the tension of the left hand, thus putting the short end of the wire at a right angle to the coil and the string. Now rotate the hook again, winding the short end up around the long portion of the wire, until you have achieved the proper length. The short end can be removed by clipping it off with the wire cutter (still in your pocket, remember? And put it back there when you finish cutting), or by simply wiggling it back and forth against the straight turns.

With the nail method, you were finished at this point, but with the hook method there is one more step. Since the far end of the wire is fixed, either in someone's hands, clamped to a bench, or tied to the bedpost, every time you rotated that hook you put some twist into the wire. If you unhook the loop now, the string will tie itself up in a Gordian knot, and you will have a terrible mess. To avoid this, simply *reverse* the rotation of the hook until you have completely untwisted the wire. Then remove the loop from the hook.

To summarize:

1. Uncoil an appropriate length of string.
2. Immobilize the coil or the far end of the string in some way.
3. Holding the short end of the string in one hand, catch the string about three inches from the hand with the hook, and pull the string into an angle of less than ninety degrees.
4. Make the loop by rotating the hook.
5. Finish off with straight turns.
6. Rotate the hook backwards to remove the twist that you put into the wire.

There are other methods of making a string loop. The easiest is to use the nail method but simply wind the loose end around the long part of the string. This probably will not look anything like your other string loops, but it is worth it if the other methods defeat you. The loop can also be made with a button hook (if you can find one) or a cup hook in an electric drill.

WINDING THE STRING ON THE TUNING PIN

Hook the string loop over the appropriate hitchpin and bring the other end of the wire to the front of the instrument, ready to wind onto the tuning pin. This must be done with care; the wire will kink easily here. Ordinarily it is not necessary to have someone hold the loop on the hitchpin; it will stay there by itself as long as you keep some tension on the wire and do not lift the wire higher than necessary. Be careful to get the wire onto the proper bridge and nut pins; this can be particularly tricky when replacing a 4′ string, so check yourself carefully and then check again.

At this point the string is too long and needs to be cut to the proper length. Look at the way in which the string is coiled onto the other tuning pins. Some makers measure a specific length of string past the pin, clip it off, and make a coil with a full wind. Others do not use that much wire, but wind on a certain amount and spiral the string down to its proper position (Figure 6-7). Since you are replacing a single string, there is little chance that a fully wound coil can be duplicated, unless your builder has provided you with a table of distances past the pin to cut each gauge of wire. As a rule of thumb, allow yourself about a foot of wire past the pin in the treble, and decrease this amount to about four inches or less in the bass. Intermediate strings will be somewhere between those extremes. If you coil *too* much wire on a pin, some trial and error may be necessary. In any event, the goal is to wind the string onto the pin so that it neither slips nor breaks. Beauty should not be the issue here. Beautiful string coils do not make a harpsichord sound better.

Before proceeding, give the string a good solid tug. This will seat the hitchpin loop and stretch the string out a little. (If the string breaks as a result of this tug, it will break at the loop, and this simply means that you wound your loop too tightly or kinked the wire there somehow. Try again.) Now cut the string to its proper estimated length (wire cutter in your pocket). Hold the end of the string in your right hand and pick up the tuning pin in your left. You must *not* reverse hands in this operation.

Threaded or tapered tuning pins with a hole. If the pin has a hole for the string do the following: grasp the bottom of the pin with the left hand and hold it horizontally, across the body, with the hole to the right. Put the wire through the pin, entering the pin from the hole closest to your body; or, if you prefer a more geographic description, enter from the south and exit from the north. Be careful with that sharp wire; if the end protrudes from the pin for any distance it will stick you and you will bleed. Start rolling the pin north, away from you, so that the top of the pin is rolling under, and the wire is under the pin. Keep the wire taut, use both hands, and roll up your coil from the top of the pin toward the bottom. Before the pin reaches the hole in the wrestplank, compare what you have done so far to some of the coils around the string you are replacing. If it looks as though your coil is about as long as its neighbors-to-be, rotate the pin to an upright position, place it in its hole, and hammer it down to the level of the pins around it. Yes, *hammer* it down, with the hammer, which you laid down next to the harpsichord. The string should leave the coil from the right.

If you have substantially more

length to your coil, you will probably have too much down-bearing, and in the bass this excess angle could break the string. You could allow the string to wind back up on itself, but this will compress the metal against its own winds and can also cause the string to break. The best thing to do is to unroll the pin, cut an appropriate length of wire off the end, and try again. Do not worry if your coil has fewer winds than its neighbors. Before you reach the hole, simply turn the pin as you wind so that you get some wider spirals toward the bottom of the pin. Then insert the pin in its hole and hammer it in.

To summarize:

1. Hold the pin with the left hand, horizontally, with the hole to the right.
2. Feed the wire in from the front.
3. Make an appropriate coil by rotating the pin away from you.

4. Hammer the pin into the hole.

Tapered tuning pins without a hole. Why, you may wonder, would anyone make tuning pins without a hole through which to put the wire? Well, that is the way it was done on the antiques, and for some, that is reason enough. Aside from that, putting holes in tuning pins takes time, costs money, and winding the string onto a holeless pin is not at all difficult (except in the bass). Later I will describe how a hole can be put in a pin that does not have one; but do give the holeless pin a fair try before you pick up the drill.

There are two ways of winding the string around a holeless pin: the "no-tech" and the "low-tech" methods.

No-tech holeless pin string winding. The pin should be oriented as previously described: horizontally, with the top end of the pin facing right. Hold the flat por-

FIGURE 6-7.
Three types of string coils.

tions of the head of the pin with the thumb and forefinger of the right hand, thumb on top. Hold the end of the string with the left hand. Lay the pin over the string, at a right angle to it, at a point about four or five inches from the string's end. Slip the wire under the forefinger. You now have several inches of free wire in front of the pin, and the wire is held in place against the flat part of the underside of the pin with the forefinger (Figure 6-8). It is essential that the coil you are about to form begins on the flat surfaces of the pin. If it does not, it is guaranteed not to hold.

With the left hand, spiral the free end of the wire *clockwise*, down onto the pin (Figure 6-9). Neatness does *not* count here; this is only to hold things temporarily in position. Now grasp pin

FIGURE 6-8.
Hold the wire against the flat part of the underside of the pin with the forefinger. Your hands will appear as in this photo when you look down at them.

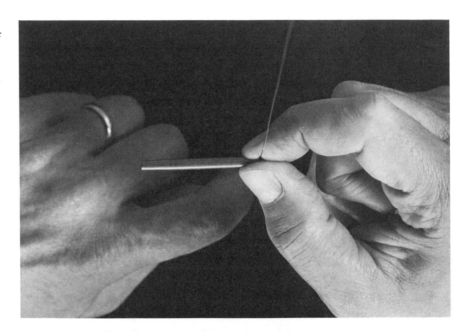

FIGURE 6-9.
Spiral the free end of the wire down the pin clockwise. Your hands will appear as in this photo when you look down at them.

and coils in the left hand, with the left index finger in contact with the top of the coil and the bottom portion of the flat of the head of the pin (Figure 6-10). Holding things together with the left hand, grasp the wire coming to the pin with the right hand, as close to the pin as is practical, and give it one wind over the pin *counterclockwise*. If you have done this properly the wire will have wound over itself once (Figure 6-11). If you have not managed to do this, back off and try again. If you still cannot do it, take another turn and see if you can get that one to wind over itself. Now take two or three more turns in the same direction, winding the string down the pin, keeping the emerging coil as tightly wound as possible. All these turns will be winding over

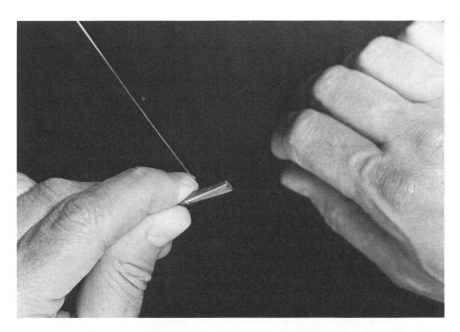

FIGURE 6-10.
Grasp pin and coils in the left hand, with the index finger in contact with the top of the coil. Your hand will appear as in this photo when you look down at it.

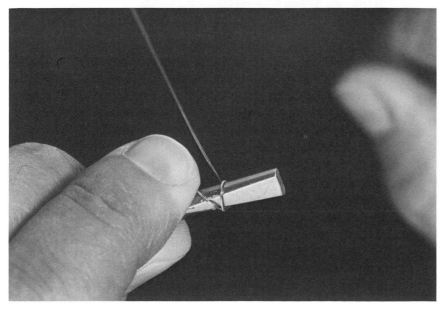

FIGURE 6-11.
The wire is wound over itself once. Your hand will appear as in this photo when you look down at it.

the string itself, as the first turn did.

Now grasp the pin and the three or four coils you have just made with the thumb and forefinger of the right hand, and with the left, wind three or four more turns onto the coil. There is a reason for the hand switch: you put three or four twists into the wire when you made those first coils; the left-handed turns take them out. Twists in the wire can result in a wire that has a strange sound and/or beats against itself.

Holding the pin now in both hands, give it another tug to seat the coil. You have now locked the coil onto the pin, and it will remain locked as long as you keep some tension on it. Turn the pin with both hands and coil down another three winds. The waste end of the wire can be removed either by wiggling it against the coil or cutting it off with your wire cutter (in your pocket). You will leave a nice sharp protruding end if you choose to cut it off, so better to twist it off if possible. Now finish the coil in the manner described for pins with holes. Remember, the string should leave the coil from the right.

To summarize:

1. Hold the pin over the wire with the thumb and forefinger of the right hand.
2. Spiral the short end of the wire down onto the pin with the left hand, clockwise.
3. Grasping the top of the coil with the left hand, use the right to take three or four counterclockwise winds back down over the wire.
4. Change hands, and make

three or four more turns to take out the twist.
5. Take three more turns, this time rotating the pin, and break off the waste end.
6. Finish the coil as previously described.

Low-tech holeless pin string winding. The low-tech method requires you to make another tool for which you need a dowel or a block of wood about ½" in diameter and about two inches long. Into one end drill a 5/32-inch hole, for a depth of ½". If your harpsichord has smaller pins for the 4′ strings, drill a ⅛-inch hole in the other end of the dowel. These are the only sizes I have ever seen for tapered tuning pins, but if your pins are larger or smaller than this, drill holes of the appropriate diameter.

Insert the end of the string into the hole in the dowel, and put the end of the pin in the same hole. The pin should lock the wire into the hole; if it does not, try drilling the hole just a little deeper. If that does not help, then the hole is too large. Get another dowel and drill a slightly smaller hole.

You are about to roll the string up the pin and back down. All motion will be in a clockwise or northerly direction.

Hold the dowel in the fingers of the left hand and the head of the pin in the fingers of the right. Rotate dowel and pin forward, winding the string quickly upward toward the head of the pin in a few wide spirals. When the spiral reaches the flat part of the head of the pin, and perhaps a little beyond, swing the dowel away from your body slightly, so that

the orientation (but not the direction) of the coil changes. Now, instead of wide spirals upward, we want to coil tight turns downward. The first of the downward turns must wind over the string of the upward spiral, and it must do it on the flat part of the pin. Of course, all the turns you make now will wind over the wire itself. After five or six turns remove the pin from the dowel, break or cut off the short end of the wire, and give the pin and dowel a tug to lock the coil onto the pin. Then proceed as in the no-tech method just described.[3]

To summarize:

1. Insert the string and the tuning pin in the hole in the dowel.
2. Clockwise, spiral up quickly to the flat part of the pin.
3. Continuing clockwise, start winding down with close turns.
4. After five or six turns, extract the pin from the dowel and break off the waste end of the wire.
5. Continue with the coil, as previously described.

Variations on these two methods are possible. One can roll the pin as in the low-tech method, but without the dowel; or one can simply lay a short length of wire against the pin and dispense with the step that spirals the wire up the pin. As long as the coil holds and the string does not break, you can, of course, use any method you wish.

We are now ready to adjust the downbearing. If the pin has been hammered down to its former height, and if the size of your coil is the same as its neighbors, the downbearing is probably correct. But check it anyway: if the string is to make firm contact with the nut, it must slant down as it leaves the nut for the tuning pin. If it does not, slack off some tension from the string and push the bottom wind down to its proper location. Use the index fingers of both hands, if you can. Pushing the coils with the fingernails is a useful technique. You can break a string doing all this if you are not careful. The trick is to slack off the string enough so that you can adjust the bearing easily, but not so much that the string loses its grip on the pin.

A steeper downbearing in the treble is of little consequence, but often the amateur string changer does not supply enough. Now is not the time to give up. Excess downbearing in the bass will lead to trouble, and the pin should be rewound. Again, proper downbearing is more important than beautiful coils and uniform pin heights.

If the pin seems loose, give it another tap with the hammer.

All that remains to do now is to tune the string up to pitch. There is no need to baby it—just bring it up there. If it is going to break it is going to break, and inching it up will not help. I am reminded of one of my customers who built a virginal kit some years ago. After stringing it, he took two weeks to bring it up to pitch. His caution was to no avail, since he had gotten his scale off in the treble. Until I fixed the instrument for him, he kept breaking strings—but all the while he thought it was because he was tuning them up too quickly!

Sooner or later you will have the experience of changing a string and finding that it will not come up to pitch. You get it *almost* there and it starts to slip. The problem is probably in your hitchpin loop: not enough double helices, if any at all. Please do not spend all day turning that tuning pin, hoping against hope that it will "catch" somewhere and hold. It will not. You must do it all over again, although there is one trick that you could try if there is enough string wound around the pin.

Get a helper to unwind the tuning pin with the tuning hammer, while you take the other end of the string off the hitchpin. Keeping some tension on the string, make another hitchpin loop, wasting as little wire as you can (obviously you will not be able to do this at the workbench). Have your helper unwind more string, reeling it out until you can reach the hitchpin with the new loop. You will probably find that you have to adjust the downbearing after this operation, but if you have saved yourself the time and effort to make another string, it will be worth it.

You may also find that nothing happens when you start to tune up the string—the wire is not winding at all. This is the unmistakable sign that you failed to lock the coil onto the flat part of the tuning pin. Pull the pin out, uncoil the wire and try again. Coiling that string a second time is not easy; it wants to go right back to where it was before. By all means try it, but be prepared to replace your replacement, if that is what your karma demands of you that day.

You may now replace the jack, jackrail, music rack, and music. The string will drop in pitch at first, as it stretches out. It can take several weeks before a brass string holds to the same degree as the others, so tune it frequently.

DRILLING A HOLE IN A TAPERED TUNING PIN

Tools and supplies needed: tuning pin, sharp center punch, hammer, electric drill or drill press, 1/16-inch drill bit, file, clamp.

You are going to deal that pin a sharp blow, so it should be placed on a surface that is sturdy, but one that will not be marred by it. It *can* mar your kitchen counter, but not if you put a piece of wood under the pin first. Clamp the pin and the piece of wood to the edge of the counter or table top. Place the center punch as low on the flat part as you can get it, and give it that sharp blow with the hammer. Now drill the hole. The hard drill steel will cut through the soft iron pin, but it takes more time than cutting through pine. A drop of oil at the point of the drilling will help cool and lubricate the process. Be sure to do the whole thing on a piece of wood, so that when the drill bit breaks through the pin, it will not drill a hole in your counter top. Doing this on a drill press is a lot easier, but not really any different. File off the metal crumbs at the exit hole, and your pin is ready for stringing.

Chapter 7 The Jacks

CHANGING A TONGUE

Tools and supplies needed: replacement tongue and jeweler's screwdrivers. If the jack is the conventional type, you will also need pliers, a straight pin, file, hammer, and wire cutter.

Tongues need to be changed because they break. Before you do anything else, find out why the tongue broke and take steps to see that it does not happen again (see chapter 11, *Jack Problems*). If your jack has a spring attached or molded to it, be careful not to break it or change its tension when you remove the broken tongue.

Tongues are of three types: those that have little nibs or protrusions designed to snap into corresponding depressions in the window of the jack; those made for axleless jacks, in which the tongue and spring are combined into a single assembly; and those for conventional jacks, made of either wood or plastic, in which the tongue swivels on an axle. The first of these would seem to present few problems—what could be simpler than snapping one tongue out and another one in? Difficulty arises only if the tongue is too loose or too tight, or does not swivel freely. If it is too loose, you can try compressing the walls of the jack's window, and if too tight, do the opposite; but the real problem may be that the tongue you picked up

was not moulded properly. Try another. If the tongue does not have the proper freedom (but is not too tight), look for bits and hairs of plastic somewhere. Check the little nibs and the depressions. They should be smooth and free of extraneous matter. When the tongue is working freely check the spring for its proper tension.

The tongues of axleless jacks also offer few problems. To remove the old tongue, place the jack on a block of wood or over the edge of a table, backside down (plectrum facing up), hanging over the edge so that the tongue will not be prevented from exiting. Push the tongue out of its seat from the back, through the little hole, with the smallest-size jeweler's screwdriver. This may enlarge the little hole slightly, but this is of no consequence.

The new tongue is simple to install, and problems arise only when the hole in which it seats is too tight or too loose. If the former, place the tongue over the hole and get it started into place with your pliers. It can then be pushed home with the largest of your jeweler's screwdrivers. If it is too loose, the little bulb-like protuberance on the tongue can be widened out with a hefty two-handed squeeze with the pliers. If it is still too loose, one might need to resort to some glue. Only something like epoxy cement or a cyano-acrylate glue (super glue) will bond plastic, and then you may someday have the problem of removing it. Glue should be a last resort and perhaps not a resort at all. If the tongue is *that* loose, try another.

The tongue should sit squarely in the window and can be straightened by pushing against the flat part of the bulb with an appropriate-size jeweler's screwdriver. Before installing a new tongue in an axleless jack, bend the spring so that tension is applied to it in the proper direction (toward the jack). As with all plastic jacks and tongues, check for bits and hairs of plastic.

The tongue is removed from the conventional jack, whether wood or plastic, by driving out the axle. This is done as follows: Inspect the axle in the jack, to see if its ends can be seen from both edges of the jack or if only one end is visible. If it can be seen from both edges, check to see if one end appears to be of larger diameter than the other. If so, set the jack down so that the edge with the narrower diameter faces up, with the axle over a hole or a slight depression; if the diameter of the pin is the same at both edges, set the jack down on either edge. Now take a common pin and cut off the first ½" (the sharp end) with your wire cutter. Smooth the cut end with the file. You have just made a pin punch. Place the punch over the axle and give it a tap with a hammer. The axle should move. Tap out ⅛" or so and pull it out from the opposite side with the pliers.

If the axle can only be seen from one edge of the jack, this means that when the maker drilled the jack for the axle, he drilled all the way through one side and only partially through the other. There are three things that you might try. First, see if you can spring the walls of the window in enough so that the end of the axle is forced out a little: it need emerge only enough to get your pliers on the end. Second, you can try pushing the axle all the way through with the pin punch, but be careful—you could split the side of the window. The third solution is the best: destroy the tongue. It is no good anyway or you would not be replacing it. Carve it to bits, break it up, or pulverize it. Then you can grab the pin in the middle with the pliers and work it out the side.

To install the new tongue, start the axle into the jack, place the tongue in position, catch the hole in the tongue with the axle, and drive it home. If you need a new axle, use a pin of proper diameter, cut off the ends after it is in place, and file the ends flush with the sides of the jack. The tongue should rotate freely on its axle—in fact, it is always a good idea to check the tongue on the axle before you put it in the jack. If it is tight, make a reamer out of a pin by cutting off its tip, setting the file down on it, and rolling it along the workbench. Now run the reamer through the tongue, twirling it around as you do. Again, check for bits and threads of material. If the tongue swivels freely on its axle while outside the jack, but not in it, this is a sign that some little bit of something in the window of the jack is in the way. Put the tongue back in and work it back and forth, twisting as you turn. Be careful not to close up the window and bind the sides of the

tongue in this way. As always, check the spring for proper tension.

CHANGING A DELRIN PLECTRUM

Tools and supplies needed: replacement plectrum, voicing block, pliers, knife, jeweler's screwdrivers.

Despite earlier statements about plectra lasting for up to a decade, they do break, usually because either the plectrum or the jack has been mishandled. But a plectrum can also get pushed through from the back of the tongue and cut back until it is too short to do any more good. An improperly cut plectrum will break, too, so when you make the replacement, try to do it correctly.

In the operations to be described, please be sure to take the configuration of your particular jack into account. If placing the jack in a recommended position will crush the spring, or damage the jack or tongue in some other way, then *stop*, and figure out another position for the jack, in which the prescribed operation can be carried out.

Removing an old plectrum from a tongue sometimes can be frustrating, particularly when dealing with a plastic tongue that has a death grip on the quill. Take your voicing block and place it behind the jack so that it supports the tongue but is below the mortise in which the plectrum is jammed. Hold this assembly firmly in one hand, thumb on the face of the jack, other fingers behind (Figure 7-1). With the other hand, take the

FIGURE 7-1.
Supporting the jack and tongue on the voicing block prior to removing the plectrum.

small pliers and grasp the plectrum tightly at a point *just in front of* the tongue—say, within $1/32$ to $1/16"$. Push forward with the pliers, and that should free the plectrum. You may have to take another purchase on it and push again, but if it moved the first time, your plectrum is as good as out.

The plectrum may not want to come out that easily. A plectrum sunk deep into the mortise, one that has been pushed through from the back several times, can be particularly recalcitrant. If the mortise is tapered, you have no choice but to push it out from the front and remove it from the rear, as just described; but if the mortise is straight-sided, it may be possible to push the plectrum all the way out from the back and remove it from the front, using one of the jeweler's screwdrivers. However, do this only to plastic tongues, and only if it appears that the tongue will not be damaged by it. Although plastic seems to have enough resiliency

to grab onto the next plectrum that is jammed into the mortise, it is not worth taking this chance with a wooden tongue. You could widen the mortise beyond usefulness, but it is more likely that you will split the tongue. In the case of a wooden tongue, the plectrum *must* be pushed out from the front and removed from the rear.

The plectrum may refuse to budge for other reasons, or the pliers may slip, or the plectrum may be so thin that it buckles. If you cannot push it through from the front with the pliers, as described, then cut off the front of the plectrum, flush with the face of the tongue. Lay the jack on the voicing block, front up, and set the block on the table, with the mortise just clearing the top of the block. Hold it all together firmly. Now push the remaining piece out from the *front* with a jeweler's screwdriver. This technique can be used with plastic tongues as well.

Some builders supply various

thicknesses of Delrin plectra. If there is any question in your mind about the appropriate thickness for the replacement, choose the larger one. Thicker Delrin can always be made into thinner quills. The new plectrum is inserted from the rear. If it has a bit of a curve, the concave side should face up. Lay the jack face down on the voicing block and push the Delrin quill home with the flat of one of the jeweler's screwdrivers.

If your jack has an adjustment screw for the tongue (or a voicing screw, as it is sometimes called), be sure that you turn it out so that the tongue can be fully supported by the voicing block when you place the jack face down. After the plectrum is in, use the voicing screw to put the tongue in a median position, and *leave* it there. A voicing screw is not really for voicing. Because these screws have been so abused by owners, few builders use them any more.

The plectrum must be tight enough in the tongue so that there is no chance of it working its way out, yet not so tight that it could not be pushed through a little more from the back. If the quill seems to be a little too wide, and resists seating itself all the way in the slot, push it in as far as it will go, and cut the rest off with the voicing knife, flush with the back of the tongue. Use some judgment here; some tongues have quill mortises that are slightly tapered, others do not. It might be smart to leave just a little of the quill protruding from the rear of the tongue. It will be just that much easier to push it through if it becomes necessary to do so. But leave *just*

a little bit: if much protrudes, the back of the quill may catch on the adjacent string, and then you will have trouble.

VOICING A DELRIN
PLECTRUM

Tools and supplies needed: The same ones you got out for changing the plectrum.

Voicing. The very mention of the word is enough to strike terror in the hearts of some harpsichord owners (and kit builders, too). Other writers have attempted to describe this process, even though it is held to be a skill that cannot be transmitted through words; but perhaps no one has attempted to be quite this detailed. I feel confident that anyone who reads and absorbs the information that follows will be able to voice a plectrum satisfactorily.

Every builder has his own way of voicing a plectrum, and I have mine. It is not my intent to tell you my way, because you will want to cut *your* plectrum so that it ends up looking like the ones in *your* instrument, not mine. And once again, I must warn you: cutting only a few quills a year, it is unlikely that you will be able to make them look as neat and beautiful as those cut by your builder. But you *can* make a quill that sounds as good to the ear, and feels as good to the fingers, as those around it. If done properly, it will last a long, long time—perhaps even a decade. There is no secret to it; in fact, all I can really tell you is, make it look just like the ones around it (yes, just like my

friend, cutting her first plectrum on her breadboard).

Let me offer some general admonitions before you make that first cut:

1. Do the voicing under a good, bright light, and angle your work as necessary so that every cut is fully illuminated. In his kit construction manuals, David Way used to say that voicing was such a tactile art that even a blind person could do it. I'm sure he was right, but I think you will do better in the light.

2. Be sure that you can see what is going on as clearly as possible. Our eyes lose the ability to focus over a wide range of distance as we get older, and many of us who wear glasses eventually find that we can see close work better by taking our glasses off. My voicing has gone through stages: glasses, no glasses, bifocals, two different types of magnifying viewers, no glasses once more, and finally trifocals. Do whatever you need to do to get up close to your voicing, with as much visual clarity as possible.

3. Brace the voicing block and the arm that holds it against the body, to provide a solid platform on which to cut. The hands should be about twelve inches away from the eyes.

4. Keep the thumb of the hand holding the voicing block as low on the block as possible. Delrin is slippery stuff, and it is easy for the knife to slip. Assume that it *will* slip, and arrange *beforehand* that no fingers will be in the way. I can assure you that you will not fail to heed this advice more than once.

5. Be sure your blade is sharp. I know I just went through that in

chapter 5, but it is worth saying again, for two reasons: first, you will ruin plectra with a dull blade; and second, it is much easier to cut yourself with a dull blade than it is with a sharp one. Dull blades slip and go out of control; sharp blades are more likely to do what they are told.

6. Hold the knife the way you hold a pencil, up close to the blade. You cut the Delrin with the tip of the blade only: put the middle finger on the side of the blade, leaving only the tip of the blade exposed. Putting your finger on the blade is not as dangerous as it sounds, and properly done, you will come to no harm. The arm holding the knife also must be braced against the body. Furthermore, the last two fingers of the hand holding the knife are braced against the voicing block. All this bracing assures maximum control of the knife; it also assures that if the knife does slip it has nowhere to go.

7. *Cut with the bevel of the blade contacting the work.* This is important! It is one of the first things learned by any craftsman who works with knives, chisels, or gouges. Unless the bevel of your blade rides on the Delrin, you will slice *into* your plectrum rather than shave off the nice, thin sliver you intended (see Figure 7-2, and remember that the bevel is that slanted part on either side of the bottom of the blade whose junction forms the cutting edge).

8. Do not attempt to cut the plastic to final form with one slice; rather, take several thin cuts, which are easier to control.

9. Look closely at the quills that your builder has cut. Aside from cuts at the very tip, it is likely that the cuts started back at the base of the quill where it emerged from the tongue. This is not always so easy to do, but it is important, since any sudden change in the cross section of the plectrum is a point of weakness, where the plectrum eventually will fail. Remember what we said in chapter 1, that the quill takes

FIGURE 7-2.
Cutting the Delrin. Note that the middle finger is pressed firmly against the blade, and the bevel of the blade is riding on the Delrin.

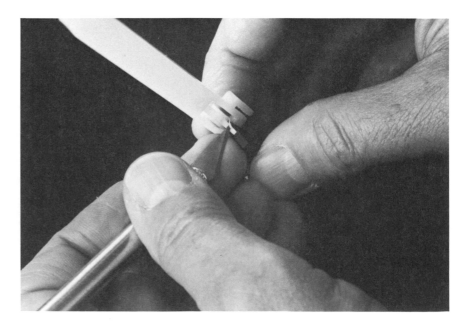

on the approximate shape of a section of a parabolic arc as it bends. It cannot do this if it is not thinned evenly from base to tip. If you cannot angle your knife blade in such a way that it starts the cut at the base of the quill, then make your cut in two parts, one cutting forward from as far back as you can, and the other from that point back to the tongue.

10. Cut the tip of the plectrum on a slant of about 30 degrees. Again, take a look at some examples of your builder's voicing.

Figure 7-3 illustrates most of these points. Note that both arms are braced against the body, that the voicing block is well supported, that the thumb is low, that the work is close to the eyes, that the knife is held close to the blade, that the middle finger is on the blade for control, that the bottom two fingers are braced against the voicing block, that only a thin sliver is being removed from the plectrum, that the cut is being made with the

tip of the blade, that the bevel of the blade is in contact with the Delrin, and that the cut has been started from the base of the plectrum.

None of this is as difficult as it may sound, and nothing should be gripped or braced with such force that tension is created. If you have the proper grip on everything, you will find that you have excellent control over the knife. I cannot guarantee that you will not waste a plectrum now and then. Occasionally I ruin a quill, and that usually starts me on a track where I destroy several until I finally get my rhythm back. If you slice through a quill, simply remove it, replace it, and start again.

One final admonition: In this section I describe common methods of holding and using tools. If you have some other way of holding the knife or bracing the voicing block that is more comfortable for you, or if it gives you better control, then do it, as long as it works and is safe. Or, if you

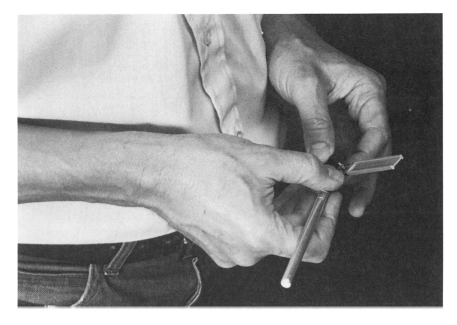

FIGURE 7-3.
The voicing position.

find that some method given herein gives you better results if you modify it in some way, then again, do it. The object of voicing is to make the harpsichord sing beautifully—*not* to see how long you can make an X-Acto knife blade last.

The voicing method I have described involves cutting toward you, which gives you more control than cutting away from you. Nevertheless, there is a way of holding the jack, block, and knife that involves cutting away from the body. I will describe it briefly because you just may find it more comfortable; or, even if not, it may come in handy for a particular cut. The jack and the voicing block are held in the same way as before, except that the thumb is now in back of the jack and the other fingers in front. Hold the knife in the manner previously described, like a pencil, with the middle finger on the blade. You may find this a useful position for bringing your cuts back to the base of the plectrum (in which case you *would* be cutting toward the body).

People who have trouble handling the voicing knife sometimes resort to scraping, rather than cutting, to remove material from the plectrum. Scraping will not give you the smooth surface you need at the tip, nor will it allow you to take material off evenly. Do not succumb to the temptation to scrape, no matter what your brother-in-law (the expert—the one who has built one kit) tells you.

Cutting the plectrum to length. Both Dowd and Herz talk about "ghosting" in the maintenance manuals they supply for their in-

struments.[1] A new quill is ghosted by turning the register *off* to the point where all the plectra just barely brush up against the strings (making only a "ghost" of a sound). The new plectrum is then cut to the same length, so that it also ghosts. Ghosting is a useful procedure when regulating an entire register, and professionals use it all the time. However, it is very difficult to cut a quill to that precise a length when you really do not know what you are doing. Distances on a plectrum look enormous when the jack is in the instrument, but minuscule when it is out; proper judgment is hard to learn. I suggest that you leave the register in its *on* position, and cut the quill longer than you think it is going to end up. It is a lot easier to cut away at the tip until it protrudes slightly past the string, than it is to estimate its length so precisely that it will ghost. Besides, as you will see shortly, there is another reason why I think you will be better off having a little length to play with.

Having estimated its proper length (and perhaps having measured or even marked it), now cut the plectrum to length. For this operation I like to use the butt end of the voicing block because it helps to have a little more surface with which to work on that first cut. Also, I suggest that you hold the blade like a scalpel, rather than like a pencil, for this step. It will give you a little more control when you cut down through the plastic (Delrin plectra are extruded under high pressure, which gives them a "grain." Most of the cutting you do will be along the grain, but

cutting off the tip is cutting against the grain). Also, this first cut should be made with the middle of the blade, rather than the tip. This part of the blade is a little more solid, and we save the sharpness of the tip for the more precise cutting.

Keeping all this in mind, and remembering my words of caution, grasp jack and block in the proper hand, jack upside down, at the back of the block, facing forward, with the top of the plectrum lying on the cutting surface. Jack and block are held in position with the thumb in front (keep it low!) and the other fingers in the back. With the other hand, place the middle of the blade on the plectrum and turn the blade at an angle (remember, we want to have an angled cut at the tip of the quill, so you might as well start now). All this can be seen in Figure 7-4. Rather than cutting off the tip by trying to slice right through, press down and at the same time rock the blade from side to side. The plectrum is now cut to length.

Thinning the plectrum. Before doing anything else, drop the jack into the register and try the note. It may be satisfactory just as it is, but miracles do not happen that often (although they happen more often in the bass, where plectra need to be thicker). However, you must try to make some estimation of its sound. It is probably too loud, but will it be acceptable when the tip is cut off a little more, to give the plectrum its proper length? Or is it raucous as well as overly loud, signifying that the plectrum is going to need some thinning?

Once again, take a look at the

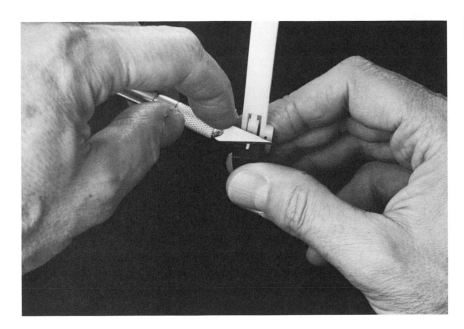

FIGURE 7-4.
Cutting the plectrum to length.

other plectra around the one you are replacing. Try to reconstruct the cuts your builder must have made in order to arrive at the plectrum's final configuration. Did he cut only on the flat surface of the quill (Figure 7-5); or did he thin the quill from the sides, thus changing its plan view (Figure 7-6); or did he thin it by taking material off the arrises (the edges, where the sides and the flat surface join; Figure 7-7)? Or did he use a combination of two or all three of these cuts? Figure it out insofar as is possible, and try to do it that way. But do it one cut at a time. If you try to cut directly to some concept of what you think the plectrum should look like, you may very well cut too much. Let your eye be your guide, but let your ear and your fingers be your judge.

A professional, who voices daily, knows exactly how much material to take off that quill, and with two or three slices of his sharp knife, the deed is done.

Someone like me, who voices four or five harpsichords a year, needs to sneak up on the desired sound and touch, so I need to cut and try. You, who may voice four or five *quills* a year, need to be very conservative with your cutting.

This means not that you should give up and settle for a louder-sounding or harder-feeling plectrum, but that you must be prepared to keep at it until you have the quill where you want it. Sometimes it is amazing how little material need be removed when approaching a quill's optimum configuration; other times it seems that you cut and cut, with no change at all. It would be fair to say that, for your purposes, every quill is a law unto itself.

You will remember that I suggested that the quill be left a little overlong. This gives you something of an insurance policy. The tendency among amateur voicers is to scoop material out of the middle of the plectrum,

FIGURE 7-5.
A cut on the flat surface of the quill.

leaving a thicker cross section at the tip. Knife and fingers seem to conspire in this direction. But there *must* be a continuous thinning; just a little thickness at the tip—so slight that perhaps you cannot even see it—and the quill will refuse to return under the string. Then you have a hanger, and no matter what you do, you will have it until you remove that thick part. But if the quill is overlong, cutting off the tip (at an angle, remember) will neatly remove any thickness you might inadvertently have left.

After you voice a few quills, you will see that the cutting is often done in two stages: the first brings the quill down, near to its final configuration; the second is a series of cuts that brings it to its finished form. So when you have finished those preliminary cuts, the ones that take off most of the meat, cut the tip to size and be very careful not to make any scoops on subsequent cuts.

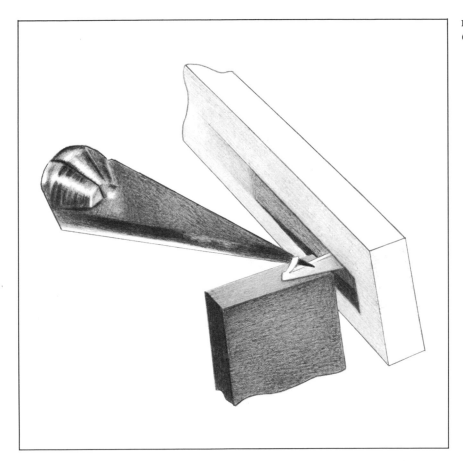

FIGURE 7-6.
Cuts on the sides of the quill.

Another place where the over-long quill gives you some insurance is in making cuts on the sides and/or the arrises. These are not easy cuts—sometimes the knife will dig in and take out more material than you really want (particularly if the blade is dull). If this does happen, you can often trim the plectrum back into some sort of shape. It may come to a point and perhaps sound too weak, but when you cut off the tip, it may be just fine. If it is still too pointed or too weak, it may yet be possible to save the plectrum by pushing it through from the back.

Pushing a little more of the quill through from the back is a handy thing to know how to do.

Lay the jack on the voicing block, back facing up, with the plectrum hanging off the edge of the block. The block can be either held in the hand (do not forget to brace the arms against the body, and the block against the chest) or placed on a table. If you have a little of the back of the plectrum still protruding from the mortise, just press it in with the flat of the blade of one of your larger jeweler's screwdrivers. Otherwise, use a jeweler's screwdriver whose blade fits the quill mortise as closely as possible. Brace your arms, fingers, and anything else you can; you will have to push, yet not push, because if you follow through on your push, you will push the

FIGURE 7-7.
Cuts on the arrises of the quills.

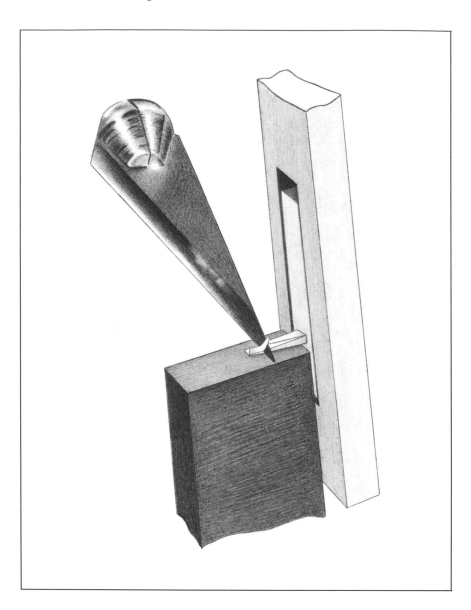

plectrum right through, out the front of the jack. It will probably happen to you more than once, but keep at it, because the ability to strengthen the quill by pushing it out and cutting it back a bit can be useful.

The perception of distance is most confusing here. Pushing the quill through by what appears to be the most minute amount results in a surprisingly obvious lengthening when the quill gets back under the string. In fact,

you may find that you have pushed too much out; then you must slice a little off the tip. Now your plectrum may be too strong, requiring a little more thinning.

Your plectrum is now voiced. It may look a little ragged; the cuts may have been minute scoops, rather than nice, long slivers; perhaps it could have been a more even thinning; it may not assume the shape of a perfect parabolic section just before it plucks. No matter—with practice you will get better at it, and even if you do not, you have learned to cut a serviceable if not a perfect quill.

But you are not finished yet. You must check the quill in its off position, check the stagger, and double-check that the quill is not hanging up on the string.

Take another look at the plectrum length. It may look fine plucking the string, but it must miss the string when the register is turned off. If it plucks or ghosts in the off position, it will have to be cut back a little. This may make the plectrum a little too stiff, in which case you will have to shave off a little more material.

If your instrument has more than one choir of strings, you need to check the stagger, also called the firing order or the timing. For example, if your harpsichord is disposed $2 \times 8'$, the two strings that sound the same pitch must pluck one after the other when the two choirs are coupled. If they fire at the same instant, the pluck will offer considerably more resistance than is necessary. Presumably you voiced your new plectrum to play with the same resistance as the one it replaced, so you should have little or no trouble with the stagger. But check it out, nevertheless: put all the ranks on and push the key down slowly. The string of each rank should be heard individually, at about the same rate, and in the same order, as those around it. If the stagger on the note in question does not feel or sound right, consult *Adjusting the stagger* in chapter 9. If your jack has a top adjustment screw, you could use it for some of

these last adjustments, as long as you do not move the tongue very far from its median position.

Finally, although you *think* your freshly voiced quill is doing a good job of returning under the string, you will never really know until you give it the slow test. Strike the note, let the string come to rest, and, as slowly as possible, let the jack down and allow the plectrum to slide around and under the string. It should do it willingly. If it cannot pass the slow test, you can be sure that it will hang up at the most crucial moments in your playing, and it will serve you right for allowing your harpsichord to get away with a hanger. If you have a hanger and you are certain that the tip is not protruding so far that it cannot return, and that there is no thickness or roughness at the tip of the plectrum, you will have to consult the section, *Hangers*, in chapter 11.

Now give the quill the ultimate test, the only one that counts. Play some music, and see how it sounds and how it feels. You may want to make it a little stronger or weaker when you hear it in a musical context, but after having done all the preceding, you should have no problem doing so.

CHANGING AND VOICING A CROW QUILL[2]

Tools and supplies needed: a supply of primary feathers from mature crows (not from crows who have died of old age), voicing block, knife.

You cannot replace a crow quill

if you have only one feather, unless you happen to be lucky. You must have a variety of sizes. Talk to your builder; if he cannot supply you with crow quill, he should be able to tell you where to get it. In contrast to Delrin, where one can use essentially the same size plectrum blank, and cut it to a strength appropriate for the string to be plucked, a crow quill is chosen for its relative strength or weakness, and little or no cutting is (or can be) done to it.

Strong feathers produce strong plectra, good for bass notes. Weak feathers are the opposite, useful for treble notes and for the 4' choir. The tip of the feather produces weaker quills; the base of the feather, stronger ones. The white part of the feather is not used at all, only the black. Replacing a single quill can sometimes be a problem if the piece of quill you want is in the middle of a feather. In that case, simply cut off the front part of the feather and save it for a time when weaker plectra are desired.

Set the feather down on the table, hold it down by the white part, and trim its sides for at least the part of the feather you are going to use for the quill. Your knife will need to be just as sharp for this as it is for slicing Delrin. Now cut yourself a plectrum in the end of the feather, and remove the pith found in the stalk. Back in the heyday of the harpsichord, people cut their own writing pens from feathers. Nobody had trouble cutting a harpsichord plectrum—you simply cut a pen, but instead of dipping it in ink you stuck it in a jack and made a plectrum out of it.

Insert the quill (feather still attached) into the tongue mortise. The feather should have been cut in such a way that the end will protrude more than actually needed, and the base of the quill will have jammed itself in the mortise with reasonable pressure. You may have to cut down the sides of the quill in order to get it into the mortise; or, you may have to leave some of the pith on the plectra intended for 4′ strings, in order to get enough pressure to hold the quill in place. If the quill is simply not wide enough for the mortise in an 8′ jack, you may have to make your quill further up the feather where the stalk is bigger. Cut the plectrum off at the rear of the tongue, leaving a little material projecting from the rear. If the plectrum needs to be a little tighter, jam this end in a little more. You now have a plectrum.

Drop the jack into the register and see how the quill plays. If it is just too weak, insert another quill from a stronger feather. If it seems all right or just a little strong, trim the tip to length on the voicing block, at the same angle (about 30 degrees) recommended for Delrin. The quill may sound loud and harsh; if so, trim the sides slightly, but only just slightly. Try to remember that any cutting you do on the quill at this point is likely to reduce its life. If it is still not sounding right, trim just the slightest amount from the underside of the quill (which is facing you at the moment). Do this as smoothly as possible, and be sure not to leave a thickness at the tip. This is about all you can do in the way of voicing on crow quill. You can cut more quill away, but if you do, you will very

soon lose the quill entirely; it will simply come apart.

The quill may not want to pass the slow test. Rub a little olive oil or mineral oil on both sides of the quill with a cotton-tipped stick (do not get oil on the damper), and wipe off the excess with a dry one. The quill should now return without any problem. This oil treatment is recommended monthly for *all* crow quills, both to ensure that the quills escape properly, and to prolong their lives. Robert Greenberg recommends mineral oil, slightly thinned with turpentine if necessary, applied *yearly*. I have heard other oils recommended as well. Whatever you use, the idea is to keep the quills pliable with a non-drying oil, and to renew them as necessary.

As always, the ultimate test is to play the harpsichord.

REPLACING A DAMPER

Tools and supplies needed: roll or piece of damper felt, knife, scissors, pliers.

Dampers do wear out; the heavier the jack and the thinner the string, the sooner the damper will need to be replaced. The most frequent problem is a little groove cut into the bottom of the damper, caused by the damper dropping on the string countless times. When this happens, the bottom of the jack sits on the key, and the damper will work only intermittently, if at all. Or sometimes the damper gets all crooked and is no longer able to do its job.

Most jacks have the simple, classical provision for a damper:

the damper slot. To replace, simply pull out the old damper. Do not cut a new one yet, but insert the end of the piece or roll of felt into the slot, pulling it down from both sides, so that at eye level, the bottom of the damper felt seems to be just above the top of the plectrum. The new damper should be noticeably longer than the plectrum. When the position of the damper cloth looks right, cut it off at the back of the jack with the voicing knife, flush to the jack, to avoid any later complications of fuzz from the back of the damper damping another string. Now drop the jack into its slot. Look at its neighbors. The damper is probably too long, and should be trimmed squarely with the scissors. It must damp the string in both the on and off positions,[3] but it must not reach over and damp the string of the next choir as well.

Some makers cut their 4′ dampers so that the 4′ strings are undamped when in the off position, allowing the 4′ strings to vibrate sympathetically. Follow the pattern of your other 4′ dampers.

Next make sure that the damper actually damps. The best way to check this is to pluck the string with the fingernail, while the jack is in its rest position, and the damper is contacting the string. You should be rewarded with a damped, dull clunk. If you hear a ringing, pull the damper down a little with the pliers or the fingers and try the test again. Now give the jack the slow test. If it hangs up, it is probably because the damper is too low, contacting the string before the quill has a chance to return. If so, pull it up a little. The damper should now be regulated; if you are still having problems with it, refer to the sections *Jack height and damper setting*, and *Leaking dampers*, in chapter 11.

REPLACING A BOAR BRISTLE IN A WOODEN JACK

Tools and supplies needed: boar bristle, pin, knife.

The jack has two fine holes drilled through it. The first goes straight through the jack, from front to back, about 1/4" below the tongue. The other is drilled through the bottom of the tongue mortise, and meets the first, in-side the jack, to form a "T". The bristle is inserted into the first hole, from the front of the jack. As it passes the second hole, which meets it at that point, it is diverted to the second hole with the pin, and emerges from the mortise. If all has gone smoothly, the bristle should now be riding in the groove on the back of the tongue, although it is too long. Cut it off at the very top of the groove with a flick of the voicing knife. With your pliers or tweezers, bend up the very end of the bristle, away from the tongue slot. This is done to prevent the point of the bristle from catching in the groove. Figure 7-8 should make all of this clear.

FIGURE 7-8.
Replacing a boar bristle.

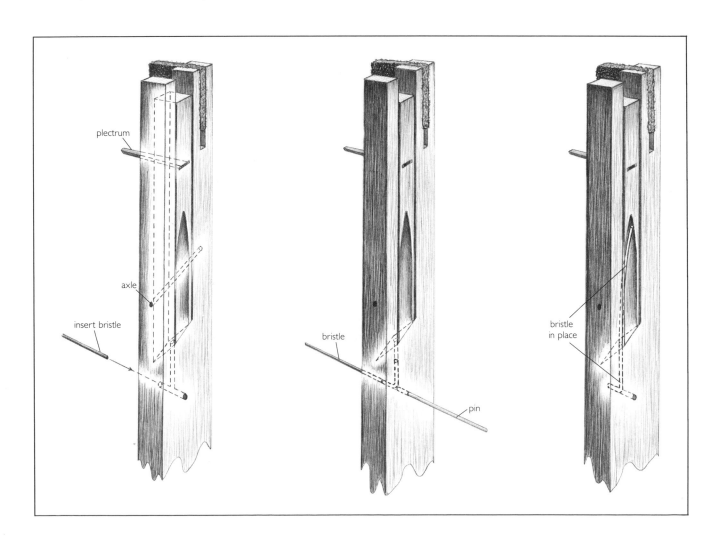

REGULATING THE HEIGHT OF THE JACK

In theory, once properly set, the length of a jack should never need further modification (seasonal adjustments should be made by raising or lowering the back of the keyboard, not the individual jacks). However, almost any kind of action regulation may call for a change in the height of a jack or two. End pins, as these adjusting screws are called, were universally employed by the revival builders and proved useful enough so that they are still found on many modern jacks. Antique jacks did not have a screw-like method of regulating jack height, and many modern builders do not use regulating screws here. Adjusting the height of a jack that has an end pin is simple: turn the screw in or out. Some require a screwdriver, some a pliers, some a turning rod, and some can be turned by hand. If you are working with a long end pin that requires pliers to turn it, be careful not to roughen or otherwise mar the pin, because it is likely that the pin itself, rather than the body of the jack, runs through the lower guide. Pad the pliers if necessary. Some builders who used to use end pins no longer do so, because their customers cranked the pins in and out with such happy abandon that the harpsichord was driven much further out of regulation than anything the end pin was designed to correct. Many builders abandoned the so-called voicing screw for the same reason. End pins and voicing screws can be useful aids but must be used wisely.

Antique jacks were usually regulated with sealing wax, a commodity then as ubiquitous as bird-quill pens. You may use sealing wax if you wish, but only on wooden jacks; it will not stick to plastic. For plastic jacks, use something that will adhere—historically unauthentic tape or something similar. Masking tape works on both plastic and wooden jacks. But mark this well: it must be masking tape purchased in an auto supply store, intended for paint masking in auto body work. The kind of tape you get in a paint store or hardware store simply does not have enough adhesive. Eventually, however, the adhesive will dry out and the masking tape will fall off. I have had good luck with masking tape, but if you have some other method of lengthening the jack, by all means use it.

To make a jack a little longer, try the following technique. First be sure that the bottom of the jack is smooth and straight. If it is not, make it so with your file. From a roll of ½" or ¾" masking tape, cut off a piece about four inches long. Stick about ½" of it to a table, the rest of it hanging over the edge. Cut the piece in half, and place the free half over the other half, forming a double thickness of tape. Cut that in half, and join them as before. Now sticking to your table is a one-inch long piece of four-thickness masking tape. Trim up one edge, then cut a strip no thicker than the width of your jack. Stick the end to the bottom of the jack, and cut the rest off with the scissors (Figure 7-9). Try the jack. If necessary, use another four-ply tape, stuck right on top of the first.

Generally, it is not worth fussing with anything less than four layers of tape at a time. The action needs to have some slack built into it if it is to continue to operate through the day-to-day changes the harpsichord undergoes. If if is too "tight," it will feel great today, but it may be unplayable tomorrow. I learned that lesson with the first harpsichord I built. The action was so tight that the instrument played if you so much as breathed on it. But the next day it was unplayable. I went through all my adjustments again, to bring it to its former state of "perfection." The next day—same thing. After three days of repeating all my adjustments, with dip, jack height, damper location, and quill lap, I finally got smart and put a little looseness into the system. It worked fine from then on.

Another way to lengthen the jack is to put card stock under the felt cloth on the backs of the keys (rather than lengthening the jack, this raises the back of the key). Although this method is more permanent than masking tape, and therefore might be considered more desirable, it cannot be used with transposing keyboards, where the tops of the backs of the keys must all be the same height.

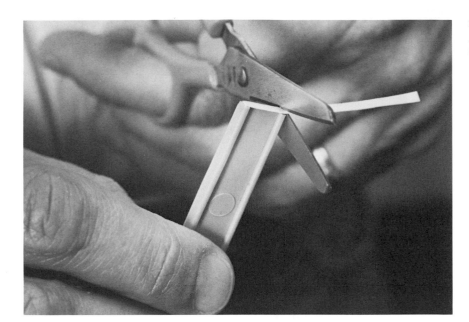

FIGURE 7-9.
Lengthening the jack with masking tape.

Chapter 8   The Action

The word "action" includes the mechanisms involved in translating the touch of the finger to the pluck of the string: the keyboard and all its parts, the jacks and their components, the registers, the jackrail, and, if a two-manual instrument, the coupler. But the word also implies a relationship between these parts, and in this wider sense, action refers to their collective functioning.

Your builder was responsible for the action of your instrument. He voiced the choirs, he set the plectrum lengths, the dip and the stagger, and he should have done these things in such a way that they would not be undone by minor changes in temperature and humidity. Nevertheless, the wood in your harpsichord is losing extractants and drying out as the instrument matures. Eventually the wood tires and is no longer capable of expanding and contracting to the degree it did when it was put into the instrument. And while these changes are taking place, the harpsichord is being subjected to the climatic extremes of North America. So no matter how fine a job your builder did, the action, which is sensitive to these changes, is going to need regulating from time to time. If you put it off for very long it will probably get worse.

REMOVING THE KEYBOARD

It may never be necessary for you to remove the keyboard, but there are some regulating procedures in which it must be done. If you have a transposing keyboard, put it in the non-transposing, or normal position. Then I suggest that you remove all the jacks. The rule of thumb is, remove the jacks from any keyboard that has a rack; but a *better* rule of thumb is, remove all the jacks, rack or not. That is the safest course, particularly if removing keyboards is a new operation for you. Nevertheless, on a two-manual instrument it may not be necessary to remove the front 8′ jacks—it depends on whether or not the upper keyboard guides on a rack. This is easy enough to see by peering into the keyboard through the slot normally covered by the name batten.

When a professional removes jacks, he places them in *jack trays*, shallow trays about the width of the length of a jack and long enough to hold a complete rank. You do not need anything that elaborate. A board of appropriate size, a piece of heavy cardboard, a shelf from a bookcase, or a small table—anything like this will do, as long as it is long enough and wide enough and does not invite the jacks to tumble to the floor like pick-up sticks. If necessary, walk the jacks one by one over to the dining room table. Keep the various sets of jacks separate from each other, and do not try to put more than one set on the same "tray." I am certain that it is not necessary to caution you not to put the jacks down on their faces, thus mashing the plectra and destroying the proper tension of the spring.

While you have the jacks out, examine them and see if your builder has numbered them. Although some builders do not do this, it is a good idea, and *you* should do it. It might save you a lot of grief sometime (like when the neighbor's kid knocks over a table full of jacks and you then have a bunch of pick-up sticks on the floor), because when the plectra are voiced and adjusted for each individual string the jacks are no longer interchangeable. Wooden jacks can be written on with pencil. Plastic jacks have to have the gloss sanded from a small area with a piece of fine sandpaper; number the jacks in the dulled space with a marking pen or a ball-point pen. Numbering jacks is a pain, particularly when that is not what you have set out to do, but the day may come when you will be thankful for it.

Now remove the nameboard or the name batten, whichever is meant to be removed. (The nameboard is that part of the case that joins the two sides and passes across the front of the wrestplank. The name batten is the narrow piece of wood, just over the keys, on which the maker usually puts his name. It is fastened to the nameboard, usually by screws.) Use the right size screwdriver or you may mar

your instrument in a prominent place. Northern harpsichords and Italian virginals usually have both name battens and nameboards, and normally only the batten is removable. Italian harpsichords, Flemish virginals and muselars, and bentside spinets usually do not have name battens, and the entire nameboard is removed by lifting it straight up. Normally it is not fastened in place.

There are all kinds of exceptions to these statements, so do not be concerned if your instrument has something other than what has been described. Put the batten or board down where it will be out of harm's way. Put it with the jacks; they should certainly be out of harm's way! Screw the screws back into their holes part way; it will be harder to lose them that way.

Now you are ready for the keyboard. On a two-manual instrument the upper manual is not fastened to the case in any way, and it can be removed by tilting it up and pulling it straight out. Early modern instruments might have some other arrangement, so be careful if your harpsichord shows some revival features. Take the upper keyboard to the dining room table, out of harm's way.

The lower manual may or may not be screwed to the bottom of the case. If it is, the screws probably go up through the bottom into the keyframe, but it could be the other way around. If you have a transposing keyboard, you probably already know if it is screwed in, and if so, how. To check, grasp the end blocks and pull the keyboard up and toward you. If it is not screwed in, it

should come right out. If not, look under the bottom of the harpsichord. Some builders will mark the keyboard screws in some way—I always identify them with a circle around the screw hole.

If you do not see any such marks, remove the coupler rail. This is the board that goes across the keys, just in back of the line of the sharps and keytails. It may be screwed in or simply held in place by friction. If you do not see any signs of screws, try prying it up with your fingers. It must come off or else you will be unable to remove keys from the keyframe.

Now look at the key levers, both in front and in back of the balance pins. Some builders will identify screw locations from the top of the keylever with a drawing of a screwhead. The screw will be revealed when that key is removed.

If you do not find these obvious clues, look under the bottom again. You may very well see screws, but be sure that they are not the screws that were used to hold the case parts together when it was glued. Keyboard screws should be in different positions from case screws, farther away from the edges of the case. If appropriate-looking screws do not reveal themselves to you, then turn to the top of the keyframe once again. Remove a key from each end of the keyframe; simply raise the key from the front until it is free of the balance rail pin, and pull it straight out. You may be rewarded with the sight of some screwheads on the keyframe. If not, remove more keys, until you have exposed the sides of the keyframe. If there is still no sign of screws, the keyboard probably is not screwed in.

Flemish harpsichords were often made with little turn buttons holding down the front of the keyboard, just behind the front rail. Check for these. On some instruments the back of the keyframe fits under some cleats fastened to the lower bellyrail. These cleats could provide a fairly tight friction fit, so you might have to give the keyboard a fairly hard tug to get it free. If it is tighter than you think it should be, sand or file down the places on the back rail that fit under the cleats. A little paraffin or wax may also help.

If the keyboard is held in place with screws, be sure you get them all. Screws can go up from the bottom into the front rail, the balance rail, the back rail, or a combination of the above. If you remove all the screws you think may be holding the keyboard, and it still refuses to budge, try some of the more suspicious-looking case screws—they may not be case screws at all. Even if they are, removing one or two of them should not damage the instrument in any way, since those screws only hold the parts together while the glue dries.

Discovering how your keyboard is held down doubtless will be easier than the process described here. The easiest way of all is to call your builder and ask him.

One more thing: after removing the keyboard give the keywell a good vacuuming. You may be surprised at the amount of dust, dirt, paper, paper clips, eraser shreds, hair, and other sorts of junk you will find, but almost everything that falls *on* the keys quickly falls *through* the keys. Pay particular attention to the left-hand side of the keywell, where it all falls when you turn your harpsichord on its spine to move it. This is particularly important with a transposing keyboard, since an accumulation of dirt on the bass side can interfere with its shifting operation.

REGULATING THE KEYBOARD

In a perfectly regulated keyboard all keys are exactly the same height, no key is canted out of level, and the spaces between the keys are visually even. That is the condition your keyboard should have been in when it left its maker's shop. With luck, it still is; but with all the punishment a keyboard takes from the weather and from players, it would be surprising if it did not eventually show slight deviations from visual regularity. These hurt nothing but one's aesthetic sense, and if your builder did his job, as he undoubtedly did, it is unlikely to get bad. But keys can warp, also. Usually they warp when first cut apart, and your builder took care of any such problems at that time. But sometimes years later a key will decide to take a strange bend.

There is a difference between leveling and straightening, although the process of putting the keyboard back into perfect regulation combines both. Leveling involves setting the position of the top of a key relative to the other keys. It is done by raising or lowering the key lever at the balance pin. Straightening involves the cant, or twist of a key lever, and the gaps between the keys. It is done by manipulating the position of the balance pin, and also of the guide pin or rack pin.

Straightening the keys. There are two possible operations involved in straightening: changing the angle of the balance pin in such a way that the top of the key is parallel to the keyframe; and reorienting the position of the head of a key so that the spaces between keys are even. The first is done by moving the top of the balance pin. Place a piece of wood against the pin and tap the wood with a hammer, thereby tilting the pin slightly from right to left or vice versa (Figure 8-1). Be sure that you do not disturb the front-to-back orientation of the pin. Obviously, tilting the pin also tilts the key, and the idea is to tilt it into its proper position. But tilting the pin and the key also changes the spacing between the keys. For example, tapping the pin from right to left, thus tilting the key from right to left, creates more space on the right side of the key, and less space on the left. This may be either good or not so good.

Perhaps the key spacing was off in the first place because the key got tilted. Then, restoring the key to its level position will also restore the proper spacing, and that is good. However, if putting the key back into its proper non-tilted position also creates a larger space on one side than the other, that is not so good. Now you must change the yaw by working with the guide.

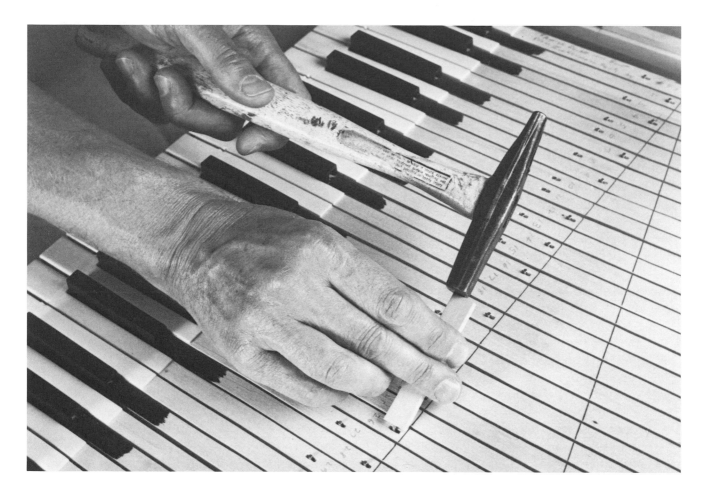

FIGURE 8-1.
To tilt the pin, place a block of wood against it and tap the block with a hammer.

If your keyboard has front guide pins, remove the key and tap the pin in the direction of the wider gap. This will close the gap slightly—hopefully, it will close it up sufficiently, because you cannot do much tapping on guide pins. They ride in slots of fairly close tolerance, and if you move the pins too much, they will bind. If this does happen, simply give the pin a tap in the opposite direction. Rear guide pins can be tapped in the same way as front guide pins, although there is no need to take the key off (tap them as you did the balance pins). Rear guide pins are tapped in the same manner as front pins, but in the opposite direction.

If your keys are guided by a metal pin in a rack, the pin can be bent slightly, either by setting the key down on its side and tapping the pin with a hammer or with a padded long-nose pliers. Be sure that the pin is bent in the right direction: toward the space you want to close up. Again, anything other than just a little change in the pin's direction may cause binding, a far worse fault than a slight unevenness between keys.

If you have wood or plastic guides riding in a rack there is not much more that you can easily do, other than remove the guide, plug up its slot, make a new slot, and reinsert the guide. Similarly, if the backs of the keys are guided *between* guide pins, you must remove wood from one side of the key and replace it on the other. These are definitely operations for a technician and should not be undertaken lightly by the amateur. If your key spacing is still a little off, you will either have to live with it or have it fixed by a professional. If the problem is a bad one, caused by warping of the key, see chapter 12 for further information.

Leveling the keys. When a key is leveled, its top is brought either up or down, so that it is in the same plane as the tops of all the other keys. It may be raised by placing paper washers under the key at the balance rail, or lowered by taking wood off the key at the balance pin. Do not attempt to level a key by working on the bottom of the back of the key. At first this may appear to be an easy solution; one simply slices off a little wood or glues on some shims of card stock. But this will change the relationship of the top of the rear of the key to the jack, and this in turn will affect the return of the plectrum, the damper, the coupler, the stagger, and the key dip.

Any piano technician or piano store can sell you some balance paper punchings, color-coded by thickness. Or you can make your own with paper of various thicknesses, a hole punch, and scissors. To raise the front of a key, lift the key off the balance pin and place a paper punching of appropriate thickness on the pin, between the balance punching and the key lever. If the level is still not right, substitute a thicker punching or add another thinner one until the key is raised to the proper level.

At that point, do yourself a fa-vor. Take the key off altogether, and remove the paper punching and the cloth balance punching. Now replace them in reverse order, paper first, cloth on top. Those thin paper washers have a habit of sticking to the bottom of the key just for the time it takes to lift the key off the balance pin. Then they drop off and are lost. In fact, that may be why you had to relevel that key in the first place.

It is less likely that a key will become higher than its neighbors, but it can happen if a key warps. Shave off some wood from the area of the balance pin hole with your voicing knife. If you have a sharp wood-carving knife or a block plane, so much the better, but the knife will do. Brace the work and the arms, and keep the fingers out of the way. Cut away from the body. Do this carefully, and keep the cut square to the key lever. If you happen to cut too much off, you will have to bring the front of the key back up with the paper punchings. You may have some success using your file here, either along with or instead of your knife. Do not attempt this operation unless you are confident of your success. It is not difficult, but done wrong it can really mess up a key.

Regulating the entire keyboard is best done out of the case. This way you can stretch a thread or string across the tops of the keys, just in back of the front edge of the naturals. The thread represents a point that every key top will be made to contact. The trick is to find some way of getting that thread to the proper height, and to get it to stay taut. If the end blocks are in the way,

remove the first and last keys (they can be leveled by eye, after you have finished with the rest of the keyboard) and work inside the end blocks. You need to get something of the proper height at each end—pieces of wood, piles of Scrabble tiles—use your imagination. Then you need to find some way to hold these things down, and to fasten your thread to them so that it will be taut. A child at each end works well, but only for a short while. Clamps work longer. Number ten cans of tomato juice may do it. Again, I leave it to your ingenuity (Figure 8-2).

The rest is easy. Set your thread so that it is just "kissed" by the highest keys. Do the straightening first, although you may have to straighten a little more as the keys get leveled. Level with the paper punchings: if the thread is positioned properly, you will be able to slip the keys off the balance rail and drop the punchings into place. The tweezer comes in handy here. When you have finished the naturals, reposition your thread and straighten and level your sharps. When you have completely finished the regulation, reverse the paper and the cloth punchings.

Before you return the keyboards to the case, check to be sure that there are no key levers binding against their neighbors. If this happens, file down the appropriate sides of the keys until proper clearance has been achieved. Check also that the cloth pads on the ends of the keys are not rubbing against each other. These can be trimmed with the voicing knife.

FIGURE 8-2.
Fastening the thread preparatory to straightening and leveling the keys. In this photo the proper height for the thread had been set by using dominos and Scrabble tiles. The thread is fixed in place by placing over it another Scrabble tile, a napkin (to avoid marring the end block), and a large can of pineapple juice to hold the whole thing in place.

REGULATING THE DIP

Ideally, the harpsichord should be regulated so that it is emitting sound most efficiently, that the touch is appropriate for the volume of sound produced (which is to say, there must be an appropriate relationship between the mass of the keylevers, the jack, and the pluck), and that this be done with the shallowest dip commensurate with good action. Actually, there is not a great deal of leeway in the dip—a change of 1/16" can make an enormous difference in the way a keyboard feels. This can affect the way in which one approaches the instrument, and in turn, the kind of music one makes with it.

There are some rules of thumb about proper distances for key dips, but I almost hesitate to spell them out. The dip of your instrument may vary from the figures given here, but that does not necessarily mean that your harpsichord has the wrong dip, or that you would be better off with a shallower or deeper dip. If there is any doubt in your mind, consult your builder. Normally, Northern harpsichords have a dip of 5/16" in the treble, often deepening another 1/16" or so in the bass. On a two-manual instrument, the dip of the upper keyboard should be about 1/4", with a similar deepening in the bass. The dip on Italian instruments and on virginals and spinets is more like 1/4". Clavichords' dips vary, but can be as shallow as 1/16". For purposes of comparison, it is worth remembering that pianos have a dip of 3/8".

These distances are measured with the six-inch steel rule, at the head of the key. Depress a key with the rule, and note the distance the rule travels as measured from the top of the next key. The key that is depressed should be at the bottom of its travel, but without any pressure on it. With pressure, it is usually possible to achieve another 1/16" of dip.

A keyboard's dip can change as

the instrument matures. To begin with, felt and action cloth get worn and packed down. Then a comparatively large amount of expansion and contraction takes place during an instrument's early years. Wood does not always want to stay where we put it, and sometimes one structural member or another decides that it wants to move to a different position from where it started. When these things happen it is possible to get the feeling that the key is "bottoming out" right after the pluck; that there is no "comfort zone"—that ⅛" or so of travel after the pluck that makes for a feeling of security.

On the other hand, too deep a dip gives the feeling that one's fingers are falling into the keys, or that it is difficult to get one's fingers out from between the keys. Either of these feelings— and they are feelings, quite subjective in nature, but real enough to the sensitive player—indicates that it is time to check the dip and, if necessary, to modify it.

As suggested earlier, regulation of the key dip may also depend on the regulation of the touch, so do not attempt to deal with one without at least being aware of the possibility that the other could also be involved.

It will be recalled that in chapter 1 we mentioned the three ways in which key dip could be regulated: at the head of the key, at the touchrail, and at the jackrail. Each of these three methods will now be examined in detail.

Head stop. To work on the dip of an instrument with a head stop, you are going to have to remove all the keys from the keyframe and replace them, at least once.

This will be much easier to do if you first remove the keyboard.

With a head stop the front rail has enough cloth or felt padding on it so that the keys contact it without the sound of wood hitting wood. But the padding also has the function of limiting the travel of the keys. If the padding consists of several strips of cloth nailed in place, the dip can be deepened by removing one of the strips. Remove the nails by whatever means necessary. If you can do this without destroying them, you can use the same nails to refasten the material. The strips can often be stapled down, with an ordinary office stapling machine. Provided that there is still enough padding so that the keys operate silently against the front rail, this should solve the problem.

Conversely, the dip can be made more shallow by adding a strip of cloth to the front rail. It need not be the same material as the action cloth; almost any fairly heavy material will do. For example, leather of various kinds is often used as action material, and you may have some in places on your instrument. Thin felt can also be used, and so can strips of masking tape placed under the cloth.

Increasing the dip when the front rail is padded with a single thick piece of felt is more difficult. It is best to simply discard the felt and substitute some strips of thinner material; you can use felt, of course, but wool flannel (not cotton, and certainly not nylon) works just as well, if not better. A single thick piece of felt can be built up, to decrease the dip, by adding a thin strip of material on top. If the felt can be

easily removed, masking tape can be used underneath.

The felt may be nailed down, but on older instruments a single thick piece was sometimes glued to the front rail. Remove the felt as cleanly as you can, and find some small tacks or brads that you can use to attach your new cloth. If the cloth or other material is not too thick, it can be stapled into place. The nails or staples should be driven down sufficiently so that they are lower than the surrounding cloth. Otherwise, the key may click when it hits the metal.

A slightly deeper dip in the bass can be achieved by omitting a thin layer of cloth, masking tape, felt, or whatever, from the bottom octave or so.

When the necessary adjustments have been made to the dip, replace the keys and measure the amount of change you have wrought. As always with the harpsichord, the only meaningful test is the one that takes place under the player's fingers; so put the keys back on the keybed, replace the keyboard and all the jacks, and play. And be prepared to do it all again if the dip is not quite right.

Rack stop. As with the head stop, it is necessary to remove the keyboard from the harpsichord, but there may be no need to remove the keys from the keyframe. There are two ways in which you can adjust the dip on a rack stop: the first involves subtracting or adding a strip of cloth or felt to the underside of the touchrail. If the padding is merely tacked on the task is relatively easy, although you will have to replace the tacks by squeezing them into place with pliers, since you will not be able to get the head of a hammer in the narrow space between the tops of the backs of the keys and the rack. Often, the padding material is sewed to the touchrail. If so, it takes little time to undo the stitching, add or remove the necessary padding, and sew it back up. If you find a single thick piece of felt here, follow the suggestions made for the head stop —in other words, replace the felt.

The second way, easier than manipulating contentious strips of cloth in those narrow quarters, is to move the rack itself up or down. This can be done if the rack is screwed, but not glued into place—and usually it is *not* glued in place, for this very reason. It is easy enough to find out: see if there are any screws under the back rail, going into the rack. If there are, unscrew them partway and see if the rack can be moved. Loosen, but do not remove, all the screws. Place shims of appropriate thickness between the back rail and the rack, and tighten the screws. The shims can be made of wood, cardboard, paper, plastic, metal, or other material. These will increase the distance between the tops of the keys and the padding and thus will increase the dip.

To decrease the dip, you will have to remove the rack, which means that you might as well remove the keys too, because you will never get the rack back on with the keys in place. Now you will have to take some wood off the bottom of the rack, and if you do not know how to use the tools to do it—a hand plane or a jointer—take the keyboard to someone who *does* know how to

use a plane, or who owns a jointer and can do it for you. You may have to use some ingenuity, but that should not include a decision that this is the appropriate moment for you to learn to use these tools. It is not. Be careful about how much you take off, but remember that it can always be shimmed back up.

It may also be possible that the touchrail is fastened to the rack in some easily removable way. If it is screwed into the rack, try the same thing; loosen the screws and see if the touchrail moves. If it can be removed, you can either shim it to raise it, or put the touchrail on the table, where you can work on it easily.

Finally, some two-manual instruments have a touchrail for the upper manual keys fastened inside the case, to the bottom of the wrestplank, near the bottom guide, rather than to the keyframe itself. This will undoubtedly be secured with screws, and should be adjustable. Remove both keyboards, so you can get your hands and your tools inside the instrument without damaging anything. Mark the location of the screws before you loosen them. When you have freed the rail, locate it in its new position by guiding it on the marks you just made. Tighten down the screws, replace the keyboards and the jacks, and give it a try.

Jackrail stop. With a jackrail stop the dip is set either by adjusting the padding on the inside of the rail, or by moving the rail up or down. If your harpsichord has some provision by which the jackrail height can be regulated, by all means use it. Otherwise, you will need to add or subtract

strips of felt or flannel to the jackrail.

Some harpsichord makers set the tops of the jacks in the various registers at approximately the same level, so that when a note is played, all the jack tops reach the underside of the jackrail. In this case, strips of padding the width of the jackrail can be used. On other instruments this does not happen: the tops of the 4' jacks are lower than the tops of the 8' jacks, and the underside of the jackrail has a correspondingly thicker center section. It is easy to distinguish which type you have, simply by looking at the jacks and the jackrail.

It should not be assumed that the tops of the jacks in all the registers are touching the bottom of their respective portions of the jackrail. Check this by coupling the keyboards (if it is a double-manual instrument) and pressing down a key in the bass. While the key is pressed down, reach under the jackrail with your voicing knife and catch the front 8' jack with the point of the knife. Push or press up, and see if you can easily move the jack up a little more. If you can, there is space between the jack and the jackrail. Do this again, for a note in the middle of the instrument, and again for one in the treble. If the front 8' jacks can be moved up by the knife the same amount on these other notes, then the jackrail has to be padded by that extra amount for the entire front 8'. If it can be moved more in the treble than in the bass, then it needs more padding in the treble; and if the jacks meet firm resistance everywhere when you attempt to raise them, then the dip is fine and no additional padding is needed. Try the same test for some appropriate 4' and back 8' jacks (or whatever registers your harpsichord does have), and make the necessary adjustments, if needed. You may find it handy to have someone hold the keys down while you probe the jacks.

The test described above should be made on any harpsichord, regardless of how its action is stopped. Although the front of the key may contact the front rail, or the back of the key the touchrail, the jacks must all meet the jackrail when the key is stopped. If this does not happen, the jacks will continue to rise. They will leave the ends of the keys in free flight, hit the jackrail, and drop back down to the key ends with some force. To the discerning player, this "jack jiggle" is distinctly unpleasant and is to be avoided.

On any harpsichord with two or more registers, where the action is stopped at the jack rail, only one of the registers is primarily responsible for stopping the action (usually the front 8' on a $2 \times 8'$, or a $2 \times 8'$, $1 \times 4'$). The rest of the jackrail should be padded only enough so that the other jacks do not give a little hop in playing. This slight distinction in the way the registers are stopped is made to avoid the sensation of a double touch, since the front and back jacks do not arrive at the jackrail at exactly the same moment. Most of the time this happens automatically, so it need not be of concern unless jacks can be felt hopping around.

ADJUSTING THE COUPLER

When the keyboards are coupled, the coupler dogs push up the bottoms of the backs of the upper-manual key levers. There should be little lost motion between the two keyboards; the upper keyboard should respond practically immediately when the lower is played. Yet there must be *some* clearance between them, or else the dogs will catch on the keys of the upper keyboard when it is slid back to couple, and the jacks that sit on the upper manual may not damp properly. This mechanism is one of the simplest on the harpsichord and is scarcely affected by changes in temperature and humidity. Thus there is little chance that one or two coupler dogs will go out of adjustment; however, as we have seen, almost anything can happen to a harpsichord.

Try the following tests if you suspect that a coupler dog is out of regulation. Get on your knees, so that your eyes are at key-top level. Rapidly couple and uncouple the keyboards, all the while watching the upper-manual key in question. If it shivers, or rises and falls as the coupling takes place, then a little more clearance has to be provided between lower-manual dog and upper-manual key lever.

To test for lost motion, press the lower manual key and note how long it takes for the upper manual key to respond. If there is lost motion between the upper and lower key that is clearly greater than that found over the rest of the keyboard, then the clearance between dog and key should be reduced.

On antique harpsichords the coupler dog was nothing more than a tapered stick of wood that rose from the top of the back of the lower-manual key, and it contacted the padded lower side of the upper-manual key lever. Most modern harpsichords also use this simple system. Clearance may be added by removing the lower manual keylever from the instrument and filing down the top of the dog the required amount. If clearance needs to be reduced, first check the felt or other material padding the underside of the upper-manual key. Replace it if it is worn, and this will probably solve the problem. If this is not the case, clearance can be reduced by building up the top of the dog with strips of masking tape applied one strip at a time. Alternately, card stock can be inserted under the cloth on the underside of the upper-manual key. Either will close the gap between dog and key lever.

A few builders make coupler mechanisms that are more adjustable. Some have little buttons that screw into the bottoms of the upper-manual key levers, and the dogs contact these buttons rather than the key itself. Clearance is adjusted by screwing the button in or out. Do not neglect to check the padding on the button. Replace it if it is worn or missing. On other instruments the coupler dogs themselves screw in and out, and that is the way their clearance is regulated. Still other instruments have more complex couplers, but they are attempting to do more than the simple classical coupler, and it is beyond the scope of this book to deal with them.

So far, we have talked about adjusting the coupling of individual keys. Although we have tried to cover all contingencies, the most likely cause for a single-key adjustment is the loss or destruction of the padding on the bottom of the key (or on the little upper-manual key button if there is one), and this should be inspected first.

It is more likely that the entire coupling mechanism, rather than a single key, may need adjusting. This usually happens because the padding between the upper manual keyframe and the lower-manual coupler tracks has been packed down or destroyed. This, in effect, drops the upper manual slightly, bringing its key levers closer to the dogs. With this clearance lost, the keys on the upper manual will shiver and shake when coupled. In this case do not attempt to deal with the dogs individually; instead, remove the manuals and locate the padding. Either the bottom of the upper manual or the coupler track (where the upper manual slides back and forth) will be padded. Even if you cannot find it, you can add some felt strips of your own (damper cloth, perhaps) where they will do the most good. If the new padding raises the upper manual *too* high it can be filed down (see *Adjusting the stagger*, in chapter 9, before you try this).

The object should be to restore the clearance of the coupler to its former condition, providing, of course, that its former condition was satisfactory. It could be a mistake for you (or your brother-in-law, the harpsichord expert, the one who has built one kit instrument) to decide that your action would be improved if the coupler worked with less leeway. That little bit of clearance was built into the mechanism for good reasons. Changing it could affect the plucking order, among other things. In this, as in all aspects of harpsichord maintenance, remember the dictum, *if it works, don't fix it.*

Chapter 9 The Touch

Unless your harpsichord lives in a climate that has a constant temperature and humidity, it undergoes a regular and normal expansion with heat and humidity, and contraction with cooler temperatures and drier air. This movement can be minimized by air conditioning, heating, humidifying, and dehumidifying, as necessary, but it cannot be completely eliminated. Winter is particularly bad in many parts of this country because it is accompanied by dry central heating (although in the far West, winter is the wet season). And many harpsichords in the South and Midwest simply stop functioning in the heat and humidity of summer. While these climatic changes affect the harpsichord in many ways, we are for the moment concerned with the string band, which is going to move in and out and up and down, as the case expands and contracts with the seasons. Like all movement of wood in a harpsichord, the effect is greatest in new instruments. Most harpsichords will settle down after a few years, and, provided that reasonable temperature and humidity stability is maintained, this kind of movement will cease to be a problem. But during those first few years, this movement can affect the touch of your instrument.

TOUCH AFFECTED BY
LATERAL CHANGES

Recently I told one of my kit builders that he could improve the touch on his Flemish double with a stronger back 8'. He called me shortly thereafter to tell me that the touch had improved all by itself, and he wanted to know how this was possible. I asked him if it was his back 8' rank that seemed stronger. It was. I then asked him if his front 8' had not gotten a little weaker. He said that it had, wondering how I could have known. There was no clairvoyance involved, since I knew how his harpsichord would react in the cool, dry fall weather of Iowa.

As his instrument lost moisture and contracted, the distance between spine and cheek decreased, and the distance between the back 8' jacks and the strings that they pluck decreased. Thus, the plectra took a slightly deeper bite, thereby making the action on the lower manual a little stronger. But the front 8' jacks pluck in the opposite direction from the back 8' jacks; their plectra pulled *away* from the strings, making the touch of the upper manual a little lighter. My builder's back 8' may have been improved by the weather, but if the touch of your instrument is the way you want it, a change of seasons is not going to help it.

We can extract some operating

principles from this. In times of expansion or contraction, the touch of some of the registers will weaken and some will strengthen. All those registers whose jacks point in the same direction will tend to react in the same way, while the registers whose jacks face in the opposite direction will react in the opposite way. The touch feels stronger or weaker because more or less of the plectrum is addressing the string. Then it becomes necessary to restore the proper lap of the plectra under the strings, and that is done by changing the point at which the registers are stopped in their *on* position.

On harpsichords of classical design, the ends of the registers themselves were stopped in both directions by contact with the case walls, and adjustments were made with shims. Today some builders provide a mechanical adjustability by using capstan screws in the ends of the registers, which bear against the case walls. Sometimes one finds the opposite: the capstan screws are in the case walls and bear against the registers. If your instrument has capstan screws, give the appropriate screw a quarter turn (one of the jeweler's screwdrivers will probably make a good handle for this) and test the results. If this has not advanced or retreated the register enough, continue with another quarter turn. It should not need more than half a turn; if it does, the touch was probably out of regulation to begin with.

Whatever you make the capstan screw do to change the lap of the plectrum under the string, you must make the capstan screw on the other side do the opposite; in other words, if you screw the capstan on the right side of the register *out* a quarter turn in order to back off the jacks a little bit, you will have to give the capstan on the left side of the register a quarter turn *in*, so that the register will be able to turn off properly.

Other harpsichords have screws that go through the window coverplate (this device will be discussed in a moment) and are turned from outside the spine. The registers bear against the fronts of the screws, rather than against the case itself. Again, try no more than a quarter turn at one time.

Many modern harpsichords do not have any such adjustment screws. Instead, like the antiques, the ends of the registers bear directly against the inside of the case—the cheek on one side, the spine on the other. On such an instrument you will probably find some paper or card stock shims at each end of the register. If you want to decrease the bite taken by the plectra, take a card or paper shim out of the *off* side of the register, and drop it into the space between the register and the case on the *on* side. This not only decreases the underlap of the quills, it also restores the *off* position to its proper place, so that the plectra will not ghost (barely brush the strings) when turned off.

Parenthetically, it might not be a bad idea to fix the shims in place somehow: use a small piece of masking tape if they poke up above the registers, or the merest drop of glue. Just something so that the shim will not fall out when the harpsichord is moved and turned up on its spine. But do not bother if you never move your instrument, or if moving it is nothing more than picking it up and carrying it from here to there.

You may find that you need more room between your register and the case wall, yet there is no shim that can be removed. The solution to this is fairly simple. Northern harpsichords usually have some sort of window—an extension of the gap through the side of the case. On Flemish harpsichords this window is found on the cheek, and the registers protrude from it. But on other Northern harpsichords, and many Southern as well, the window is on the spine, where the gap would be if it extended through the case. There you will find a coverplate.

That plate is actually the outside of a plug, which fits in the window. On the spine side the registers bear against the plug rather than against the case itself. To provide a little more room for the register to travel, simply loosen the screws holding the coverplate to the case, and insert strips of card stock between the coverplate and the outside of the case wall, one on each side. This will draw the plug out of the case the distance of the thickness of the card. This should be sufficient to give you the added room for the additional motion the register needs on the left side; if not, insert additional strips of card stock between coverplate and case.

You will have to work a little harder if the room between the register and the case is needed on the right side, at the cheek. First, move your harpsichord so that there are about four feet between the spine and anything else, such as a wall. Remove all the jacks from the register involved. Unscrew and remove the plug from the window. Draw the register right out of the case, through the spine. Mark the treble and bass sides on the register, and write its name on it (e.g., "back 8").

Now draw a line about 1/32" from the right end of the register. Somehow, you must remove that 1/32" of wood. You can slice it off with your voicing knife and trim it up with your file; or you can walk down the street to your friend with the disk sander, and ask him to take it off for you. No need to worry if you take off a little too much—it can always be shimmed back with card stock.

For a Flemish harpsichord, whose registers protrude through a window in the cheek, the solutions are practically identical, though reversed. Something will limit the travel of the registers on the right, and that is what you must work with. If you need to take some wood off the left side of a register, reverse the instructions given above.

Not all harpsichords have windows. Northern harpsichords do, but Italians often do not. Virginals and spinets do not. To remove a register from one of these instruments, if it is removable at all, it is almost necessary to take off the strings. But before you do, satisfy yourself that you know how the registers are held in place. They may be removable in a less-than-obvious way.

All this may sound complex, but the normal adjustments take only a moment. Imagine, for example, that winter is almost here. For some time you have noticed that the touch on the lower

manual of your year-old French double is getting stiffer, and that the two 8's together pluck much harder than they used to. Ornaments are increasingly difficult to play. At the same time, the touch on your upper manual has grown weaker, offering too little resistance. In a burst of insight, you realize that it is time to winterize your harpsichord. You stop playing. You remove the music, the music rack, and the jackrail.

Checking out the registers, you note that the back 8' and the 4' point to the left, and the front 8' points to the right. Using your tweezers, you slip a card stock shim out of the right side of each of the three registers and place them on the left side, between register and spine. You replace the jackrail and play some music. The registers are even once again. The proper plucking order has been restored. Ornaments flow off your fingers. There are no hangers. You have winterized your harpsichord, and you should not have to fuss with that regulation until spring, when the opposite will happen. When it does, simply reverse the procedure.

After several years you may find that shifting a shim the thickness of a mere piece of paper, rather than a card, is all the adjustment necessary. And a year or so after that no adjustment at all may be necessary—provided that you keep the temperature and humidity under control.

Do not be confused by any slight and perhaps unnoticeable unevenness that might already exist in your action, such as a somewhat weaker or longer quill. As the weather gets cooler and/or drier, all the notes on the back 8' will become a little heavier to

the touch, but some may become even heavier than the others, while others will not change much and thus appear to be weaker. Meanwhile, on the front 8', the touch will be weaker, but jacks with slightly longer or stronger quills will seem stronger. The normal reaction may be to think that you have a problem with a few strong or weak notes, but what is really required is that the registers be moved a bit.

Virginals and spinets are special cases, because on these instruments alternate jacks point in opposite directions. Thus, when the case expands, one string is drawn closer to its jack, while the next string is drawn away from its jack. This can result in a disconcerting strong-weak, strong-weak pattern. There is not much that can be done with Italian virginals, since in its classical construction the box register is immovable, glued to the bottom of the soundboard, with slots cut through the soundboard for the jacks. Check to be sure that the lap of the plectra under the strings is not too short, since that will tend to exacerbate the strong-weak feeling; if the quills are underlapping as much as possible, commensurate with good touch, sound, and plectrum return, the problem will probably disappear after a few years. In the meantime, you will have to deal with the individual jacks, softening down some plectra, pushing others through the tongue mortice to make them a little longer.

Flemish virginals and muselars may have some provision for register adjustment. On these instruments the top register is nothing more than a piece of leather glued to the soundboard, with slots punched in it for the jacks. But it is possible to provide an adjustment for the bottom register in some way. There are two ways you can find out if your virginal or muselar has such an adjustment: remove the nameboard and look inside, or call your builder and ask him.

Bentside spinets usually have some provision for moving the box register, which, like a harpsichord proper, drops into a gap. Look for shims on either side of the register. Sometimes the register fits tightly, held in position by friction, and shims are not needed. If this is the case, try to move the register by inserting something thin at one end, like a knife blade. I hesitate to put that suggestion in print—I can just see broken strings, slashed soundboards, and blood all over the place. Please be reasonable if you try this. If a little pressure gets no results, work with the individual jacks.

If your harpsichord has a full plywood bottom it probably is not going to expand and contract in the way that has been described. Plywood tends to expand in all directions, rather than across the grain, as with plank wood. If your instrument expands or contracts in such a way that the bass gets weaker than the treble, or vice versa, you must set the register, with shims or with the capstan screws, so that the middle octave ghosts. Then you must adjust the quills on any jacks that do not do the same. Use voicing screws if your instrument has them; if not, you will have to push out and/or trim back plectra. When the entire register ghosts like the middle octave, it can be set to its on and

off positions. At that time, any notes that are particularly strong or weak can be handled individually. And be of good cheer. Plywood also will cease its expansion and contraction after some years.

TOUCH AFFECTED BY VERTICAL CHANGES

This is another aspect of the touch of your instrument that may be affected by the weather, particularly when it is new. In the summer the soundboard is likely to pick up moisture and to rise, taking the bridges and the string band with it. The case also expands a little in the vertical direction. The strings are now slightly higher than they were, which means that the jacks now appear to be shorter. Or the opposite may happen, if your harpsichord was finished during the hot, humid summer months. Now, in colder and drier weather, the soundboard drops, and the jacks appear to be too long.

Though less likely, the soundboard can also drop, rather than rise, when it expands in the summer. Soundboards are supposed to rise, not fall, when they take on moisture, but sometimes it just does not happen that way. This should not be a problem unless there is a consequent loss of bearing, and/or the strings buzz against the soundboard. If either of these things happens, you will have to take the instrument to someone who can repair it. It can probably be made as good as new.

In either case, up or down, the change makes itself felt in the touch, which can become a little unpleasant. With the rising

soundboard, the distance the key travels before the strings are plucked is increased. With all registers on, the keys may almost seem to bottom out before the strings pluck. The sensation is one of a heaviness of touch and a decrease in the dip, and you will undoubtedly get out your six-inch steel rule to measure it. However, the fault lies not in the dip, but in where the pluck occurs.

When the soundboard falls, dampers may leak and plectra may no longer return properly. Notes can seem to go off by themselves, and the player may feel that he has lost control of the keyboard. These changes probably will not occur by themselves, but rather in association with the lateral changes just described. It may seem that a beautifully adjusted action suddenly has deteriorated seriously. We have discussed the remedy for the shifting registers. The remedy for vertical changes is not quite as simple, but it is as necessary.

For a rising string band, first remove the keyboards from the instrument. Shim up the back of the lower keyboard by putting some sort of material under it, such as squares of damper felt, glued to the two far corners of the keyboard. More than this should not be required. If it is, glue another square on top of the first. When the glue is dry, the felt can be filed down, if needed, to the proper thickness. Now all the jacks will be raised by the amount of the felt shims.

When drier, cooler weather sets in, and the soundboard drops, the jacks may seem too long. The dampers may leak and some of the plectra may refuse to return. All you need do is remove the keyboards and pull the squares of felt off the bottom. Again, do not try to deal with this condition by manipulating the dip, changing the height of individual jacks, revoicing plectra, adjusting dampers, or tampering with the firing order. At least, do not do these things until after you have accounted for the temperature and humidity changes; then it may well be that a few notes need attention in some other way.

When a string band has dropped before it has had a chance to rise, one assumes that there are no shims that can be removed from the keyframe. But this is merely an assumption, and it is possible that your builder may have put them in. You will never know until you look, so remove the jacks and take out the keyboard. Or take the direct approach and ask your builder. If there are no shims to remove, you have no choice but to lower the height of the jacks—all of them (see *Regulating the height of the jack*, in chapter 7). In six months, when the soundboard rises again, you will have the opportunity to install some shims.

Some builders provide two screws that go through the bottom of the case and bear up against the bottom of the rear of the keyframe, just in the spot where you would put your shims. If you have such adjustment screws, you need only turn them in a little to raise the keyboard, and turn them out to drop it.

Virginals and bentside spinets are prone to the same problem of rising and falling soundboards.

The consequences are not as severe here, because you are dealing with only a single register. Nevertheless, if the dampers start to leak, lower the jacks; and if the dip seems to diminish, install some shims under the key frame.

Let me say it once again: like all kinds of expansion and contraction in your harpsichord, the effects are felt most keenly early in its life. After some years you may find that the instrument no longer needs as much shim adjustment, or that it is no longer necessary to fuss so much with the capstan screws. The keyboard shims may not be required after a while, or your harpsichord may find that it likes the little felt squares there as permanent fixtures. Let your fingers listen to your harpsichord, then do what they tell you to do.

ADJUSTING THE STAGGER

Your builder did the hardest part of the stagger adjustment in his shop, before you got the instrument, but stagger needs to be touched up from time to time. Registers shift and jack heights change. Replacing a quill can also affect the stagger. Then there are the changes that take place over a period of time, as the instrument settles in, the felts pack down, and the plectra work-harden. It is unlikely that you will ever have to undertake a complete adjustment of the stagger, but there will be notes here and there, now and then, that will require some work. You will probably not have any trouble knowing when that time has come; it does not take many

notes with poor stagger to make the entire keyboard feel overly stiff when everything is on, or even when just the two 8's are played together.

The four things that affect the stagger are the coupler adjustment, plectrum strength, plectrum lap, and jack height. Let us discuss these one at a time, again using our French double as an example. When coupled, the 4' jacks will usually fire first, since their quills are normally the weakest and the shortest. Next to go will be the back 8'. The front 8' will fire last, because its jacks have to deal with the coupler motion and the necessary clearance between the dogs and the upper-manual keylevers. Thus it can be seen that the more play in the coupler mechanism, the later the front 8' jacks will fire. It is well worth remembering this if you find it necessary to replace the felts under the upper manual keyframe (see *Adjusting the coupler*, in chapter 8). An indication of how much padding to replace may very well come from any change in the stagger. Although this should be kept in mind, it is unlikely that this is an adjustment that will be made with any frequency.

Not every instrument will want to fire in the order I have suggested; they can sometimes be very individual that way. Builders sometimes can be very individual about it also, insisting on some firing order or other that they feel is better, or better suited to their instruments. The important thing is that the harpsichord *has* a firing order, and that it works. Sometimes a perverse note or two will insist on firing differently from the rest of the instrument. If it works, and if the individual registers are not bothered by it, I suggest that you leave it alone.

The stronger the plectrum, or the more the plectrum laps the string, the more resistance it offers to the string, and the later it will pluck. And the shorter the jack, the more time it is going to take before the plectrum even contacts the string. Assuming that the coupler mechanism is in order, the stagger can only be adjusted by working with the strength of the quill, the length of the quill, and the height of the jack. Problems concerning stagger should be addressed in that order.

Stagger is tested by pressing the key in a slow, controlled manner, with all the stops on and with the manuals coupled. Try laying your forefinger along the top of the rail in front of the keyboard, and press the key with your thumb, as if you were squeezing the very tip of the key (Figure 9-1). If you can develop the simple skill to do this, you can figure out a way to test the stagger on the sharps. Tested properly, the notes will sound one at a time: 4', back 8', front 8' (or whatever the firing order is on your instrument). The timing should be similar to the word "certainly," spoken deliberately: cer-tain-ly. It is very difficult to explain proper stagger with words. Every instrument wants

FIGURE 9-1.
Testing for stagger.

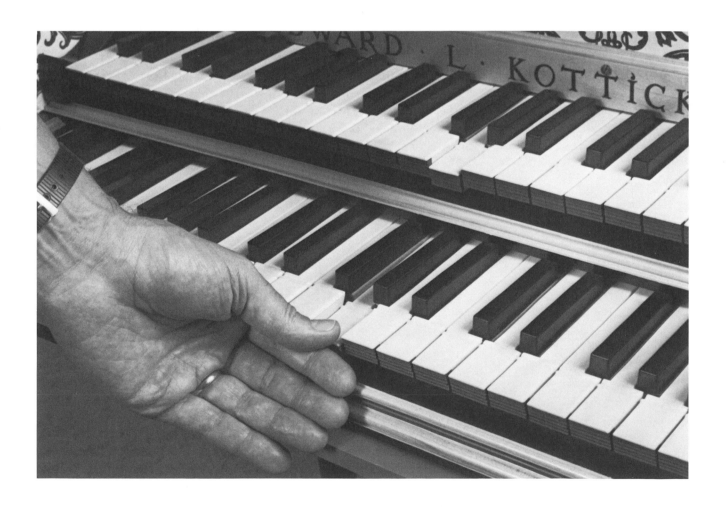

to do it its own way. Some do well on a narrow stagger, others demand a wider timing. Perhaps the best way to determine the stagger rate appropriate to your instrument is to find the coupled notes on your instrument that seem to play easiest, and attempt to duplicate that timing on the notes that need adjustment.

When the stagger is properly adjusted, you should be able to separate the individual notes with the unaided finger. This is the final test, and it is the one that counts.

Although it is impractical to go through the steps necessary to adjust the stagger for every possible combination of circumstances, an example may suffice to illustrate the process. Suppose you find that the three jacks of a certain note all pluck at the same time. First check the 4' jack, to see if there is any reason why it is not plucking sooner. Since it is not any louder or softer than its neighbors, check the plectrum length. It also looks very much like its neighbors.

However, by pressing down on the top of the jack, you discover that you have to push a little more than on the jacks around it before you see any response from the key. The jack is a little short; if it were a little longer, it would fire a little sooner. You lengthen the 4' jack and find that it now speaks first. Before proceeding to the other jacks, test the damper and the quill return to be sure that you have not lengthened the jack too much. You test and find that the damper does its job, and that the quill returns without any problem.

The two 8's are still firing together. You check the back 8' jack for strength, quill lap, and jack height, and find nothing out of the ordinary. If this last assessment is correct, you must now figure out how to make the front 8' fire later. Here you find that although the strength of the pluck is fine, the quill appears to be a bit too short. You push some quill out from the back of the jack, or turn it out with the adjustment screw (do not attempt

to push a quill through the back of a wooden tongue—the mortice is too fragile). Now the lap of the plectrum is just like its neighbors, but it is going off too late because the quill is now a little too strong—which means that the note itself is stronger than its neighbors. It seems that you have solved one problem but created another. But you know that you can decrease the strength of a plectrum by shaving some material off the quill. You slice off a curl with the voicing knife and, behold, the proper firing order is restored, and the front 8' is of proper strength.

You try the note coupled, and compare it to the notes around it. Although the firing order now *seems* to be all right, the note still plucks a little harder than its neighbors. If only you could make that front 8' pluck *just* a little later! You can. You shorten the jack just a bit, and that does it. The note now plays beautifully, both coupled and when the registers are played individually.

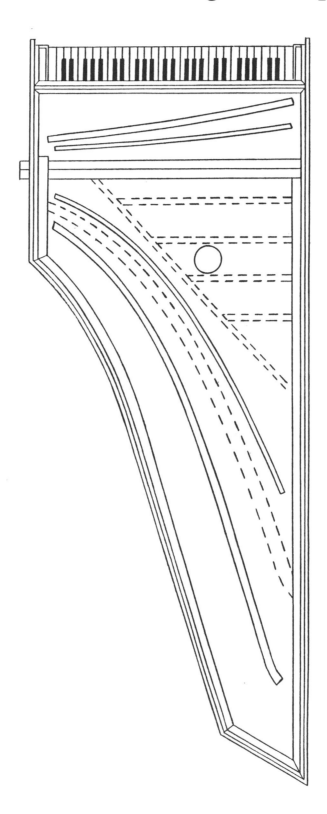

Chapter 10   String Problems

Strange string sounds can be divided into four categories: strings that beat against themselves; strings that are damped when they should not be; strings that buzz against something; and strings that are false.

Strings that beat. A beating string is usually discovered while tuning. If you find it impossible to tune a note to its octave or unison, listen carefully to each note individually. One of them is probably going wa-wa-wa-wa. That string may be beating against itself.

First things first—you still have to get the string tuned. Simply tune the octave or unison so that it beats at the same rate as the beating string. This has little to do with the ability to hear or count beats. You already heard the beats, or else you would not be aware that the string was beating. And you do not have to count anything—play the beating string by itself, then the two notes together. When they both do the same thing, you have tuned the octave.

Now—why is that string beating and what can you do about it? It is most likely beating because a twist was put into the wire when it was strung. But the string may also have some kind of imperfection—something that has set up a node in a position where the string would rather not have one. This imperfection could have occurred when the instrument was strung, or when that string was changed, or it could have happened later (perhaps something was dropped on the string). Or it can simply be a flaw in the string.

There are three courses of action you can take. First, you can change the string. Second, if the beating is not too bad, and if it is only noticed while tuning, you might just leave it alone, with the observation that you would be happy if the flaws in the rest of your life were as minor as this one. Third, you can try to remove the beating. One way is to run your thumb along the length of the string with considerable force—not enough to break the string, but enough to provide localized pressure that may just remove the blemish. Another way is to take a piece of wood—it could even be an edge of your voicing block—file a smooth notch into it with a fine, round needle file, and run the notch over the string a few times, again, with considerable force. These methods may not entirely succeed in removing beating from a string, but they can minimize it.

Strings that are damped. Sometimes dampers damp strings other than the ones to which they are assigned. Suddenly a string that used to sing no longer has any sustaining power, or it sounds different in some way from its neighbors. This can happen inadvertently when some sort of regulation change is made to the registers: when the back 8′ is moved forward, for example, it moves not only plectra, but also dampers. If a damper is moved far enough it can slightly damp the next string. Thus the note b on the upper manual might be slightly damped by the damper belonging to the jack for the lower manual c′. Conversely, if the damper for the upper manual b is too long, *it* could reach over and damp the lower manual c′. And, if the 4′ dampers are too long, they can touch the 8′ strings when the 4′ jacks are in the on position.

The backs of the dampers, and even the backs of the jacks, can also participate in this inadvertent damping, and again, a regulation change is often responsible. If either the back 8′ or the 4′ register is moved away from its strings, the backs of either of their jacks could contact the front 8′ string of the same note—the right-hand string of the wide pair. The same thing can happen with the backs of front 8′ jacks that are set too far over.

Your instrument was undoubtedly regulated properly in the builder's shop, with provision made for normal minor adjustments. However, perhaps your builder did not figure on the range of temperature and humidity to which your harpsichord has been exposed; or the dampers may have been mishandled by you or someone else. Then again, there is that maturation process

through which every instrument must go.

Whatever the cause, the solutions are relatively simple. If the damper is reaching over too far, trim it back a little with your scissors, although not so much that it will not damp in the off position. If the back of the damper is at fault, either pull the damper out of its slot a little more, thus causing the back edge to retreat into the jack, or trim the back of the damper with your voicing knife. Then be sure to check that the front of the damper is not now too long. If it is, cut it back. Check also to be sure that the back of the damper has been cut cleanly. Little bumps or threads can sometimes make an adjacent string "oink" a little. If you find these, trim them off with the voicing knife.

If the problem is not solved by cleaning up the back of the damper, you may have another problem. Get some good light on your register, jacks, plectra, and dampers. Look carefully at the register of jacks that contains the offender. If it is only one jack, or perhaps a few others as well, and if they are close enough to the strings to cause the problem, file the jack at the point at which it contacts the string. Do not overdo this, because this is not really the best solution, and will only work if the contact between string and jack is minimal.

It is also possible that the jack may be warped, and is leaning backward farther than it should. Warped plastic jacks will be discussed in chapter 11.

If there are more than just a few jacks whose backs look as if they are dangerously close to the

wrong strings, then your jacks are simply set too far back from the strings they pluck. You will have to advance the register a little. That will solve the problem with the backs of the dampers, but it may create a problem with their fronts, and you may now have to re-regulate all of your plectra. That will be too bad, but probably it cannot be helped and you will have to deal with it with the voicing knife. There is only so much room between those strings, and the off-on tolerances cannot be exceeded.

Strings that buzz. A string buzzes because it is hitting something else as it vibrates. Almost anything that falls onto the strings can buzz. We have all had the experience of playing a harpsichord with the lid stick lying across the strings, or a piece of music, or the metronome, a pencil, and so on. Sometimes the offending object is not so easily spotted: a piece of paper, a bit of debris. But these buzzes are easily fixed: sight down the string to locate the offending object, and remove it.

Less easily rectified is the buzz that occurs when the tongue of a jack slaps against the next string as it returns. This can happen for several reasons. A weak tongue spring (see *Poor return of the jack spring*, chapter 11) is sometimes to blame. A jack whose back is too close to the next string can also allow it, and this may even be combined with some unwanted damping. Both of these conditions can be corrected; adjusting the spring tension will be found in the next chapter, and jacks that are set too far back have just been discussed.

A third cause, more or less built into the harpsichord, is the tendency for a string that is vibrating with a wide amplitude to fling the tongue back with some vigor when the plectrum contacts the string on its descent. If it gets flung back far enough, it buzzes against the string behind it. This can happen with a string that is overplucked; that is, one whose jack is plucking with a greater force than necessary. Your instrument should not be overplucking; if it is, you have a regulation problem. Overplucking or not, the vigorously flung tongue is most likely to happen on bass strings, which vibrate with the greatest amplitude.

This can be a real problem on the Italian virginal or the muselar, where the plucking points in the bass are farther from the nut than they are on the harpsichord. The amplitude of vibration at those points can throw the tongue with considerable force. You could voice the harpsichord down. It will sound softer, because the strings will not vibrate with as much amplitude, and that will probably solve the problem of the vibrating string flinging back the tongue.

Late eighteenth-century English harpsichord builders had another solution. To keep the tongues from buzzing on the strings of their strongly plucked instruments, they limited the travel of the tongue by inserting a staple in the back of the jack, or by gluing a thread around the back of the jack. Please, do not attempt to drive a staple into

your jack. On wood jacks you can use the thread, as the English did. On plastic jacks, where glue would not hold thread, the effect can be obtained by tying a thread around the entire jack, about $\frac{1}{16}''$ below the plectrum. The part of the thread that goes in front of the jack has no effect on anything, but in back it stops excess motion of the tongue.

How tightly you tie this thread depends on the kind of jack you have. The back of the tongue should have *some* room to move or else the plectrum will not be able to return. On some jacks the tongue is set into the jack so that the back of the tongue is at a lower level than the back of the jack. In this case the thread should not be too loose, since the top of the tongue will do a certain amount of pivoting on its axle before it reaches the plane of the back of the jack. On other jacks the back of the tongue and the back of the jack are in the same plane. In this case the thread needs to be loose enough to allow sufficient movement.

Use a piece of heavy-duty thread, about twelve inches long, and clip off the excess close to the jack after the knot is tied. If the thread is to be tied fairly tightly, simply notch the four arrises of the jack where the thread will wrap around (you can use your voicing knife for this), and tie it on. If it is to be tied more loosely, notches will not hold it in place; use the merest drop of super glue or household glue on each side. Figure 10-1 shows several jacks with threads tied on.

A number of builders make plastic jacks that limit the back-

ward motion of the tongue with a stop of some kind. If your jacks are of this type you should not have the problem described. If you do, something other than the amplitude of the tongue movement is causing it, and it will do no good to limit the tongue even more by tying on a thread.

In conditions of high humidity the soundboard can sometimes rise into the 4' strings, causing them to buzz. This happened years ago to a French double that I had sold to a university in another state. Their piano technician called me to discuss the problem, explaining that during the most humid time of the year they had lost their air conditioning, and that they were going to need the instrument for a concert in two weeks. He wanted to cut a hole in the bottom of the instrument, sink a hook into the 4' hitchpin rail, and hook a cable between it and another hook in the bottom. I told him, with more certainty than I really felt, that he should do no such thing. "Put it in an air-conditioned room," I said, "and in two weeks it will be fine." They did, and it was.

In this case the owners were fortunate, because the high humidity did not last that long. However, sometimes the soundboard can undergo plastic deformation and refuse to come back down. Then surgery may be required, and in that event you should call a professional.

False strings. A false string sounds—different. It does not beat, it is not damped, and it does not buzz; nevertheless, it does not sound right. A false-

FIGURE 10-1.
Jacks with threads tied on to limit the travel of the tongue.

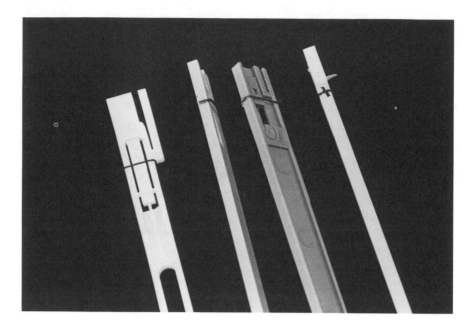

sounding string may be due to one of two causes: either a loss of bearing, or a loose bridge or nut pin. These both have to do with the way that one end of the sounding length of the string is fixed: a false string *sounds* as if things are not right at the ends.

A string must be in firm contact with its bridge and nut pins if it is to do its job of transmitting the string vibrations to the soundboard. That contact is provided by "bearing" the string against the pin in two planes. Your builder determined the *side-bearing* of the strings at the bridges and nuts when he built the instrument, and, barring some catastrophe, there is practically no way for it to change.

Downbearing, or downdraft, as it is sometimes called, is another story. You might have changed it yourself when you changed the string—remember the discussion of downbearing in chapter 6. Downbearing at the nut is the first thing to check if you suspect

a string is sounding false. Next, check downbearing at the bridge. Harpsichord strings are under low tension, so a string may not be contacting a pin as firmly as it appears to be. To check, push the string down and to the side, from behind the bridge or nut pin. This will provide firm contact, and if that contact was missing before, you will hear the difference.

If your soundboard goes down so far that downbearing is lost, you have a sunken soundboard and you have troubles whose solution lies beyond the realm of this book. But a sunken soundboard (or, for that matter, a raised soundboard) can be repaired. As stated earlier, it is not a difficult task for a professional, and properly done it will not hurt the harpsichord.

There is practically no reason why a bridge or nut pin should come loose, but I have seen it happen. If the bridge or nut is fine except for the loose pin, pull the pin out. Get a round toothpick, and put a small amount of glue on the tip. Push the toothpick firmly into the hole and break off the rest. While the glue is drying, go to that well-stocked hardware store and buy a number 57 drill bit. A 57 should work; bridge and nut pin diameters seem to be standard, at least in this country. If there is any question in your mind, bring the pin with you to the hardware store. Redrill the hole to an appropriate depth. I cannot tell you what that is because I do not know how long your pin is. You can make a stop on your drill bit with some masking tape.

If the pin came out of a nut, just hammer it back in to the appropriate depth. If it came out of a bridge, do *not* hammer it back in; if you try to do that you will very likely break your soundboard. Instead, you must *push* it in as best you can. In the absence of a specialized pushing tool, a small vise-grip pliers will work. A little soap on the pin will help it go in smoothly. Do not worry if it sticks up a little further than its neighbors; you will have forgotten about it tomorrow, and no one will ever notice.

The pin may have become loose because the bridge or nut has split in that place. If so, remove the pin and work some glue into the split. Hold it closed with your fingers for at least fifteen minutes, or figure out some other way to clamp it. Let it dry overnight, then proceed as above. If the pin is still loose, plug the hole with a toothpick and redrill.

SLIPPING STRINGS

In chapter 6 we talked about two of the reasons that a string might slip in pitch: a hitch-pin loop without the double helices, or an improperly wound tuning pin. Another possible reason is that the tuning-pin hole has become so enlarged that the pin is loose.

A tuning pin is not considered to be loose if you cannot turn it with your fingers. Tell that to your piano technician, and he'll give you a strange look. A loose pin on a piano is serious business, calling for pin doping, shimming, or even replacement of the wrestplank, all at an expense ranging from considerable to enormous. The strings on that piano exert about twenty tons of tension on the wrestplank. No wonder a loose pin is cause for alarm! But on the harpsichord—no problem, unless you can turn it with your fingers, and even then it is not really a problem.

Tapered tuning pins can loosen up from time to time, and they can work their way out of their holes if you allow them to. Think of these pins as a violinist thinks of his tuning pegs, and keep them tight in their holes as you tune. Bear down a little with the hammer in order to overcome the natural tendency of the pins to work their way out of their holes. If a pin does seem to be getting loose, rather than wait for it to loosen completely and allow its string to unwind, simply give it a tap with a hammer. Tuning hammers made for tapered tuning pins usually have a little hammer on the end for that very reason.

A threaded pin becomes loose because its hole has been en-larged from removing and replacing the pin more than just a few times. This can happen if you have to replace a particular string frequently for one reason or another, and sometimes only a few times will do it. This is not serious, and can be fixed easily. First, try knocking the pin in just a little deeper. That will probably work, at least for a while, perhaps for longer than that. If it is really loose it will have to be shimmed with some paper. Cut a thin strip of paper from a sheet of bond stationery or something equivalent, push it into the hole, and follow it with the pin. If the hole ever needs to be shimmed again, use a heavier piece of paper.

Loose pins can also result from putting lateral pressure on the tuning hammer. This is like swinging on the gatepost; eventually you will work it loose. Rock the pin, and before very long you will enlarge the hole. If you do, shim it and promise yourself to use proper tuning technique from now on. There are other things you can do as you tune that will result in slipping strings, and they will be covered in chapter 13.

So far, the reasons for slipping strings have been minor and easily fixed—a tap here, a shim there. Strings are most likely to drop in pitch with the approach of cold weather, as the harpsichord contracts, and obviously this is nothing to worry about. But it *is* something to worry about if the treble alone drops persistently, particularly if the drop seems independent of the weather. It may be an idiosyncrasy of your harpsichord, but it may also be a sign that the bellyrail and/or the soundboard is being drawn into the gap. "How can the soundboard be drawn into the gap when it is glued to the bellyrail?" you ask. It can—it is called "cold creep," and it happens. If it happens to your instrument you have a lot bigger problem than slipping strings. Take the tension off your strings, go directly to the next chapter, and read the section on *Frozen registers*.

BREAKING STRINGS

If there really are parallel universes, as some science-fiction writers claim, I hope the harpsichords in the one next to ours have strings that never break. Nothing that can happen to the harpsichord seems more disconcerting than that snap! of a breaking string, and it always happens at the most inopportune moment. In chapter 6 we listed the usual reasons why strings break: too high a pitch level, turning the wrong pin, hitting the string with something, and what we might call natural or internal causes, as when a soft brass string stretches out and finally exceeds its breaking point. Now let us examine some of the less common causes of breaking strings.

The less a string is moved when it is tuned, the longer it is going to last. This means that when you tune you should move the pitch around as little as possible. This does not really make any difference on most strings (*except* that it is also true that the more the string is moved when it is tuned, the sooner it will go out of tune. Chapter 13

explains that). It does make a difference, however, on those brass and bronze strings. That soft metal work-hardens as it slides over the pin, and work-hardening makes the string brittle. Brittle strings break. If you have not already reached it, one of your goals as a harpsichord tuner should be to tune with minimum movement of the tuning pin. Lest there be any doubt, this is not to be interpreted as a reason to tune less frequently; on the contrary, frequent tunings are necessary to avoid violent pitch changes.

There are some stupid things you can do when you replace a string. You can replace a broken iron string with a brass one of the same gauge, because you forgot to check when you looked at the stringing schedule. Or you can misread the schedule altogether, and simply use the wrong string. Or you might try to replace a steel string (the kind used in pianos) with a soft iron string. Any of these probably will break.

It can happen that the string you are trying to use is not what it says it is. A few years ago I bought some .014 brass wire. When I tried to use a piece—snap! I figured I did something wrong, and tried another, but—snap! At that point I got out my string gauge and discovered that I had been sold .016 gauge, the wrong stuff.

Finally, you might just get some bad string. I do not have any idea how this can happen, but it does. I built a fortepiano some years back, and strung the bottom of the instrument in bronze. No sooner did the piano settle in when those bronze strings began to break. It soon

became obvious that they were *right* at the breaking point—one false move with the tuning hammer, and—snap! It got so that I feared tuning it. I finally got some new brass wire, restrung that section, and the instrument has not had a broken string since.

Sometimes it can be difficult to know why strings break. I am reminded of the conversation I once had with the harpsichordist at a small college in a neighboring state. He told me that his institution had a harpsichord made in the Zuckermann shop, and that they were very unhappy with it because it was breaking strings so consistently that it was unusable. I found it difficult to believe that the shop could have produced such a flawed instrument, but as an agent of the company I felt a responsibility for the instrument. I asked my colleague a series of questions whose answers might have revealed the problem to me, but I was unable to make a diagnosis. I told my colleague that I would visit the instrument as soon as I could. A few weeks later he called to tell me that the harpsichord had been examined by a harpsichord builder in his area, who only confirmed his bad impression of it. Again I was skeptical, this time because I knew the local builder to be an autodidact, and I did not have much faith in his diagnostic abilities.

Some months later I was passing through my colleague's state and was able to examine the harpsichord. One look at the instrument, which was kept in a basement room, was enough to reveal that it had undergone some structural damage. The cheek was cocked, the wrestplank was tilted forward, the hitchpin rail was pulling away from the case, and the tuning pins had loosened so that they were being yanked out of the wrestplank. I asked him if the harpsichord had ever experienced some high humidity, and he said it had, several years back. In fact, that very room had been flooded for a week, and the harpsichord had *sat* in it! The poor instrument had swollen so badly that it had undergone severe plastic deformation, and would never return to its original dimensions. The wonder was not that the strings were breaking, but that the instrument stayed together at all. But my colleague did not connect the flood with the breaking strings, and he put the blame on the builder rather than the water.

Chapter 11   Jack Problems

The jacks, their components, and the registers in which they ride are the most trouble-prone parts of the harpsichord. If chapter 7 did not convince you of that, this chapter will. Yet, despite all the things that can go wrong with jacks, once they are put into proper shape they usually stay that way and cause little grief. But unless those things are set right, jacks can drive you *crazy*!

STICKING JACKS

How do you know when a jack is sticking in its slot? You do not— you only know that something is sticking, and it could be the key as well as the jack. Remove all the jacks that are operated by that key and try the key again. If it operates smoothly, then it is indeed the jack that is at fault. But just to be sure, watch the way the jack operates in the register slot. If it sticks, you should be able to see it stick.

The jack must have been working in the recent past, so it is unlikely that anything serious has gone wrong. Most likely the problem is caused by one or a combination of four things: dirt, humidity, the shape of the jack itself, or something interfering with the operation of the jack. Before you even try to determine the cause, try the direct approach. Grasp the head of the jack and work it up and down in its slot, at the same time putting pressure on one side, then the other, with a twisting motion. Do this vigorously, but carefully—you could break a tongue or a plectrum if you get too violent. Nine times out of ten, this will open the slot, knock off the dust, or otherwise solve the problem, and it will never occur again. If this does not work, then you must try to pinpoint the cause.

Dirt. Airborne dust reaches every surface of your harpsichord, whether covered or not, and this includes the jacks. On the antique instruments, jacks usually fit in their slots with some degree of play, and a modern instrument built in this way is not likely to have jacks that stick from dust. Some builders like their jacks to fit in their slots as tightly as possible, and it will not take much dust to make such a jack feel sluggish or even to halt its operation altogether. And if the dust does not do it, specks of material from the dampers, dog hair, cat hair, human hair, eraser fragments, and bits of food from your child's fingers can do it just as well. Fortunately, the solution is simple: wipe off the jack with a clean, dry, lint-free cloth.

Older harpsichords sometimes have jacks riding in metal registers. Other instruments have jacks with long metal end pins, and these, rather than the body of the jacks themselves, ride in holes in the lower guides. The metal from the registers or the end pins can oxidize, depositing a coating on the register slots in one case, and on the end pins in the other, and this can cause the jack to stick. Again, all you need to do is wipe off the jacks or the long end pins, although you may have to rub fairly vigorously.

Humidity. Here it is again. By now I trust that you are thoroughly convinced that excess humidity is your harpsichord's most vicious enemy. You paid a lot of money for that instrument, and if you do not protect it against excess humidity you are not protecting your investment. Even if you care nothing for yourself, your furniture, your dog, or your children, put an air conditioner in one room of your house, if it is needed, for the sake of the harpsichord. This advice is for everyone, but particularly for those in the Midwest, where people seem to make a virtue out of burning wood in the winter and *not* running their air conditioners in the summer. On the hottest and most humid days of August, I hear my friends testing each other's righteousness with remarks such as, "Well, it reached 103 degrees today, but we really didn't think we needed the air conditioner." Personally, I run my air conditioner constantly in such weather. It is the price to be paid if one is a harpsichord owner, a furniture owner, or a body owner. I humidify my house in the winter for the same reason.[1]

Humidity can affect the parts of wooden jacks; tight or stuck tongues will be discussed later in this chapter. Plastic jacks are immune to humidity, but the jack slots in the upper and lower guides are not. If jacks and/or slots swell from humidity, do nothing until you get the humidity back to normal (whatever that is), and everything has had a chance to dry out. If the swelling was not too bad, and if the excess humidity did not last too long, the slots will probably go back to their original size and the jacks should work fine. But if the swelling was worse than that, the wood is likely to have undergone some plastic deformation. This means that it will *never* go back to its original condition. Now you have a problem, but like most problems on the harpsichord, as long as it is not structural it can be fixed without too much trouble.

It is possible to enlarge the slots, with a properly shaped file and a great deal of care. Although some builders prefer that you file the slots, it is difficult to control the file and at the same time avoid filing a string. It is usually better to work on the jack. If you have French-style leather-covered registers you have no choice but to work on the jacks.

Go to your well-stocked hardware store and get some fine sandpaper, around 300 grit. Get a full 9″ × 11″ sheet, so that you can lay it down on a table and rub the jack over it if necessary. Sand the front and back of the jack with moderate vigor, taking care not to break the plectrum or ruin the spring. Check the jack in its slot—the sides may need some sanding, too. Then round off the arrises a little. Sand only in the direction of the length of the jack, keep the jack smooth, and wipe off the dust you have

created by sanding. This can be done on both plastic and wooden jacks. A file can also be used if you wish, but that requires more care. Remember that the idea is remove only what is binding, nothing else.

The shape of the jack itself. It is unlikely that a well-made wooden jack will have any swellings, projections, roughness, or burrs. The very process of making a wooden jack removes any such flaws. However, such is not the case with plastic jacks, which are made by injection moulding. This process can result in jacks with bulges, twists, warps, projections, hairs, splinters, and burrs. Many times these must be dealt with or removed before the jack can be made to work; then it usually will operate without any trouble. But if the registers swell a little, a bulge in the jack, formerly benign, could now cause it to stick.

In such cases take the bulge down with the file, carefully, working in the direction of the length of the jack. Do not change the angles of the jack's sides, and do not make it so thin that it has more play in the register than it should. Sometimes it is best to lay the file down on a table and move the jack over it, rather than the reverse. If you do take too much off you will have to shim things back to where they should be. You can glue paper or card stock (or even stamps) to a wooden jack, but such materials will not stick to plastic; with plastic jacks, use transparent tape or shim the register. If you have leather-covered registers, try the following ploy, recommended by Dowd,

You will need a hardwood block that *just* fits inside the wood part of the mortise in the bottom of the register. Place the register face down on a hard, flat surface. Place the block inside the mortise that has the problem and give it a solid blow with a hammer. This should squeeze out the leather slightly, thus reducing the size of the slot in the leather.[2]

It is possible to put a bulge in a jack yourself, when you try to free a sluggish tongue by prying open the window or slot in which the tongue pivots. If you overdo this you can bulge out the walls of the jack and it can stick in the register. Undo the damage by squeezing the walls back in, gently. If for some reason it is impossible to do this without affecting the operation of the tongue, then file the sides of the jack.

A tiny plastic hair or a splinter or a burr can catch on a string and interfere with the jack's operation. Cut these off with the voicing knife.

Plastic jacks sometimes warp as they cool off from the injection moulding. There is little harm in using a jack that has a slight warp or twist; however, when the registers swell slightly, or when seasonal register adjustments are made, the warp could become a critical factor and then the jack may stick. If the sticking portion of the jack can be identified, and if filing it off does not make the jack too loose otherwise, try taking it down with the file. If this does not seem possible, it will be necessary to remove the warp from the jack.

Hold the jack under the hot water tap for a few moments—just long enough so that it will retain a bend in the opposite direction, but not so long that the plastic loses any of its firmness. It is impossible to say how long to hold it under the water or how hot the water should be; that depends on the particular plastic from which the jack is made and on the thickness of the jack. Bending it in the direction opposite from the warp for just a few moments should be enough to bring the jack to its new and, we hope, better configuration.

Interference with the operation of the jack. Aside from the hairs, burrs, bulges, etc., on the jack itself, there are only two things that normally will interfere with the operation of the jack: the gap spacers and the jackrail.

Gap spacers are little slips of wood (sometimes metal), about $\frac{1}{8}$" thick, that span the distance between the bellyrail and the wrestplank. Depending on your harpsichord and your builder, you may have anywhere from one to five gap spacers, and they are important structural members. The pull of the strings tends to pull the bellyrail into the gap; the gap spacers transfer that thrust to the relatively massive wrestplank. In addition, the tops of the gap spacers are on the same level as the little shelves on either side of the case on which the registers sit. Thus, they also function as little beams over which the registers run, preventing them from sagging into the gap.

Many harpsichord owners are unaware of the existence of gap spacers because they are hidden by the registers. But if a register is moved over far enough in any one direction, eventually a jack will contact a gap spacer, and it will stick. This should not happen—there should be plenty of room for register adjustment without hitting the gap spacers. But if the harpsichord has been in a lot of humidity, and/or is really out of regulation, the problem could arise.

Be sure that the instrument is in its normal state before attempting to deal with this problem. If it persists, see if it cannot be ameliorated by filing down the surface of the jack that is sticking on the spacer. If the jack is warped in such a way that the bend contributes to the problem, then unwarp it. That should be all it needs; if it needs more, you should give serious consideration to the regulation of your harpsichord. Perhaps this is the time to return the registers to a more normal position and to give the jacks a thorough going over and a revoicing.

If things have really shifted so that the placement of the gap spacers is a problem, or if the gap spacers were installed improperly to begin with, then you have another one of those problems that is beyond the scope of this book. The gap spacers will have to be moved, and that is a job for a professional.

Harpsichords with box registers normally do not have gap spacers, since the solid box register prevents anything else from crossing the gap. However, there are some antique Italian instruments that have thin gap spacers under the box guides, and some modern Italians may also have them. To check, remove the keyboard and get a hand up into the gap from below. Antique Flemish harpsichords often had iron rods

—sometimes no more than one— across the gap as spacers, and some modern builders follow that practice; other Flemish harpsichords may have conventional spacers.

Interference with the operation of a jack by the jackrail is hard to spot. A jack sticks, so you remove the jackrail to observe its operation. It seems to work fine, so you replace the jackrail. It sticks again. Again, you remove the jackrail, and so on. Finally, you realize that the jack works perfectly without the jackrail, but sticks when the jackrail is on. Thus, it is sticking on the jackrail. Perhaps the jackrail position has shifted for some reason; if so, shift it back. On a harpsichord that has plenty of room between registers, one of them could get moved out of line for some reason: then a jack or two could graze the sides of the jackrail, and catch. Move the register back into its proper position.

Two jacks operated by one key. This rare event is caused by a jack that overlaps onto the next key. Pressing the key raises not only its jack but the overlapping neighbor as well. This could occur on a harpsichord with transposing keyboards, and it means that the keyboard has only partially been moved to its transposing or non-transposing position. Thus each key is probably straddled by two jacks. Set the keyboards properly.

The problem is more likely to occur on a virginal or bentside spinet, where the jacks sit crosswise on the keys. If things shift slightly, a key just might pick up its neighboring jack. File the side of the lower part of the jack, at an angle, in order to make its base a little narrower. Be sure to file the side that is responsible for the problem.

WEAK AND INCONSISTENT NOTES

The regulation of entire registers was dealt with in chapter 9. This section will deal with notes that play normally one moment, but are weak, or even missing entirely, the next. This is another one of those problems that can be very frustrating. Part of the time the note is satisfactory in every way, balancing beautifully with its neighbors; but the rest of the time it is barely heard, emitting only a whimper. The wise owner will rightly suspect the plectrum, but a quick inspection reveals that its string underlap looks just like the ones around it. There is no damper interference to be seen, and the jack works smoothly in its register. The plectrum returns without any problem. Played slowly, the note is just fine. But repetitions reveal that it is indeed inconsistent.

Let us eliminate from consideration a note that is *consistently* weak. Through normal wear and tear, or normal expansion and contraction, this is a note that is just weaker than it used to be. Simply push the plectrum through a little with the proper jeweler's screwdriver, and cut back the tip if necessary. Check also to be sure that the fulcrum screws on the register stop levers are tight enough; or, if your registers emerge from the side of the case, that they have been provided with enough friction. In any case, you should check frequently to be sure that the stop levers are *all* the way on or off: you never know when someone might have pushed something out of curiosity and did not put it back exactly the way it was.

Normally, there are only three reasons why a note plays inconsistently: first, the plectrum is cut too short, and is plucking with the very tip; second, the register slot is too wide, thus leaving the amount of underlap to chance; and third, the jack tongue is not returning all the way.

Plectrum too short. Harpsichords do not operate so precisely that a plectrum whose tip *just* plucks the string will work every time. If a plectrum is that short, push it through from the back and do some voicing. If that is not possible, cut a new quill, and be sure it is long enough. The quill must underlap enough so that it will pluck consistently, despite moderate day-to-day changes in temperature and humidity. If it does that, it will certainly pluck consistently with a variety of touches.

Register slot too wide. It has been noted that the register slots on antique harpsichords were wider than strictly necessary, and that it is thought that they were so because the slots had worn over time. Thus many early twentieth-century builders made slots whose jacks fitted with great precision. But with the slightest swelling of the registers, the jacks were sticking—which meant that the jacks were sticking often. This was one of the reasons that revival instruments so often had metal registers. Then, when it was realized that wooden jacks and wooden registers needed that play in order to function properly, some builders went the other way, making registers with slots that were wider than they needed to be.

Even with the best of intentions, slots can turn out slightly wider than planned, jacks slightly thinner. There should be few problems if these departures from normal tolerances are minimal; but if a slot gets just a little wider than it really should be, and if a slightly narrower jack gets in that slot, trouble can follow, and you have a case of "jack jiggle." The note usually does fine if the key is struck sharply. Then the jack tends to shoot straight up, and the string is attacked by the full tip of the plectrum. But when you try to play with a slow attack, the jack has time to slant away from the string, and thus plucks with less of the quill tip.

The easiest way to cure this is to glue a card stock shim on the side of any slot that is too wide— or on all of the slots, if they need it. Think carefully about which side of the slot you want to shim. Remember that the jack should be either upright or leaning slightly *away* from the string it is going to pluck. Remember also that shimming the slot may change the plectrum underlap, perhaps for better, but maybe for worse. Take into consideration also the location of the back of the jack—remember the discussion of strings buzzing against the backs of jacks, in the last chapter. And remember that

leathered registers are a special case. If you cannot shim the jack, you must try to narrow the slot in the leather by the method described a few pages ago; if you cannot do either, the register should be sent back to the maker for releathering.

Poor return of the jack tongue. The symptoms of "tongue jiggle" are just about identical to "jack jiggle," but the culprit in this case is the strength of the spring rather than the width of the register. Again, visual observation confirms that the plectrum underlap is good, the return is fine, the jack works smoothly, and there is no damper interference. And, of course, the register slot is not too wide.

With tongue jiggle, the spring is not strong enough to make the tongue contact the stop on the jack. *Something* must stop the tongue: a voicing screw, a bridle, or a ledge. On wooden jacks it is the slanted part at the bottom of the tongue that stops against the slanted part of the jack's mortise. Whatever it is, something stops the forward thrust that the spring gives to the tongue. If the spring is not strong enough to do its job, there will be a little gap between tongue and jack—a little play, a tiny space where the tongue will jiggle back and forth. The strength of the pluck, therefore, will depend on where the tongue is located in that space at that moment, since the plectrum is attached to the tongue. If it happens to be up against the jack, where it should be, the pluck will be normal; and if the key is depressed slowly it is also likely to be normal, because the friction of the string on the plec-

trum will draw the tongue into the jack. But if the tongue is away from the jack, or if the pluck is made swiftly, so that the tongue does not have time to be pulled into the jack, the pluck will be light or perhaps it may miss altogether.

A misguided solution to tongue jiggle is to set the jack, or even the entire register, to a heavier pluck. To eliminate any chance of a weak note the jack must be set to *overpluck*, but then the note will play strong or stronger, rather than strong or weak, and that is almost as bad. Furthermore, the combination of the weak spring and the force of the overpluck can fling the tongue back far enough so that it catches under the adjoining string. If that happens you will really have problems, because this makes the spring even weaker, the jiggle greater, and the note even more unreliable. It is also a good way to break tongues. (Obviously, this cannot happen to a jack with a thread or a built-in stop of some sort.)

The proper solution is to reset the tension of the spring. With jacks that have plastic, wire, or hog bristle springs, the spring tension can be manipulated with the tweezers. Grasp the spring with the tweezers and bend it so that it has a little more of a bow. Please try not to ruin the spring, but if you do, replace the tongue, or jack, or spring, and worry not. A well-regulated jack is worth the few pennies you wasted. Setting spring tension can be overdone, of course; it must be set so that the spring returns the tongue smartly to the jack, but not so tight that the plectrum cannot return smoothly when given the slow test. If the spring is set too strongly, it can be weakened by manipulating it in the opposite direction with the tweezers.

Axleless jacks are a special case, since the functions of tongue and spring are carried out by a single assembly. Punch the unit out of the jack (see *Changing a tongue*, in chapter 7), and bend the spring in the proper direction with the fingers. Then reinsert the unit, being careful not to bend the tongue in the wrong direction as you do so. If the spring has been set too strongly, such that the plectrum will not return, it can be weakened without taking it out of the jack with the following maneuver: push the tongue back by pressing in on the front, on the plectrum, with the index finger. Catch the back of the tongue as it emerges from the jack, with the index finger of the other hand. Draw the tongue back and release it, so that it flips back to the jack. The spring strength can be set precisely with a few properly released flips.

Finally, it is not enough that the jack tongue now returns—it must do it at a rapid rate of repetition. The proper test is the "four-finger flip," the fingering technique with which keyboard players learn to play rapid repeated notes. If the "four-finger flip" is not in your technical arsenal, try three fingers, two fingers, rapid mordants, and rapid trills. The adjustment for this last refinement is usually in the strength of the spring.

HANGERS

A hanger, as every harpsichordist knows, is a note that will not play because the plectrum is hanging on the string instead of returning under it the way it should. It is one of the easiest problems to diagnose (particularly by those who sit down to play *your* harpsichord), but finding the proper treatment can be elusive. As always, the first thing to do is to give that jack the slow test and find out what is causing the hanger. This is important, because hangers of all sorts tend to be overridden in rapid playing and quick releases, where the vibration of the string itself tends to fling the tongue back. In slower passages, and in releases where the string is no longer vibrating, hangers are more likely to show up. Of one thing you can be certain: if you have a hanger, it will reveal itself at precisely the wrong moment.

Hangers most often occur because of some problem with the plectrum. Next most frequent is a malfunction of the tongue or the spring. Hangers may also be caused by improper jack height or damper setting, and they can also happen because of some sort of interference with the jack's proper operation.

Interference. Let us discuss interference first, because most of the things that happen under this rubric, such as the sticking jack, have already been discussed. Sometimes the offending jack sticks in its register *just* at the point where the plectrum is about to return under the string. This looks for all the world like a plectrum problem, but you can

tell with certainty if you gently pull the string out of the way of the plectrum. The jack is now free to fall to its resting point, and it will, if it is not sticking and if the jack is not too long. If it does not move, give it a helping push with your finger. If it now descends to its resting place, it should be considered a sticking jack problem and treated as such. If it will not move at all, or not far enough, see below under *Jack height and damper setting*. Please note that when the problem of the sticking jack is solved, there still may be a problem with the plectrum or something else.

Little hairs or protrusions formed when the jack was moulded can cause hangers. In the front of the jack, they can hang on the string and actually hold the jack up, preventing the tongue from returning. On the back of the tongue, they can contact the adjacent string, refusing to allow the tongue its required range of motion. Sometimes the smallest nib can make a problem if it is strategically placed. Some good preventative advice is to remove the nibs, hairs, protrusions, burrs, or splinters from a jack or a tongue any time you have it in your hand for any reason.

The plectrum. Nine times out of ten a hanger means that there is some problem with the plectrum. The quill is likely to hang up if the tip has not been cut at an angle. It will certainly hang up if there is a thick part at the tip of the quill. It can also hang up if the tip was not cut cleanly —the results of a dull knife and/or a messy cutting surface. The knife must be kept sharp, and the top of the voicing block dressed flat, if the cut is to be clean. The *slightest* little unevenness in that cut—so slight you may not even be able to see it—can hang up the quill. A curl of the plastic at the tip will also hang up the tip. This can develop over time with a very thin quill, but it can also be put into the plectrum with that cut at the tip. Keep your knife sharp and your block flat—the harpsichord supplies plenty of problems for you to solve; there is no need to provide additional ones if they can be avoided.

A plectrum can hang up if it is too long. Then it requires a large backward movement of the tongue to allow the return of the quill. To accommodate that large a movement, the spring will have to be so weak that the result is tongue jiggle. The only solution is to reset the spring tension, cut off some of the tip of the plectrum, and revoice.

The tongue and the spring. The one time out of ten that the plectrum is not at fault, the hanger will probably be caused by the tongue. And if it is the tongue, it will probably be because you have just replaced it or have done something to it. A tongue can be tight and not rotate freely on its axle; it can also get stuck in the window or mortise, if the walls of the jack close in on it. But it is practically impossible for these things to happen by themselves. These problems were discussed in chapter 7, under *Changing a tongue.*

Spring problems have been covered earlier in this chapter. Once the spring is set to its proper tension, it is not likely to give problems. The one exception

could occur if the setting of the register is changed to the extent that the plectrum is taking a significantly larger bite of the string. This is, of course, what can happen when the seasons change, and normal maintenance should take care of most of these sorts of hangers.

Jack height and damper setting. You will have a hanger if the height of a jack is such that it does not permit the plectrum to return freely. You may have a leaky damper at the same time. Jack heights do not change, but we know that the string band can rise and fall with climatic changes. Since there is only so much that can be done to minimize these changes, residual problems will have to be taken care of by other adjustments. In chapter 9 we discussed the possible need for raising and lowering the keyboard with shims. But if only a jack or two is having problems, shorten the jack until its length is such that it permits the quill to return.

A damper can interfere with the plectrum return if the bottom of the damper is set too close to the top of the quill. Then there simply is not enough room for the proper things to happen. A damper does not set *itself* too low; somebody set it there because the damper was leaking, because the jack was too high, because the string band had fallen, because the soundboard had dropped, or because the temperature and humidity went down. Under these circumstances the damper will probably leak if you raise it. If it does, shorten the jack a little.

Crow quill. Changing and voicing crow quill were treated in chapter 7. Crow quills and Delrin quills are just about complete opposites: voicing Delrin is difficult, but when properly done the plectra seem to go on forever. Voicing crow is no more difficult than cutting a pen point, but the quills do degrade and need maintenance. In contrast to the inert Delrin plastic, crow quill changes as the climate changes. In humid weather the quills will take on moisture and get soggy; in drier weather they will dry out and tend to split. The two most important things to do with crow quill are, first, to keep them oiled, and second, to keep the temperature and particularly the humidity as constant as possible. One can, of course, voice them down by thinning them on the sides and the bottom, and bring the volume up by pushing the quills through and cutting them back, but the quills are not going to last very long that way.

Crow quill hangers are most often caused by broken, bent, or otherwise damaged plectra. If doing so will solve the problem, and *if it is possible* (a wooden tongue is pretty delicate, and pushing a quill through from the back may put more pressure on its walls than it can take), push it through from the back and cut a new tip; otherwise, replace the plectrum. Unoiled plectra tend to hang up, and you should take this as your signal that it is past time to oil. Also, be sure that no pith has been left at the tip of the plectrum. If nothing else helps, rub the tip of the underside of the quill with a lead pencil. Quill really is not that hard to care for, but you do have to be prepared to ignore sudden, quirky changes in humidity.

LEAKING DAMPERS

A great deal has already been said about the cause and cure of leaking dampers, most of it in connection with the length of the jacks.

Jacks, tongues, and Delrin may not wear out, but dampers do. Time after time they come down on those thin metal strings, and eventually grooves are worn in them. Then they start to leak—the strings continue to sound, even though the keys have been released. The cure is obvious: replace the dampers. However, a case of leaking dampers is often misdiagnosed as "singing tails" disease.

Almost every harpsichord has an after-ring—a high-pitched note that persists after the keys have been let up and the dampers let down. This after-ring represents some sort of resonance in the instrument and normally is heard by no one but the player. The string tails—those sections of the string between the bridge and the hitchpin rail—vibrate sympathetically with the sounding portions of the strings, and some of them may produce part of the after-ring. The amount of sound they produce is minimal and usually inaudible, and, in any case, it is part of the sound of the harpsichord.

When dampers begin to leak, tails are often suspected, and listing cloth is wound through them, piano style. There may be a psychological benefit to the listing cloth, but in practical terms it does nothing to stop the leaking dampers. Nevertheless, I have found it difficult to convince people that the root of a leaking problem did not lie in the tails. There have been times when I have had to be high-handed about it. I just removed the listing cloth, told the owner to accept my explanation on faith, and promised to replace the cloth if I was unable to cure the problem by other means.

There is a simple, reliable test for leaking dampers. It should be used to test the damper any time it is changed or any time the length of the jack is changed. Simply pluck the string somewhere between the jack and the nut with a fingernail. If the string is properly damped, you will produce something akin to a plink—high- or low-pitched, depending on the string, but a plink nevertheless. If there is any leaking at all, you will hear a note sing. It may be a full tone, or it may only sing softly, and perhaps even an octave higher (it is the presence of those upper partials that leads to winding listing cloth through the tails). You must be hard-nosed about this—if it does not plink, it almost certainly leaks.

Given a well-designed jack and the proper thickness of material, a damper should not move once it is set. If it does, there are many ways of dealing with it, including using thicker dampers, shims, and various kinds of glues. But a specific recommendation depends on the kind of jack you have, so if you have this problem, you should contact your builder and ask him what to do.

FROZEN REGISTERS

With each passing day it becomes harder to get the registers in your instrument to move from their on or off positions. Thinking that the fulcrum screw on your register lever has been driven down too tightly, you keep reminding yourself that one of these days you will have to get out the screwdriver and loosen it up. Finally the day arrives when you can scarcely move the registers at all. You loosen the fulcrum screw, but it makes no difference at all. Your registers are frozen.

There is only one problem that leads to frozen registers, and it is not an easy one to deal with. It was alluded to in the last chapter, under *Slipping strings*; it is a result of either the bellyrail or the soundboard, or both, being drawn into the gap. The gap gets narrower, diminishing the room needed for the registers to move smoothly. Finally the registers are pressed together, side by side, and cannot be moved except with difficulty.

I do not know precisely why your gap is closing. I would hate to blame your builder, but it is possible that he did not get his *boudin* (4' hitchpin rail) glued into the case properly in the treble, or that he erred in his scaling or in the design of his case. He may have done a poor job of gluing. On the other hand, you must ask yourself if you have abused the harpsichord in one of the ways that could lead to this condition: if you subjected it to extreme humidity for a long period of time, or kept it at a higher pitch than it was designed for, or perhaps both.

The gap closes because the

force generated by the tension of the strings is greater than the structure's ability to resist it. Either the wrestplank, the soundboard, or the bellyrail must move. Usually it is the bellyrail, but if the wrestplank is not securely fastened in, it can rotate, tipping up toward the gap. The soundboard can surrender to the pull of the strings, sliding right across the bellyrail without the two members losing their glue bond—a condition known as "cold creep." Inevitably, a shear crack in the treble portion of the soundboard accompanies this movement (a crack in the treble portion of the soundboard is common, and by itself does not mean that you have a problem). Sometimes when this happens the 8′ hitchpin rail will start to pull away from the bentside, and the cheek-to-bentside joint will open up. That is an advanced state of this syndrome, called a cocked cheek or cheek disease.

If you can help it, do not let this problem progress to the point where you have a cocked cheek. The first thing to do when you notice the gap closing is let *all* the tension off *all* the strings. If the 8′ hitchpin rail is pulling away, or if the wrestplank has tilted, or if the cheek-to-bentside joint has opened, you need the services of a professional. If the problem is only in the gap, you can fix it yourself, if you have the nerve.

Think carefully about the operations to be described. Individually, they are within the capabilities of most people. But if you are all thumbs when you pick up a tool, and have doubts about your ability to do these things,

then do yourself, your harpsichord, and your builder's reputation a favor by calling in a professional.

Let the harpsichord sit for a week or so with the tension off. It needs to regain its composure. So do you. If it was only the soundboard that was pulling into the gap, it may have done all the moving it intends to do. Remove the jacks and the registers and check the extent of the soundboard incursion. Usually, the worst of it is the first six inches or so of the treble. Remove the strings from that area. Throw them away; it is possible to put old strings back on, but usually more trouble than it is worth.

Using your knife, your file, and any other tool you may be handy with (such as a violin maker's plane, a chisel, or a wood-carver's knife), trim the soundboard back to the bellyrail (be sure that your soundboard does not normally overhang the gap). Restring as needed, bring all the strings back up to pitch, replace the registers and the jacks, tune it up, and watch it carefully for the next month or so. The soundboard may pull in yet a little more, but that is not necessarily a cause for alarm. If it continues to pull in to the extent that it is impossible to keep the treble in tune, and if the registers start to freeze again, then let the tension off the strings and call in the professional.

Bellyrail movement needs to be treated in a different manner. Again, let the tension off the strings, remove the jacks, registers, and the necessary amount of string from the treble, and let it sit for a week. During that time

take a good look at the gap spacers, because you are going to put an additional spacer in the treble. After a few days with the tension off, if you are lucky, the bellyrail will start to move back to the position from whence it came. Do everything you can to help it. Put wedges in the gap. You may be able to find a small machinist's jack in your well-stocked hardware store. Use it to help open the gap. Put these wedges, machinist's jacks, or whatever you use in such a position that they will not interfere with the location of the new gap spacer. Try to open the gap just a bit, day by day. Measure it with your six-inch ruler, and see if you can get it to equal the width of the gap in the bass.

When the bellyrail is back in its original position, or at least as close to it as you think it is going to get, make the new gap spacer. It should have the same thickness and height as the others. It can be made out of hardwood, brass, or even iron or steel. Whatever its material, the ends should be flat and smooth, so that the spacer does not sink itself into the softer wood of the bellyrail when tension is reapplied. Look straight down at the existing spacers, and note their position in relation to the strings directly above them. Put your new gap spacer in the position where you think it will do the most good and in the same relationship to the strings as the others. Make sure it is at the right level, because the registers have to slide over it. Run a register through the gap and drop some jacks in, on either side of the new spacer, just to be sure that you are not putting it in a spot where it is going to interfere with anything. Then remove the jacks and the register.

When the new gap spacer is in position, nicely held by friction, squeeze some glue out on a piece of paper. Picking up what you can with a toothpick, spread glue on the spacer-to-bellyrail joint, and the spacer-to-wrestplank joint. Tension alone should be enough to keep it in place, but the dried glue offers a little added insurance. If the soundboard has crept past the bellyrail, cut it back, as described above, before you put in the gap spacer. Do not attempt to repair the crack in the soundboard. It hurts nothing and is of no consequence. If you simply cannot stand to look at it, have a professional shim it—but be prepared to have it crack again.

When the glue has dried, restring as necessary, replace all the parts, and tune it up. If you have not been able to get the gap opened enough, and the registers are still tight, remove them and take them down the street to

your friend with the plane. Have him take one light pass off each side of each register.

If your problem is still not solved, console yourself with the thought that you made a valiant effort, and call in the professional. If you have succeeded in conquering frozen registers, pat yourself on the back. But do not get so cocky that you now feel ready to take on any repair job! The next one may not be that easy.

In writing this section on frozen registers, I am reminded of a repair I did almost twenty years ago on the registers of one of those little blonde revival Wittmeyers. Its registers were box-like affairs, made of metal, and metal was also used to line the gap. The theory was that metal would be immune to expansion, and indeed, there was none; nevertheless the gap was frozen, and I could not understand why the problem existed.

I used as much force as I thought I could to unfreeze those metal registers, but nothing seemed to work. Finally, I de-

cided to call the owner and tell him that I was going to have to cut a window in the spine in order to get the registers out; but before I did, I made a supreme effort to free the registers, and this time I succeeded. The next day, however, to my surprise, the registers were frozen again. Once more I was able to free them, and this time I squirted some graphite in the gap, to lubricate the metal surfaces. That worked fine, and I found that things would continue to work smoothly as long as the graphite was applied once a week.

When the owner came to pick up the instrument, I asked him if anything had ever been spilled in the gap. He admitted that a glass of orange juice had landed there some years ago. Evidently the citric acid in the juice had eaten at the metal, finally welding it together. I handed my customer a tube of graphite and instructed him to use it weekly. That instrument is still functioning, and it still gets an occasional shot of graphite!

Chapter 12   Action Problems

In chapter 8 we went through normal maintenance routines for the action. In this chapter we look at the nasty things that can happen to an action.

STICKING KEYS

A key can stick because it has warped, and an accidental can stick because its front catches under the back of the head of a natural. But when a key sticks, suspect our old enemy humidity first, before you look elsewhere.

A keyboard needs to be adjusted so that it will play without any problems under *normal* extremes of temperature and humidity. It may take several years before it is so regulated, and you may have to do part of that regulation yourself. Or, as happened to one of my instruments several years ago, it may get moved to a climate more humid than the one in which it grew up, and then it will require further adjustment.

A lot of humidity can spell trouble for a light, unbushed classical keyboard. Some months after that harpsichord just mentioned was moved to its new home, I received a call from the owner. She was living by a lake, it was the most humid time of the year, and her basement had been flooded for a week. She said that a lot of her keys were sticking, and she didn't know what to

do. I told her to get the instrument out of the humidity immediately, and to get it dried out. After that much moisture, some parts of those keyboards had undergone plastic deformation and never returned to their original dimensions. But with a little instruction over the phone she was able to make the keyboards operate smoothly once again.

Be sure that it is the key, rather than the jack, that is sticking. Use the test described in the last chapter: remove the jacks that are operated by the sticking key and try the key again. If the key still sticks, that is indeed where the problem is. It will be sticking either at the balance pin, at the guide, or at both. Easing the key is relatively simple and the repair is usually permanent.

Sticking at the balance pin. First try to ascertain that the key is sticking at the balance pin, rather than at the guide. This is not always easy to do, but sticking at the guide is more obvious than sticking at the balance pin; so if it works freely at the guide, suspect the balance hole. You will need an easing tool like an ice pick or a small awl. Try that well-stocked hardware store again, and bring the hole in the key with you so that you get the right size tool.

Ease the hole from the top and from the bottom. Be firm, but please be gentle. The hole should not be visibly enlarged. If easing the hole a little does not produce results, suspect the fulcrum mortise next. Ease that from the top with a more vigorous back-and-forth motion, taking care not to jam your tool as hard as you can all the way into the key. If the key works freely but will not come back to its resting position, check the front-to-back angle of the balance pin. Sometimes tapping it back or forward a little (in the manner described under *Straightening the keys*, in chapter 8) is all that is needed.

Sticking at the guide. No matter how a key is guided, it is safe to assume that it is sticking at the guide if you moved the guide while straightening the key. Ease a front or a rear guide hole with your easing tool, and that should do it. Rear guide holes can sometimes be sensitive to the back-and-forth position of the pin, so if the key tends to get hung up at the top of the pin, try tapping it slightly back or forth.

If the key is guided by a metal pin in a rack, it is possible to unstick it either by enlarging the slot in the rack or by filing the pin. Enlarge the slot only if the pin is so thin that filing it would be dangerous; otherwise, file the pin. Lay the key on its side on a table. Take one good solid pass over the side of the pin with the file. This is done by setting the front of the file on the pin and pushing forward—a file only cuts in one direction. Turn the key over and take a pass over the other side. Do not think that you are filing a round pin into absolute flatness; your filing will not be that precise, and you will naturally tend to make an oval shape. Put the key back and try it. If necessary take another pass, and perhaps another. After each pass check that you have not filed too much off. Put the key back in place, grasp its head, and rock it gently back and forth. You should barely be able to feel the sides of the pin contact the sides of the guide slot: but there must be that little bit of play, or else the key will stick every time the humidity goes up slightly. If the play is not there, file off a little more. You do not want this filing to roughen the surface of the pin. If it does, either use a finer file or sand it smooth.

If the pin feels right in its slot but the key still sticks, see if it is sticking in some particular spot —perhaps at the top of the rack. If so, carefully widen the slot with a pencil point, working it up and down in that area. Do not worry about the graphite left behind; it is an excellent lubricant.

Sticking keys that are guided by wooden, plastic, or bone guides are treated in the same way, except instead of filing a metal pin, you file a wooden, plastic, or bone slip. All of these are softer than metal, and filing them can easily be overdone, so be careful. In any case the guide, whether metal, wood, plastic, or bone, can be replaced if you ruin it.

Some keyboards are guided by pins between the backs of the keys. Here the sticking key is eased by sanding, filing, or cutting a little of the wood away on each side, where it contacts the guide pins. But file just a little— or at least, a little at a time. If you have a number of these to do, it will be worth it for you to buy a medium half-round needle file, the tool of choice for this operation.

Before returning the keyboard to the instrument, check the sides of the keys and the action cloth on the ends of the keys. They should not be rubbing against each other.

Warped keys. Keys can warp after they have been cut out of the key blank, but your builder took care of all that when he made your keyboard. Nevertheless, one day you may find a key, formerly well behaved, now curving in toward its neighbor. If it is just a little out of line and not really bothering anything, I suggest you leave it alone. But if it has warped to the extent that it is rubbing against another key and affecting the action, you must take out the warp.

Like putting in a gap spacer, this takes a little nerve, skill, and knowledge; so go to a professional if you doubt your ability to do it yourself.

Cut a slot in the side of the key, about one inch forward of the balance hole, on the concave side of the warp. You want to make a fairly wide kerf, so do this with a band saw, table saw, or hand saw, rather than some fine-blade saw, like a backsaw or a jeweler's saw. Prepare a wood shim, slightly wedge-shaped, so that it will slide into the slot without any trouble but will exert increasing pressure as it penetrates the slot. The grain of the shim should run at right angles to the grain of the key, or else the shim will break when you try to force it in. Put glue in the kerf and hammer in the shim. If you have chosen the width of the shim wisely, it will open up the warp and straighten out the key. Even if it is not completely straight, congratulate yourself for a job well done. When the glue is dry, trim the shim to the key. The back of the key may still be warped and rub against its neighbor. If so, carve or file the appropriate amount of wood off the side of either or both keys. The key should now operate without sticking. Figure 12-1 shows a formerly-warped key that has been straightened by this operation.

Another method of straightening a key consists of wetting it, applying heat, and bending it in the direction opposite from the warp. Although this may sound easier, it is much more difficult to control, and I do not recommend that you try it.

Naturals that catch sharps. On keyboards where the front of the sharps are very close to the rear of the key-cover heads, things can shift a bit and the sharp may get snagged on the natural key cover. This does not happen often and for this reason may be hard to spot. It may be accompanied by a clicking sound as the two surfaces pass each other, so that could be your clue. File back the rear of the key-cover head a bit, until proper clearance is provided. Would that all problems on the harpsichord were solved so simply!

SQUEAKY, WIGGLY, AND
NOISY KEYS

Squeaky keys. These can be annoying but usually only to the player. The problem often lies in the guides, whether pins, wood,

bone, or plastic. Remove the keyboard from the instrument, and remove the keys from the frame. Insert a pencil point in each guide slot and, without enlarging it, lubricate the sides of the slot with graphite. Balance points can be lubricated in the same way. If you object to the mess that a pencil point can make, any sort of dry lubricant or wax will do.

Wiggly keys. Squeaky keys can be confused with wiggly keys, since the latter often set up a mild clatter. Wiggly keys are caused by guides that are *too* loose. They can get that way because you or someone else filed the guides too much, and now in cold, dry weather, they are too thin; or they can get that way because whoever is playing the harpsichord is beating up the keyboard. Hard, sloppy playing can put a lot of lateral force on the keys, and eventually that can open up the guide slots. It is within the rights of every harpsichord owner to refuse to let a heavy-handed player touch his instrument.

Wiggly keys are not easily fixed. Guide slots can be shimmed, but if you have many to do, it can be a painstaking operation. Before you start glueing in shims, try putting a drop of water on each slot. This should swell the slot enough to tighten up the key. If a slot swells up too much, ease it by working the key up and down, bearing against one side of the slot and then the other. Try to avoid filing the guide pins or slips if you can; but remember that guide pins and wood, bone, or plastic slips can always be replaced, if it comes to that.

If you must, shim the slots with thin, gummed paper, such as the return address labels many charitable organizations send at Christmas time. And remember that putting something on one side of the guide slot is going to move the head of the key to that side, so think before you shim.

I once tightened up a keyboard that was loose on its rear guide pins by wrapping each pin with pressure-sensitive graphic tape, placing the seam of the wrap where it would not bear against the walls of the guide holes in the ends of the keys. I see no reason why this treatment should not also work on front guide pins as well as on keys that are guided between pins.

Noisy keys. Keys and jacks should operate relatively silently. They do make some noise, but it is well masked by the sound of the harpsichord. If you start to hear sharp raps when you play, you must track down the sound and eliminate it. The following are some of the more common causes of noise but by no means the only ones.

Probably the most frequent reason for the knocks that some notes seem to produce is that the jackrail is slightly loose. In an action whose dip is limited by a jackrail stop, the jacks hit the rail with considerable force. The rail must be fastened down securely to absorb all that force, and it probably was when your instrument was new; but now, through wear, something is *just* a little loose—a hook, a shelf, or whatever it is that is supposed to grip that jackrail. Now, the jackrail is taking a little hop every time a jack hits it, and

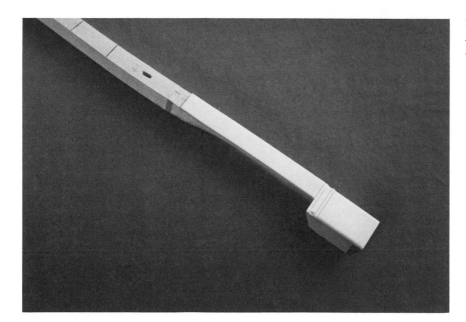

when it comes down it clacks against the ledge on which it sits. The case itself obligingly resonates to the knock, amplifying the unpleasant noise.

Have someone hold down the ends of the jackrail as you play. If the knocking sound is no longer heard, you have found the cause. Tighten up the connection between jackrail and case with some kind of shim: card stock, damper felt, or masking tape will handle just about any situation of this sort.

It is possible for the action to knock only when coupled. If you use your coupler a great deal, the lower-manual dogs can wear off the felt or cloth that covers the bottom of the end of the upper manual key levers. Wood hitting felt is silent; wood hitting wood makes a knocking sound. Replace the felt.

Knocking can also be caused on a double-manual harpsichord by the back end of an upper-manual key hitting the lower guide. It usually will not happen unless the key is played with some force, but it should not happen under any conditions. It may occur if you have overdone the shims under the keyboard (see chapter 9, *The Touch*), raising the keyboard to the point where the upper manual keys are too close to the lower guide. This situation exceeds the bounds of normal adjustment, and you must pay the penalty by lowering the keyboards and readjusting the heights of all the jacks.

The noise could come from the lower-manual key hitting the coupler rail, but this could only happen if in leveling the lower-manual keys, you built up the balance felt punchings and/or the paper punchings well beyond reason. If you did indeed do this, it was undoubtedly in response to some other problem, and you chose the wrong solution. Get the keys down where they belong and call a professional.

A clack can also be produced by the front of the key hitting the front rail. If the action is stopped at the head and it clacks, you do not have enough padding there to stop the noise. But why do you not have enough padding? Did you remove too much when adjusting the dip? If so, once again your problem lies else-where. And if your action is *not* stopped at the front rail and it clacks, you have a different prob-lem, and given the fact that your keyboard *had* been working fine before this, I cannot guess what it might be. Call the professional.

If the front of a key is really close to the molding in front of the keyboard, it is possible for something to shift enough so that the very tip of the key cover knocks against the molding. A careful pass over the front edge of the key cover with the file should fix it.

The keys can be pounded so hard that they are made to bounce off the balance rail and hit the bottom edge of the name batten. One way of fixing that is to glue a strip of felt to the bot-tom of the batten. The better way is to learn to play the harpsi-chord without pounding the keys. By pummeling the keys al-most any harpsichord can be made to rattle the jack rail and produce action noise. This is an abuse of the instrument, and it will damage the keyboard. It should not be permitted.

LOOSE AND LEAKING BUFF PADS

Repairing a leaking or a loose buff pad is simple: just pluck the pad off the buff rail with your fingers or the pliers. Turn the buff stop on. Hold the loose pad with the tweezers and put a little glue on it. Put the pad back in place on the rail, and press it in against the string. Play the buffed note. If it is satisfactory, leave ev-erything alone for an hour. The pad should now buff perfectly.

Part Four   Care of the Harpsichord

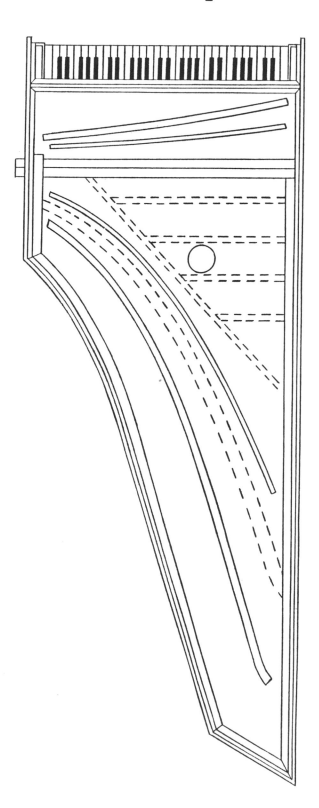

Chapter 13

Tuning, Temperaments, and Techniques

Tuning your harpsichord should be a joyous task. What better way is there to spend a few moments than in tuning? What gives a greater sense of accomplishment than bringing order out of chaos? What is more gratifying to the ear and to the soul than a well-tuned and sweetly singing harpsichord? Few things in life are so worth learning to do well, because they make you feel so good, as tuning your harpsichord.

But tuning can be approached negatively, too. It does nothing to improve the instrument; it merely puts it in the condition in which it should have been anyway and from which it will depart as soon as the tuning is finished, if not sooner. Furthermore, tuning is inherently unfair: a good tuning effort stays in tune no longer than a poor one. Every once in a while I get lucky and set a beautiful temperament, one worthy of a master tuner. Then sometimes I have a bad day and cannot for the life of me set a decent temperament. Does the first last any longer than the second? It does not! Nevertheless, I never complete a tuning without a sense of satisfaction and accomplishment. The music never sounds as good, and I never play as well as at that moment.

The harpsichordist is also faced with the apparent dilemma of temperament. When I built my first harpsichord, back in 1963, I taught myself to tune it in equal temperament. What else *could* I tune it in? I knew that other temperaments had been in use before the nineteenth century, but practical information on how to set them was nonexistent. I remember laboriously working out some sort of meantone, which may or may not have resembled anything historical. I set it on my harpsichord and invited my students over to hear its arcane intervals. I retuned it in equal temperament as soon as they left.

Today one reads instructions on tuning this or that temperament in every other issue of the various keyboard and early music magazines, and books have been written on the subject.[1] What is not generally understood, though, is the reason that these temperaments existed in the first place. The section in this chapter on the history of temperament is intended to help put the all-important relationship between the music and the tuning in perspective. When this is properly understood, temperament becomes a matter of choice rather than a dilemma.

Those reading this chapter probably fall into one of three broad classifications. In the first are the experienced tuners, those who know what temperament means and are capable of setting one or more historical temperaments with some accuracy. These are the professional harpsichordists, the technicians, and the many, many knowledgeable and capable amateurs. Those in this class need do no more than skim this material.

To the second class belongs that large number of people who have a fair idea of what temperament is about, but who more or less move the notes around when they tune. They achieve some sort of arrangement that seems to work, but in all honesty it cannot be identified with a particular historical temperament. This is the way my friend, the one who carved her first plectrum on her breadboard, tunes her harpsichord. For the large number of people in this group—undoubtedly the vast majority of harpsichord owners—it is hoped that this chapter will remove the mystery from tuning and temperament.

The third group encompasses those who take a dim view of the entire tuning process. To them, it is the prelude to the demise of the instrument—it is that "kaboom switch" we talked about in the Introduction. These people feel helpless and frustrated at their inability to hear intervals, beats, or pitches, and they lack confidence in handling the tuning hammer. I remember a couple who purchased a small instrument from me a few years ago. They were particularly concerned about tuning, so I gave them a long tutorial with some hands-on experience. Visiting the instrument a year later, I found it badly out of tune. I asked them when they had tuned it last, and they admitted that it had not been touched since it had been delivered. They were afraid that they would only make it worse,

that it would take an enormous amount of time, and that they lacked the necessary skills anyway. I tuned the instrument for them, but I also suggested that they invest in an electronic tuner. They took my advice and found that it did indeed give them the confidence they needed to keep their harpsichord tuned.

Others in this third group seem bewildered by the need to tune at all. Living in an electronic, transistorized world, we have come to expect things to work perfectly after they have been adjusted. So why does a harpsichord not work that way? It was delivered in perfect tune, yet now it is unusable; thus as a modern product it is somehow faulty! David Way tells about a phone call he received from the president of a small college that had just taken delivery of their new French double. "Mr. Way," said the man, "we just unpacked your instrument, and it certainly is beautiful. But it is *out of tune!*"

Those in this third category may or may not benefit from this chapter; it depends on how much confidence my words will give them. I hope it gives them a great deal. But it must be recognized that some people simply are incapable of hearing pitches in the particular kind of way that is needed for tuning. There is no point in berating yourself if you do not have this ability: you undoubtedly have other positive characteristics that the rest of us lack. Instead, buy an electronic tuning aid. Considering the many thousands of dollars you spent on your harpsichord, another hundred or so is little enough to pay for the reward of

having an instrument in tune; and with an electronic tuner to help you set a temperament, you may be able to train your ear to the point where the aid itself becomes superfluous.

While this book was still in the planning stages, I was urged by some builders and technicians to include detailed instructions for tuning four or five useful temperaments. It seemed like a good idea at the time, but when I talked with the people in the second and third classes who were going to do the tuning, it became clear that what most harpsichordists need is the ability to set *one*, or at the most, *two* temperaments with a modicum of skill. Thus, my discussion of temperament will focus on attaining this ability. Having achieved it, the would-be tuner should be able to adapt it to any reasonably presented tuning system.

TUNING AND TEMPERAMENT

These two words are frequently confused, and the relationship between them is not always understood.

Tuning. In the context of keyboard instruments, tuning is a multi-step process by which an instrument's pitches are brought into a predetermined relationship with one another, usually in reference to a specific standard. By way of example, note the steps your technician goes through when he tunes your piano. First he matches a single note to the pitch standard to which all the other notes will be related. On the piano this is normally the internationally recognized a' = 440 Hz. Harpsichords, of course, are often tuned to some other standard, such as the generally accepted "low pitch" of a' = 415 Hz, one half-step lower than a' = 440 Hz. Second, the tuner sets the temperament. We will define temperament shortly, but for now let us simply say that he tunes the pitches to which all the other pitches on the piano will relate. This is done within an octave somewhere around the middle of the piano, called the *bearing octave*. Third, he tunes all the other notes by octaves, matching them to the notes he has set in his bearing octave; finally, he tunes all the unison strings. The same sequence of events is followed in harpsichord tuning.

Temperament. Temperament is a way of setting the bearing octave so that the Pythagorean comma is divided in some way. That, of course, is no explanation at all: what is a Pythagorean comma, why does it have to be divided, and what happens if it is not?

Suppose you decide to tune your piano by setting twelve pure, beatless fifths upward from the lowest CC. These are the notes you would tune: CC - GG - D - A - e - b - f'-sharp - c''-sharp - g''-sharp - d'''-sharp - a'''-sharp - e''''-sharp - b''''-sharp. Seven octaves later, when you arrive at the b''''-sharp, you might assume that you had reached some point of closure. Logically, one should be able to regard that b''''-sharp as the enharmonic equivalent of c'''''. But just to check, to make sure that you are right, you ascertain the frequency of the pitch of

the b''''-sharp (say, with a frequency counter), and divide it by seven. If things were indeed perfect in this world of ours, the resulting number would be exactly the same as the frequency of the first CC. But, as you already know, it is not. Perhaps it happens otherwise in that parallel universe, but in this one, the frequencies of the pitches we use in music do not form a closed system.

The difference between those two numbers is called the Pythagorean comma, which is equivalent to about one quarter of a semitone. There are other commas, derived by means other than tuning pure fifths, but they lie outside our immediate area of interest.

Now the meaning of temperament becomes clear: it is the division of the comma and the placing of each of those divisions on specific intervals. This is easily understood if one thinks of it in terms of equal temperament, the one your technician sets on your piano. Here the comma is divided into twelve parts, and each fifth, rather than being tuned pure, is mistuned by the amount of one-twelfth of a quarter of a semitone. If you have grasped the idea that your tuner tunes by mistuning, you have made the conceptual leap necessary to understand temperament.

You must also understand that only instruments of fixed pitch, such as keyboard instruments, the harp, and the xylophone, can be tempered. String and wind instruments and the voice are instruments of flexible pitch; fretted strings are dependent on temperament to some extent, but instruments like the gamba and

the lute have movable frets, and on these instruments pitches can be bent somewhat. Elsewhere I have coined the term semi-temperament to describe the phenomenon on those instruments.[2]

The answers to the other questions raised at the beginning of this section, why does the comma have to be divided, and what happens if it is not, require that we look at the relationship between temperament and the music it serves.

A SHORT HISTORY OF TEMPERAMENT[3]

Pythagorean tuning. Polyphonic music, or music of more than one part (which is to say, just about all the music played on the harpsichord), was developed in the West around the tenth century. At the core of its harmonic basis was the rationale of the *perfect* intervals: the unison, the octave, the fifth, and its inversion, the fourth. These perfect intervals were the building blocks, the buttresses of multi-voice music. Between their more-or-less regular appearance was to be found a great deal of free dissonance.

All the other intervals—seconds, sevenths, augmented and diminished intervals, and major and minor thirds and sixths were considered to be dissonant in medieval music. Thirds and sixths are the sweetest-sounding combinations that *we* have, so it is a little difficult for us to understand how medieval theorists could call them dissonances. Even more to the point, composers *treated* them as dissonances, often using them as tendency tones that resolved to perfect consonances. How could thirds and sixths be consonant to us and dissonant to them? The explanation of this seeming paradox requires another conceptual leap.

Fifths and octaves have a hollow purity that greatly appealed to the medieval sensibility. As much as we may appreciate the harmoniousness of thirds, there is no question that they thicken musical texture and destroy the purity of the perfect intervals. With perfect intervals as building blocks, individual lines tend to be isolated, exposed, and separated one from the other; thirds and sixths, on the other hand, tend to blend the individual lines and glue the texture together. Thirds, therefore, break down the leanness of the texture and blend what should be separated. Thus it is no surprise that thirds appeared in a dissonant context between the buttresses of the perfect intervals and at cadences.

Now let us connect this bit of information with our discussion of temperament. Medieval performers had the same division of the octave that we do. All twelve notes of the scale were available to them, and were either called for by the written notes or applied in performance by the demands of *musica ficta*—accidentals implied but not written down. When it was invented in the fourteenth century, the harpsichord was tuned in the same way as the organ, the harp, or any other instrument of fixed pitch: *the comma was not divided in any way, but was placed all on one interval*.

In other words, the medieval keyboard player did not temper his comma at all. He tuned pure

fifths and fourths in one direction (tuning a fourth down, fifth up, fourth down, fifth up and so on, is equivalent to tuning successive rising fifths), then some fifths and fourths in the opposite direction, all within the bearing octave. This method of tuning gives precisely the same result as the rising fifths we tuned earlier in this chapter: the Pythagorean comma of a quarter of a semitone. The harpsichordist knew full well what he had done. He tuned his instrument in such a way that the comma was tucked into a fifth that he and the composer (undoubtedly the same person, anyway) avoided. That particular fifth was called the wolf.

There were good reasons for using Pythagorean tuning. Since perfect intervals were the most important intervals in the medieval tonal system, their purity was crucial: Pythagorean tuning yields pure, beatless fifths and fourths (pure octaves, too, but every conventional system produces pure octaves), except for the wolf. Pythagorean thirds, however, are anything *but* pure: they are quite wide and they beat rapidly. Their sound is almost unpleasant. In other words, they *were* dissonances, in sound as well as in theory and practice.

Here, then, is the answer to the second of our questions: what happens if you do not temper the comma? Pythagorean tuning turns out to be the ideal tuning (it obviously is not a temperament) for medieval music. It emphasizes the beauty, the purity, and the hollow, restful quality of the perfect intervals, and it intensifies the vibrant dissonance of the third. These two qualities are played off against

each other in the keyboard music of the late middle ages, as the music oscillates between consonance and dissonance.

Meantone temperament. The Renaissance, which began about 1450, had a different way of looking at musical space and texture; in fact, this outlook is one of the major characteristics that distinguishes Renaissance music from that which preceded it. Now it is thirds and sixths, the former dissonances, that are the building blocks of music. And they were considered to be consonant, although, in truth, not as *perfectly* consonant as the perfect consonances. All other intervals were considered dissonant, including the fourth when it appeared above the lowest-sounding note.

Because thirds and sixths became so important, the purity of *these* intervals became paramount. To achieve it on keyboard instruments musicians had to trade the purity of the perfect consonances for the purity of thirds and sixths. Instead of tuning pure perfect consonances, and allowing the thirds to beat as they would, the thirds were tuned pure, and the fourths and fifths were allowed to beat roughly.

The best known of these meantone temperaments, as they are called, is the quarter-comma meantone of Pietro Aron. In this temperament, one-fourth of the Pythagorean comma was placed on four of the fifths, which, by general agreement, were usually avoided. Actually, the loss was not that great, since it was not the intent of Renaissance music to explore all possible tonal areas.

We often read that quarter-comma meantone is useful in keys up to three flats and two sharps, or vice versa, depending on which thirds you tune pure. This statement is true, but it is misleading. Neither functional tonality nor the closely related major-minor key system, both of which we take for granted, were fully developed until well into the seventeenth century. Thus, for most of the period in which this temperament was used, music was not written in "keys." True, we can discuss the *tonal areas* of a Renaissance keyboard piece, and even assign it a tonality; but the distinction between being in an F *tonality* and being in the *key* of F is a crucial one.

The glorious thing about quarter-comma meantone is that the thirds are pure. They are not enharmonic. G-sharp and A-flat are two different notes, and the performer had to tune one or the other, according to the demands of the music he was to play. Of course, retuning a few G-sharps to A-flats was no problem and probably was done regularly. It will be recalled from chapter 2, however, that there were instruments with split sharps—particularly in Italy, where they seemed to regard the purity of the third with great seriousness. With such a keyboard one was spared from taking even the few moments to retune an occasional accidental.

Just as Pythagorean tuning fits medieval music, so quarter-comma meantone fits music composed from 1450 to 1600 and well beyond. It is ideal for the keyboard entabulations of fifteenth-century chansons, for the fantasias of the English virginalists, for the toccatas of Frescobaldi, the variations of Cabezón, the suites of Froberger, and the variation sets of Sweelinck. Now, instead of the consonant effect of the music depending on the purity and static quality of the fifth and octave, the pure third overwhelms the emptiness of those intervals and binds them together for a quite different but equally pure and static effect. Dissonance is also achieved differently, with careful preparation and resolution of the dissonant intervals.

Modified meantone temperament. The garment of meantone temperament that cloaked Renaissance and early baroque music was a beautiful one, but it presented increasing problems for harpsichordists playing the functionally tonal, key-centered music that everybody was writing by the middle of the seventeenth century. Modulation is one of the cornerstones of functional tonality, and modulation to any key, including those in which meantone was unacceptable, is one of its possibilities. With this new tool at their disposal, composers refused to be restrained by the limitations of meantone temperament. True, a great deal of the difficulty could be gotten around by clever retuning, and an instrument with two or three split sharps per octave could handle most situations, but these solutions were at best annoying. It is not unreasonable to suggest that most players just put up with the "bad" intervals, rather than spend time retuning accidentals.

To meet these new musical demands a new kind of temperament was developed. It had many forms, all slightly different one from the other, but they all were some variation of a fifth- or sixth-comma temperament. Collectively these are known as the modified meantone temperaments, or the revolving, or unequal temperaments. With the comma divided into more than four parts, even intervals with a fifth or a sixth of a comma were usable, and the accidentals were now enharmonic. The most important thing about these temperaments was that they were usable in *all* keys; but since the intervals were not uniform, every key sounded different and each had its own character.

This versatility did not come without its price: in exchange for the ability to sound "in tune" in all keys, these temperaments sacrificed the purity of the thirds and sixths. The pure, static triads of meantone were gone; thus, instead of purity there were only degrees of impurity. It was for this very reason that there were so many of these temperaments: each attempted to address the issue of the impurity of the thirds in a slightly different way, changing one element or the other in order to favor certain keys. Often the differences between them are minimal, and in a musical context, inaudible. Furthermore, since the revolving temperaments were more difficult to tune than meantone, many versions were proposed simply for ease in setting the bearing octave.

To musicians brought up on the purity of the imperfect consonances, the sounds of the new temperaments must have been jarring; it is hard to accept anything else once the sounds of meantone thirds are in the ear. We can sympathize with those more conservative performers who refused to give up quarter comma and relied instead on retunings and on cleverly ornamenting the offending notes to minimize their dissonant quality. Their intransigent attitude was at least partially responsible for J. S. Bach's writing *The Well-Tempered Clavier*, with its two sets of preludes and fugues in all keys. Bach wanted to demonstrate the potentialities of unequal temperament, and the version he favored evidently was known as *Wohltemperatur*, or well-temperament.

For a long time it was believed that *Wohltemperatur* referred to equal temperament, and generations of pianists were brought up believing that Bach championed equal temperament.[4] There can be little doubt that Bach, an educated musician, was aware of the theory of equal temperament, since by that time it had been around for at least two thousand years. But the hallmark of equal temperament is its sameness of all keys, since all like intervals are exactly alike. This is definitely not what Bach and his contemporaries wanted.

It was part of the aesthetic of seventeenth- and eighteenth-century key theory that each key should have its own *Affekt*—that each key should have its own character and sound different from all the other keys. Thus, the distinction between keys that was made by the revolving temperaments was something to be prized and sought after rather than merely tolerated.

The same sort of distinction was found on almost all other instruments as part of their playing technique as well as their physical characteristics. It was not until well into the nineteenth century, when musical taste changed and it became desirable to minimize distinctions between keys, that equal temperament took hold. Thus, not only did Bach and his immediate predecessors play their keyboard instruments in a modified meantone temperament and write their music with its particular sound in mind, but so did Mozart, Haydn, and, for the part of his life in which he could hear it, Beethoven.

Equal temperament. The harpsichords built at the beginning of the harpsichord revival and for the first three-quarters of our century were tuned unquestioningly in equal temperament. With all its intervals "mistuned" by one-twelfth of the comma, this temperament appealed to the rational side of the twentieth-century mind. Also, we inherited the nineteenth-century tendency to ascribe all change to an evolutionary process. The progression seemed clear: at first the comma was not divided at all; then it was divided into fourths; then sixths; now, finally, it is divided so that every interval gets its equal share.[5]

With hindsight, things now appear a little clearer, and we have come to realize that equal temperament makes good sense on the piano, but *only* on the piano. During the time that the harpsichord (or the early piano) was the dominant keyboard instrument, the musical aesthetic demanded that all keys sound different. It

was not until almost the middle of the nineteenth century that this aesthetic would be overturned, to be replaced by precisely the opposite view that all keys are equal and should sound the same. It is no coincidence that most instruments underwent design changes at that time, sometimes fairly drastic, to have them conform to this new sound ideal. Viewed in this way, equal temperament is ideal for the piano.

Another reason for its close connection to the piano had to do with that instrument's constructional features. The early piano, which was lightly built and lightly strung, had a tone rich in upper partials. In common with the harpsichord, this richness of sound also tended to produce something of a jangle, so it would make little sense to tune these instruments in equal temperament, where every interval but the octave adds its own jangle by virtue of its being out of tune by one-twelfth of a comma. But more and more volume would be demanded of the piano, a demand met by heavier actions, hammers, and strings, and a heavier frame to support the whole thing. In turn, the more massive instrument required yet heavier action, hammers, and strings, which called for a heavier frame. The culmination of this spiral was the invention of the cast-iron frame around the middle of the nineteenth century. At that time the modern piano, with its heavy strings under great tension, was established.

Hitting those taut strings with a wide, soft hammer tends to repress their upper partials. Thus the piano became an instrument capable of great dynamic range but with a relatively dull sound. It makes sense to tune the piano in equal temperament, so that the slightly out-of-tune intervals can give some shimmer and life to the tone. But the harpsichord has plenty of this shimmer already, and does not need more added by the temperament.

TUNING TECHNIQUES

Tuning a harpsichord is a simple task, easily mastered and quickly executed; but to someone who has never done it, it may appear to be utterly impossible. The reasoning goes something like this:

First, you, the expert, tell me, the neophyte, that I must tune my own harpsichord, although very few people tune their own pianos; thus it seems obvious that tuning is a job for a professional. Second, the piano technician has that mysterious ability to count beats (whatever they are), and everybody knows that you cannot tune unless you can count beats. I can't even hear beats—I don't even know what they are, so how can I tune? Third, the technician spends years learning to set a temperament—they even have schools to teach you how to do it—so how can you expect me to set one merely with the help of a few written instructions? Fourth, as if setting a temperament is not difficult enough, you expect me to set one or more varieties that have not been used for over a century or more—temperaments even my technician cannot set. How can I possibly do it if he cannot? Finally, it takes the piano technician hours to do a de-

cent tuning job on my piano, yet you are telling me that I can tune my three-rank harpsichord in less than thirty minutes. How can I believe that?

Let me try to put your mind at ease. Many thousands of harpsichord, clavichord, and fortepiano owners have learned to tune their instruments, and the majority of them do at least a passable job. What may have seemed obviously impossible becomes obviously doable when the facts are known. And the facts are as follows:

First, tuning a piano is much more difficult than tuning a harpsichord. Your technician must use a skilled tuning-wrench technique that simply is not required for the harpsichord, and he must exercise the skill constantly if he is to retain his touch. Second, to tune the harpsichord the ability to count beats, though useful, is not necessary. What *is* needed is the ability to hear *beatless*, that is to say, *pure* intervals, and this is relatively easy. Third, if you want to set equal temperament you probably *should* go to school. It is a difficult temperament; it takes skill and constant practice; and it *does* require the ability to hear and count beats. Fourth, it is *because* you are setting those older temperaments that the job is made so much easier. Equal temperament is not only difficult, it leaves practically no margin for error. The temperaments to be presented here are much easier to set, and even if they are a little off, the tuning can still be usable.

Finally, your piano technician takes so long to tune your piano because he has to "set" each

pin—something you do not have to worry about. Furthermore, he has to do a *very* careful job, since it will be six months before he returns. But *that* careful a job is not required on a harpsichord. Harpsichords do not have iron frames and thick soundboards, and their tuning is more affected by changes in temperature and humidity than the modern piano. And since the piano's sound is so much plainer than the harpsichord's, even the same degree of out-of-tuneness is less annoying on the piano. Thus the harpsichord is going to demand more frequent tuning, but it will also be more forgiving.

How frequent is frequent? That is a question that neither I nor anyone else can answer for you. How stable is your instrument? What kind of climate do you live in? What climatic extremes will the instrument have to endure? How well do you control the internal temperature and humidity? How far out of tune will you allow the instrument to get? How much out-of-tuneness can you stand? When you tune, do you turn the pins or only twist them? Are you as fussy about the 4' as you are about the 8's? Give me the answers to those questions and I will hazard an answer as to frequency of tuning.

I *can* tell you that you will have to tune more frequently when the seasons change. Sometimes I have to tune my instruments on a weekly basis during spring and fall, when we have spells of warm, humid weather followed by periods of cooler, drier air. At other times they go for months. I used to have a little fretted clavichord that I tuned once a year, whether it needed it or not, but my larger instruments are much more responsive to climate. Other factors affecting stability will be discussed in the next chapter.

All of this applies to casual tuning. For concerts, the harpsichord, like the piano, needs to be tuned before each and every use and touched up during intermission.

Some admonitions about tuning are in order. Although this may seem like a lot of information, some of it you already know, some of it is self-evident, some will be so obvious that having read it once you will never forget it, and the rest you will remember after a few tunings.

1. *Get comfortable.* Sit at your usual playing height. Rest the tuning arm on top of the nameboard.

2. *Get things quiet.* Put the dog out in the yard. Send the children to the other end of the house and forbid them to play loud music. Give your spouse a good book. If you have problems with traffic noise, tune at a time when traffic is light or move the instrument to a back room. Turn off the cuckoo clock and, if need be, unplug the refrigerator.

3. *Get realistic.* How long did it take you to become a competent keyboard player? Certainly not a few days. Tuning is not nearly as difficult as playing, but even so, it is a skill, and it will not be learned overnight. Do not get impatient—just recall that you were happy to make steady progress when you learned to play.

4. *Tune frequently, and do not worry about the accuracy of any one tuning.* If the tuning is not as good as you would like, just see if you can do better the next time. A tuning session is a practice session, not a recital! How long were your practice sessions when you first started an instrument? Probably not more than an hour or so, depending on your age. Learning to play an instrument involves a lot of muscle training, and the amount of exercise muscles can tolerate has to be built up gradually. Tuning exercises yet another set of muscles, those in your ears. People are sometimes told that they have a "good ear," but whatever that means it has nothing to do with the ear muscles you must train in order to tune.

5. *If you spend more than an hour tuning, it will only waste your time.* You will no longer be hearing accurately and you will only frustrate yourself. You must *force* yourself to do a *complete* tuning in that hour. You may think you could do a better job if you spent the hour all on a single rank or all on the bearing octave. My experience says that you are wrong. Although Eric Herz does not impose my one-hour time limit, he does say that if you spend an entire minute tuning one interval in the temperament, or thirty seconds tuning an octave or unison, you have spent "an inordinate amount of time" on one note.[6]

6. In either of the two temperaments that are given in this chapter, fifths are tuned narrow, or *inside* pure. For example, to tune f, a fifth down from c', first tune it pure. Then move the f *up* just a little to where you want it to go, thereby *reducing* the size of the interval. To tune d', a fifth up from g, first tune it pure and then *drop* the d' a little, again reducing the size of the fifth.

7. Similarly, fourths are tuned wide, or *outside* pure. To tune g down from c', tune it pure and then move the g *down* a bit to its proper place, thus *expanding* the fourth. To tune d' up from a, tune it pure and then raise the d' a little, again expanding the fourth.

8. Do not try to use that "good ear" to determine if an interval is wide or narrow; very few people can hear so accurately that they can detect when an interval is a few beats on one side or the other of pure. Instead, tune the interval pure—beatless—and then tune to one side or the other as required.

9. Strike the two notes of the interval to be tuned simultaneously, and keep striking them at intervals of around two or three seconds as you turn the pin.

10. A marker of some sort on the back 8' a or c' pin, to identify your reference pitch, is a good idea; but it is not necessary to put felt punchings, dabs of paint, fingernail polish, or bits of colored paper on the tuning pins in order to identify the ones to turn. Instead, lightly touch the string you *think* should be vibrating with the tip of your tuning hammer, somewhere between the nut and the jackrail. If you have touched the right string you will hear a nice "twang" and a cessation of sound. If not, try the string to one side and then the other until you have located it. Then put the tuning hammer on the pin on which that string is

wound. The whole process only takes a second and only needs to be done when tuning the bearing octave.

Be particularly careful with virginals and spinets, where the tuning pin and the key are not lined up. On these instruments it is a good idea to make a tuning aid consisting of a piece of cardboard the length of the bearing octave and about two inches wide, with holes punched in it that correspond to the tuning pins of the bearing octave. Write the names of the notes next to the appropriate hole and drop the device over the tuning pins. Now you can clearly see which note you are tuning in the bearing octave.

11. This has been said before, but it is worth saying again. The pins must be *turned*, not bent. It will help to grasp the handle of the tuner as close as possible to the shank. Do not put any sideways, front, or back pressure on the pin, but put only direct, downward pressure. Downward pressure will also help keep tapered pins tight in their holes. To be certain of what you have done, remove your hand from the tuning hammer before you accept the tuning of the interval. Then remove the tuning hammer from the pin by lifting it straight up. Sideways pressure, in which the pin is twisted more than turned, is one of the major causes for a tuning that does not hold. If you twist the pins the harpsichord will be out of tune before you finish.

12. Turn the pins as little as possible. This is easy to say, but not so easy for the unskilled tuner to do. A lot of turning of

the pins, which coils and uncoils the strings, is the other major cause of a tuning that does not hold. Since it is practically assured that you will do a lot of pin turning in the early stages of your tuning career, you will automatically provide yourself with plenty of opportunity to practice your tuning skills. Do *try* to limit the amount you turn the pins; and never fear, you will improve in time.

13. Several sources recommend that you first drop the pitch of the note to be tuned, and then tune *up* to the proper pitch.[7] This is probably a good idea, if for no other reason than that it will keep you from breaking a string if you have the tuning hammer on the wrong pin. However, if you then inadvertently bring the note above pitch (which you will inevitably do at first), do try to come down to it, rather than dropping below and starting all over again. Remember, you want to move the pins as little as possible.

14. Having told you several times to move the pins as little as possible, I feel it necessary to say that if you do not move them at all you will never get your tuning done. Some people approach the tuning pin as if it were an egg that might crack under the pressure of the tuning hammer. Better to turn a lot at first and refine later, than to hardly turn at all.

15. Since you only have an hour, you might as well accept the fact that you probably will not be able to do a great tuning—there simply is not enough time. But soon your accuracy will improve, and so will your speed.

When you can tune a five-octave, three-choir instrument in thirty minutes or less, you can consider yourself a competent tuner. This does not mean that you are ready to do concert tuning—work so accurate it could be used for a recital or a recording—but you should be good enough to do a job that will satisfy until it is time to tune again.

A TUNING AND TWO TEMPERAMENTS

Historically, Pythagorean tuning, quarter-comma meantone, and modified meantone temperaments followed one another, and each is more difficult than the last to tune. Readers who have not tuned before should learn to tune all three—not for some fusty historical recreation, but for important pedagogical reasons. Tuning Pythagorean will put the sound of pure intervals in your ear. Without this you will find it difficult to get into the other two tunings. You need not set this tuning more than two or three times, then you can move on to meantone. If that temperament is appropriate for all or most of the music you play, you need not even learn modified meantone; but if you do go on to that temperament, you will find it fairly easy after you have the practice of the first two under your belt.

The reference pitch. Back in chapter 5 it was recommended that you get a good loud tuning fork. I hope you did. If not, I trust you have an electronic tuner or some other good source for a reference pitch.

If you are tuning a virginal, a spinet, or a 1 × 8' or 1 × 8', 1 × 4' harpsichord, you have only one 8' register, and the bearing octave will be set on it. But if you have a 2 × 8', or a 2 × 8', 1 × 4', you have a choice of setting the bearing octave on either the front or the back 8'. Although some people like to set the front 8' because they feel that its more penetrating quality makes it easier to hear the intervals, most (including me) feel it is easier on the back 8', with its somewhat plainer sound. Try the back 8', at least for a while. Then, if the peculiarities of your ear or your harpsichord, or both, make it easier for you to do the front 8' first, do it first.

Setting the reference pitch with a tuning fork is something of a trick. Ideally, one hand holds the fork against something that will amplify its sound, one hand strikes the key, and one hand turns the tuning pin. Since this cannot be done without a third hand, try to learn to manage the first two tasks with one hand.

If the fork is really loud, or if your harpsichord happens to have some particularly resonant key covers, you can strike the base of the fork on your knee or the heel of your shoe and use its end to depress the key. If this does not work, try holding the vibrating fork against the front molding or against some part of the front of the case with the thumb and forefinger. Then strike the reference key with one of the other fingers. If this is not possible for you, then you will have to strike the fork, hold

it against some other resonant part of the harpsichord (such as the soundboard), remember the pitch, and pick up that hand and use it to depress the reference key. Then strike the fork again and see if it matches the pitch you set. With practice this trial and error method can be surprisingly effective, but that may take a while.

Another method is to grasp the vibrating fork between the teeth. Through bone conduction, the pitch will ring loud and clear. Keep your lips off the fork; they will damp it.

Do not be afraid to explore all of these methods. I frequently use two or three of them as the circumstances demand and as a means of checking myself. And if you are a beat or two off the mark (sorry, but those beats *are* there, whether you hear them or not), it makes little difference as long as you are not going to be playing with another instrument.

Now for the pitch itself. Although we talk about using a' = 440 Hz (or 415 if you are tuning low pitch), that is the frequency of the tuning device, not the note to be set from it. The A we set is an octave lower, 220 Hz (or 207.5), the a below middle c'. The same holds true if you are using a c" fork (a b' fork is usually used to tune at low pitch when the reference pitch is C). There is nothing for you to do with this information except remember it so that you will not get confused between what you are told (tune a' = 440 Hz) and what you actually do (tune a = 220 Hz).

Pythagorean tuning. Although you probably will never use Pythagorean tuning, it will be worth your while to set it a few times, since all the fifths and fourths are pure, and it is pure, beatless fifths and fourths that you want to learn to hear. Even if your tuning skills are advanced, set it once, just to hear what it sounds like.

Set the reference pitch with either a C fork or an A fork. If the C fork is used, proceed with the tuning as shown in Figure 13-1: tune a pure fourth down to g, a pure fifth up to d', and so on, until you reach the g-sharp. If A is the reference pitch, consult Figure 13-2, which is exactly like Figure 13-1 except that you go backward from a to c', then forward from a to g-sharp.

The one problem with telling you this, rather than showing you, is that I cannot demonstrate the pure, beatless intervals for you. That *sound* you will have to learn yourself; nevertheless, the quality of the beatless interval is so pure and full of repose, that you will have no trouble recognizing it when you hear it. In this early stage of your tuning career do not be afraid to turn those pins. You will not *know* the beatless sound until you first hear the rough quality of the beating interval.

Now tune the second part of the series, Figure 13-3, from c' to f to b-flat to e-flat. Complete the bearing octave by tuning the f', an octave up from f. Octaves must be as pure and beatless as the fourths and fifths. Check your tuning by playing parallel fourths and fifths in the bearing octave. They should all be pure, hollow, and beatless, except for the "wolf" fourth e-flat-g-sharp. The entire comma is placed on that interval, and it *sounds* it.

The next step is to tune the rest of the keyboard by octaves and then tune the unisons: that will be discussed later, under *Completing the tuning.*

If you have been able to do a Pythagorean tuning, no matter how rough, you have gotten the hang of it and need only practice now to improve your accuracy and speed. In the meantime, you *can* play your harpsichord in Pythagorean tuning, although some things may make you shudder. But that should only spur you to learn meantone temperament.

Quarter-comma meantone temperament. Set the reference pitch. If you are using an A fork, consult Figure 13-4, which contains the four intervals that receive the quarter of the comma: tune a-d', d'-g, g-c', and c'-f. The last f-f' is tuned to round out the bearing octave. Refer to Figure 13-5 if you are using a C fork. It contains the same intervals, but set in a different order.

Your task is to place one quarter of the comma on each of those intervals. The fourths, you will remember, get tuned *outside* of pure, the fifths, *inside.* It is not possible to discriminate a quarter of a quarter of a half step just by listening, so do not even try. Instead, slightly *mistune* these four intervals, all in the same way. Now—how much is *slightly* mistuned? Fortunately, there is a way to tell. If you have distributed the entire comma— no more, no less—the f-a interval, marked "check" in Figures

13-4 and 13-5, will be a pure, beatless third. If you have been able to recognize and set pure fourths and fifths, you will recognize the pure third with no trouble.

Now go back and check the *quality* of your four intervals. Play the fifths f-c', g-d'. The quality of the roughness should be about the same. Now play the two fourths, a-d', g-c'. They also should have the same quality of roughness and, in addition, that quality should be pretty much the same as the quality of the fifths. The two checks used at this point, then, are the pure third f-a, and the similarity of the sound quality of the fifths and fourths. If you have set these four intervals with some degree of accuracy, you have accomplished the hard part of quarter-comma meantone. Note, however, that these checks are independent of each other, since it is entirely possible to mistune the fourths and fifths. You can even get the wrong ones inside or outside of pure and still end up with the beatless third f-a.

The second and last step in setting the bearing octave is to tune the thirds. Since these are all set pure, this step is easy, as promised. First, however, tune the c an octave below from the middle c' (because the pure third c-e will be easier to hear in that octave), and the d from the d' (because it will be easier to hear the d-f-sharp third) (Figure 13-6).

Consult Figure 13-7: tune the e pure to the c, then tune the upper e' to the lower to fill out the bearing octave. Now tune the f-sharp pure to the d. Continue by tuning thirds upward: the g-sharp

FIGURE 13-1.
Pythagorean tuning from a C fork: part one.

FIGURE 13-2.
Pythagorean tuning from an A fork: part one.

FIGURE 13-3.
Pythagorean tuning: part two.

check

FIGURE 13-4.
Meantone temperament from an A fork: part one. The same sequence is used for both quarter-comma and modified meantone.

check

FIGURE 13-5.
Meantone temperament from a C fork: part one. The same sequence is used for both quarter-comma and modified meantone.

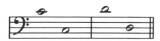

FIGURE 13-6.
Quarter-comma meantone temperament: tune d' and c' down an octave.

FIGURE 13-7.
*Quarter-comma meantone
temperament: part two.*

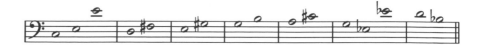

from the e, the b from the g, and the c'-sharp from the a. Now tune down, e-flat from g, then e'-flat up an octave, and b-flat down from d'.

The bearing octave is now set; the rest of the tuning will be discussed under *Completing the tuning*. Before leaving this section, however, it should be remembered that the sharps are not enharmonic in quarter-comma meantone. If you are playing a piece that calls for, say, an A-flat rather than a G-sharp, you will have to set *that* note, a pure third down from c'.

Modified meantone temperament. I have set many of the unequal or modified meantone or revolving temperaments, and find that there is little to distinguish between them (at least on the harpsichord; the differences are more easily noticed on the sustained tones of the organ). Begin by setting the temperament I am about to describe. Later you may find one that for some reason is easier for you to set, or that you like better; but if you have conquered this one, you should not have any trouble with others.

This temperament was described by John Barnes some years ago.[8] Barnes presented what is to me convincing evidence that this temperament is a useful one for Bach, although he does not claim that it is indeed Bach's *Wohltemperatur*. This aside, it is an easy temperament to tune.

Set the reference pitch and refer to Figure 13-4 if you are using an A fork or Figure 13-5 if you are using a C fork. Set the sequence of fourths and fifths given in these examples, but tune them a little closer to pure, a little less rough, than you did when tuning quarter-comma meantone. Again, you have two checks: the first is the third f-a, which should now beat three times per second. Oops! I said earlier that you would not have to learn to count beats! Well, that is true, but if you can count them here, so much the better. If not, you will have to learn what the *quality* of three beats per second sounds like. I should add that the f-a third must be wide, *outside* of pure. It is entirely possible (I have done it many times myself) to tune those first four intervals in such a way that the f is set a little higher than you want it, and three beats per second inside pure sounds exactly the same as three beats per second outside. But there is a check for that which I will describe shortly.

The second check for your first four intervals is, as in quarter-comma meantone, the quality of the intervals. Test them as directed earlier, remembering that they will be smoother in this temperament. Then, as in quarter comma, the hard part of the temperament is finished.

Now tune the sequence of fourths and fifths given in Figure 13-8. They are all tuned *pure*, just as in Pythagorean. Tune b-flat up from f. Test the b-flat against the d'. This wide third should beat fairly rapidly—about twice as fast as the f-a third. If it beats slowly or not at all, this is a good indication that your f-a third was tuned inside rather than outside pure. You could go back and start all over again, but remember, you only have an hour! Best to go on and try to do better next time. Your temperament will be usable, although not too happy in keys with many sharps or flats.

Continue with Figure 13-8: b-flat up to e'-flat, e'-flat down to a-flat, a-flat up to d'-flat, and d'-flat down to g-flat. These are all tuned pure. Now tune the fifth a up to e', also pure, then tune e' down to b (see Figure 13-9). If you have done a perfect job you can place that b between the e above and the f-sharp below in such a way that each interval has exactly the same quality, that the b will make a good third above g, and a usable third to d-sharp. If you have not achieved that level of perfection, put the b where it will do the most good. You may also find that you have to raise the f-sharp a little to get acceptable B-major and F-sharp major and minor triads. But do not sacrifice the usefulness of your D-major triad to get those less-often used combinations better in tune; remember, the accidentals are now enharmonic.

The bearing octave is now set.

Completing the tuning. Two steps remain: the first, to complete the tuning of the register; the second, to tune the other registers to it.

Tune chromatically by octaves, from the bearing octave down to the bass, then from the bearing octave up to the treble. You can do treble first and then bass if you wish, but that is the only leeway you have. I once had a student who tuned out of the bearing octave by tuning all the F's, then all the E's, then the E-flats, and so on. This is poor practice. First, it makes you jump all around, instead of moving smoothly from one pin to the next. Second, the sound quality changes over the octave jumps, forcing the ear to work harder. If you have bad habits like this, now is the time to discard them.

The octaves all are tuned pure. You can check yourself by playing notes two octaves apart: if the octave is beating the beat rate will be doubled two octaves away, and hence easier to hear (no need to count the beats—all you have to hear is that the interval is not pure). This is a particularly useful procedure in the extremes of the bass and the treble, where it becomes more difficult to assess purity.

If you have a virginal or a spinet or a single 8' harpsichord you have finished the tuning.

If you have a 2 × 8' or a 2 × 8', 1 × 4', turn on the other 8' and tune it in unison to the completed register. This is not as simple as it seems. It is relatively easy to set unisons when two sounds are identical in character (like two flutes or two violins or even two unison strings on a piano), but more difficult when the sounds are different (like a flute and a violin). Such is the case with the two 8's of a harpsichord. If nothing else, one string is longer than the other (look at your harpsichord if you doubt this), and they are plucked at different points. This distinctive-

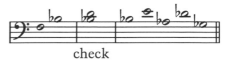

check

FIGURE 13-8.
Modified meantone temperament: part two.

FIGURE 13-9.
Modified meantone temperament: part three.

ness of sound is desirable on instruments such as the French doubles, where the plucking points of the two 8's are separated even more by the 4' jacks, but it does create some difficulty in tuning the unisons.

Start tuning unisons chromatically from middle c', either up or down (I prefer up, but it makes no difference). Tune the first five or six unisons as best you can, but as you tune, go back to middle c each time and play the notes you have tuned (Figure 13-10). Inevitably you will notice one or more unisons that are less rough than the others. Take the quality of that note or two, and make it your model for the quality to be achieved by the other unisons. Again, testing for purity by playing notes two octaves apart can be helpful. On a two-manual instrument it is also helpful to test the purity of the octaves of the front 8' alone, on the upper manual (assuming that you started your tuning on the back 8').

Let me remind you once more, however, that you have only an hour. The ability to tune well will come more from refining your technique over time than it will from an over-meticulousness of detail, so try to avoid spending a great deal of time on the unisons. On the other hand, try to be aware of what you have done wrong. Perhaps it may even be worth writing down, so that the attempt can be made to avoid it the next time you tune.

A warning: Do not tune your back 8' and then tune your back 8' to your out-of-tune front 8'. That is tuning a tuned register to an untuned one. It will happen, but I hope you spot it before you get too far (I confess—I *still* catch myself doing it on rare occasions).

The final step is to tune your 4', if you have one, to the register you first set. If you have a $2 \times 8'$, $1 \times 4'$, turn off the front 8' or uncouple the manuals, and turn on the 4'. As with the unison 8's, start with middle c' and tune either up or down (again, I prefer up). Those 4' pins need very little turning, particularly in the extreme treble, and overshooting can be a problem. Again, practice will help. In the extreme treble the in-tune 4' tends to have something of a flat sound. To me, it resembles a high-pitched whistle. Here one must listen for purity rather than for pitch.

As long as you ascend or descend chromatically you will have no trouble putting your tuning hammer on the right 4' pin; but if you interrupt that sequence (perhaps to fix a note elsewhere), you will have to find your way back to the proper pin. Simply touch your tuning hammer to the string you think is vibrating to find the proper string.

The harpsichord is tuned.

FIGURE 13-10.
An aid to tuning unisons.

etc.

THE NEED FOR FREQUENT TUNING

Like most people, you bought your harpsichord to play it, not to tune it. But it is a mistake to let the tuning go until the instrument is so cacophonous that even the dog cannot stand to be in the same room with it, because a harpsichord that is allowed to go badly out of tune cannot be put back into tune easily.

Although harpsichord strings do not put the piano's twenty tons of tension on the frame, there is tension enough. Suppose you let the overall tuning go a half-step flat. Now you want to bring it back up to pitch. But there are two reasons why the instrument and the strings do not *want* to go back up. First, the strings like that nice, relaxed lower and less strenuous tuning, and will try to go right back there after you tune. Second, when a string is tuned up it does not stretch evenly along its entire length. The tail—that section of wire between the bridge and the hitchpin—will be drawn up less tautly than the speaking length of the string. But the wire seeks equilibrium, so before you know it, both parts are at the same tension, and the pitch is now flat.

You and the instrument will have to strike a compromise. You will bring it up a half step, and it will drop back down a quarter step. If you are lucky, it will almost let you finish the tuning first. If you have let your harpsichord get that far out of tune, plan on tuning it twice in a row if you expect it to be usable. Even then, it will not hold for very long and will have to be tuned again within a few days. In dealing with an instrument allowed to go flat, it is worth raising the pitch of the string just a little higher than needed, then letting it down.

On the other hand, if you make an effort to keep it up to pitch at all times—or *down* to pitch at all times if that is the case, string tension will remain constant and the harpsichord will stay in tune for much longer periods of time. Thus, the more you keep your harpsichord in tune, the less you have to tune it. And if you bought your harpsichord to play on it, it is infinitely more satisfying to play on it when it is in tune.

Yes, I hear you. There is music to learn, concerts and recitals for which you must prepare. Even if you are strictly a recreational harpsichordist, there is only a limited time available at the keyboard—to be spent *playing*, not *tuning*. You admit the truth of my statements, but you simply cannot be fooling with tuning all the time. Well, I agree with you. That is why I am about to make a final statement about tuning speed: *when you are learning to tune, speed of tuning is more important than accuracy.*

Maintaining the harpsichord may be something of a chore; nevertheless, at least you can hope that any adjustments you make will last a while and will be needed less frequently as the instrument matures; but tuning must be done again and again. One can only hope, if that parallel universe really does exist—the one where harpsichord strings never break—that at least there, a good tuning lasts forever.

Chapter 14

The Harpsichord as Furniture

As a piece of furniture the harpsichord demands little. Unlike other furniture, we do not sit on it, pile things on it, put things in it, or eat things off it. Yet it does require some care beyond the ubiquitous "Don't bump the harpsichord!"

LOCATION

It used to be one of the iron-clad rules of the piano trade: never place a piano against an outside wall. This made a good deal of sense when the exterior walls of most houses had little or no insulation. Such a wall is almost transparent to outside changes in temperature and humidity, and an instrument sitting next to it is immediately exposed to these climatic changes. Placing the piano next to a single-pane window is even worse: heat and cold sweep through the glass almost as if it were not there. Draperies help, but not enough.

Given a choice, this rule is still worth following, for harpsichords even more than for pianos. But it can be safely ignored if exterior walls are well insulated and if fitted with double-pane windows (or at least tight-fitting storm windows). Even so, a harpsichord placed by a window or an outside wall should be kept about six inches away from the wall; the room air itself will help insulate the instrument from temperature changes.

These precautions are of course unnecessary when the harpsichord sits by an inside wall. (Many an older harpsichord, built when it was the practice to attach the legs directly to the instrument, is kept from falling over by leaning it against a wall. I have a friend with one of those old harpsichords whose legs are so shaky that he *screwed* the instrument to the wall!)

It is wise to cover the windows with draperies and, normally, to keep them closed. In the winter they provide a buffer against the cold, and in the summer, against the heat. They also protect the instrument from exposure to direct sunlight. Shining through a window on an instrument, the sun warms the spine, thereby putting the bass end out of tune. Beyond that, direct sunlight, and, for that matter, any kind of light, darken and deteriorate paint, varnish, or any other finish. For this reason it is a good idea to keep the lid flap down, so that the entire lid covers the instrument when it is not actually being played. This way the inevitable color change will occur evenly, over the entire surface. Otherwise you run the risk of finding after a few years that the lid has darkened except for the part normally covered by the open flap. Then you will *have* to keep the flap open all the time, in order to hide your bi-shaded lid.

This does not mean that your living room must be shut up like a tomb, with only dim light allowed. True, sunlight eventually destroys wood, but it will take hundreds of years of bright light to really hurt the instrument. Nevertheless, there is no point in hurrying up the process by giving your harpsichord a daily sun bath.

The harpsichord should not be placed near an air-supply vent blowing heated air, dry air, air-conditioned air, or any other kind of air *directly* on it. Proximity to hot-water or steam radiators and electric baseboard heaters is also to be avoided. In other words, try to insulate the harpsichord from sudden changes in heat or cold or wet or dry, keep it away from drafts, and keep it out of the hot sun. Doing this faithfully can be something of a problem, since in most climates in this country there are times of the year when the furnace is turned up during the day and down at night, or the air conditioning is on during the day and the windows are open at night. I do not think that we should allow our lives to be ruled by a harpsichord; certainly you may turn your heat down at night when you retire and open your windows during the summer when the evening is pleasant, but you must also realize that you have an investment to protect, which requires that you avoid extremes as much as possible.

Sound is another consideration for location. The typical living room, with its parallel surfaces, its stuffed chairs and sofas, its heavy draperies, and its thick carpet, is a terrible acoustical environment for a harpsichord. Much better would be a high, vaulted ceiling, angled walls of wood paneling, an absence of fabric-covered furniture, and a hardwood floor. Although you may not have a room such as this, it could be that some place other than the living room would serve the harpsichord better; or, perhaps some judicious furniture moving could create a more sympathetic acoustical climate than the one you now have.

Finally, mention should be made once again of the importance of having a small table near the harpsichord on which you can keep extra eyeglasses, pencils, paper clips, metronome, tools, knife, coffee cup, etc. These things do not belong anywhere on the harpsichord.

CLEANING THE SOUNDBOARD

You may keep the lid of your harpsichord closed when it is not played, but eventually you will find a fine coating of dust on the soundboard. After a while that fine coat becomes a thicker coat; the dust forms into balls; other bits of dirt and gunk drop on the board and get trapped in the dust. It is time to clean that soundboard.

Buy a soft two-inch paintbrush. Brush the dust from the front of the instrument toward the tail, getting the bristles down between the strings. The section of the soundboard between the 8′ bridge and the hitchpin rail is difficult to do, because the tails of the strings run at an angle to the board. Another problem area is the place where the tails of the 4′ strings run at an angle to the 8′ strings above them. Take your time and work your way down the soundboard. Leave piles of dust behind, if you must. Then vacuum up the dirt piles, using your vacuum cleaner's softest brush. Unless your builder tells you differently, you should not have to worry about loosening or removing a soundboard painting with either the paintbrush or the vacuum cleaner.

Vacuuming the soundboard is something to be done *before* you tune.

SPILLS ON THE SOUNDBOARD

The things that most often get spilled on soundboards are water, coffee, and alcoholic drinks. Even if your soundboard does not have a painting, any of these can do serious damage to its appearance. If you do have a soundboard painting, any of these can be *disastrous* to its appearance. Serious or disastrous, the consequences can be avoided by quick action on your part; but the action *must* be *quick*! Think about the following steps and be prepared to put them into effect should need arise.

First, reach your hands into the harpsichord and rip out the strings that cover the area of the spill. Yes, *rip them out*, with your bare hands! If you try to reach down between the strings to wipe it up you will only make it worse. Do not stop to look for a wire cutter or, even if one is handy, to clip the strings one by one. Time is of the essence, since the fat in the coffee cream is seeping into your soundboard, threatening to leave an eternally ugly stain; or the water or alcohol is dissolving the tempera paint of the soundboard decoration, to leave behind large discolored areas around now splotchy-looking flowers.

Second, blot the spill, *up and down only*, with smooth paper toweling. Do not blot with your shirt tail, your handkerchief, or any thing else that is not really absorbent and lintless. Do not wipe sideways or in circles. Be gentle if you have a soundboard painting, but blot it, up and down. This prompt action will most likely save your painting, although it probably will not be as crisp as it was before. (If the detail has softened to a noticeable degree you might think about having your builder or his decorator touch it up.)

Although most soundboard painters use gouache or water color with an egg yolk or gum arabic binder, some use acrylic paint, which is a plastic and therefore impervious to the solvents under discussion. Nevertheless, unless blotted up immediately, the liquid will stain the soundboard even if it does not dissolve the painting.

Now, of course, you must replace the strings you ripped off the harpsichord. Consider yourself lucky if you have gotten away with only the time and expense of some restringing. The alternative could have been to sand down and refinish the entire soundboard. That would be really messy and far more expensive.

CLEANING THE KEYS

Harpsichord keys can get pretty dirty. From time to time they should be cleaned, using one slightly dampened cloth for the naturals and another for the sharps. Naturals and sharps are most often made from different materials, and staining one with the residue of the other is to be avoided. A few drops of liquid dish-washing soap can be added to the water into which the cloth is dipped, if water alone is not enough. If the keyboard is really dirty, add some denatured alcohol to the dampened cloth. Again, wring it out well. I recently serviced a French double I had sold to a university that shall remain nameless. Evidently it was the custom of the harpsichord students there to eat lunch while they practiced; how else could one explain the dried-up food I found coating the keys. Damp cloths and denatured alcohol took it all off, although I almost gagged in the process.

The cloth should be just *slightly* dampened; otherwise you risk getting water between the key lever and the key cover, and that could cause the cover to loosen. Avoid other cleaning substances, including soapy water, unless you know the material from which the key covers were made, what glue was used to fasten them on, how they were finished, and what the effect of your cleaner is on all this. Whatever you do, use no abrasives. Polish the keys with a soft cloth when dry.

Note that bone will darken from the absorption of fats excreted by the fingers. This "antiquing" is a natural process and

can be neither avoided nor reversed.

CLEANING THE CASE

For the most part, the harpsichord can be treated just like any other piece of fine furniture. Dust it from time to time, and do not forget the keywell and the keys. Any dirt, food, or other foreign substance that gets on the case should be removed with nothing more than that soft, damp, lintless cloth, with that drop of liquid soap if necessary. Do *not* dip the cloth in denatured alcohol to clean the case unless you are certain of the finish material and your ability to deal with it. Generally speaking, anything that is safe for polishing or cleaning your furniture should be safe for the harpsichord, and alcohol is not considered to be one of those safe substances.

Gold bands and moldings, if you have them, need not give you undue concern. The gold should be on tight, and normal maintenance of the case will not remove it. On the other hand, there is no need to do anything to the gold unless it actually has dirt on it. Concentrated rubbing will remove the gold.

Since there are many different ways to finish a harpsichord, it is impossible to know if you should wax or polish the case or not. You must get this information from your builder. If in doubt, do not do it, despite those advertisements that talk about the need for wood to be nurtured and moisturized. Wood certainly needs moisture when it is alive, in the tree, but the wood in your harpsichord, although it may be acoustically alive, is dead lumber. Wax will not prevent it from drying out; to do that, you would have to cover every single square inch of surface, both inside and out.

MOVING THE HARPSICHORD

From room to room. Harpsichord owners often are wary about moving their instruments, thinking that doing so will upset some delicate internal balance. This concern, while understandable, has little basis in fact. Owners would be amazed to see how many harpsichord builders have shops on two or more levels, requiring that the instruments constantly be lugged up and down stairs. Moving a harpsichord from one place to another in the same house should not cause undue concern, but it should be done with a little common sense.

First, be sure that the harpsichord will make all the bends and turns required; it almost always can, by carrying it spine down or even straight up. Second, be sure that it will fit the new spot. Third, note that while it only takes two people of normal strength to move almost any harpsichord, a third person is probably going to be needed to carry the stand and hold doors open. Otherwise, be prepared to put the harpsichord down somewhere—the floor is fine and so is the dining room table (make sure that the leaves are securely propped)—move the stand, and then come back and get the instrument.

That moving will put an instrument out of tune is another unfounded concern. It is not un-common for an instrument, well wrapped in protective covering, to cross the country and arrive at its destination in almost perfect tune. But as soon as the cover is taken off, the instrument is exposed to a different temperature and humidity, and it starts going out of tune within minutes.

To somewhere else. A harpsichord should never be taken out of its normal environment, put in a vehicle, and taken elsewhere without covering it in some way. If the instrument is only going to be moved once a year or so, you can get by with wrapping it securely in three or four blankets and banding the whole thing with masking tape or large rubber bands. But this is only minimum protection against the elements and perhaps a gentle jolt. If the instrument is regularly taken out you need a special padded cover.

Buy a cover if you did not get one with your instrument. Good padded covers are not cheap, but this is not the place to stint: your harpsichord needs *protection* when it is moved. Check with your builder and see if he can supply one or if he has a source he can recommend to you. Failing that, check the ads in the early keyboard and early music magazines for cover makers. A suitable sturdy cover has a soft inner pad, a thick, durable middle pad, and an outside cover of heavy duck or some similar material. The seams are reinforced, and there is additional padding at all the corners. Heavy loops are fastened firmly to the bottom every few inches, and a rope, usually nylon, runs through the loops. Anything less than this sort of strength and protection ultimately will prove unsatisfactory.

To move the harpsichord do the following:

1. Remove the lidstick and anything else that is loose. No matter how secure you think that stick is, it will rattle around and can cause damage. What you can do, however, is fold a thick pad of foam rubber over each end of the stick and secure each with a rubber band. Then you should be able to jam the stick tightly in the keywell, between cheek and spine. Do not allow the music rack to remain in the instrument unless it was specially constructed to be there during moving.

2. If you have a transposing keyboard that is normally not screwed down but which can be screwed down, then screw it down. Screwed down or not, position the board to the left, with the transposing block to the right. This is simply insurance against damaging your keyboard or some of the jacks when the instrument is carried on its spine. If the keyboard is screwed down it should be perfectly safe to carry the harpsichord upside down if this becomes necessary, unless your builder has instructed you otherwise.

3. Place the padded cover over the harpsichord. With the help of an assistant, lift the instrument, turn it on its spine, and set it back down on its stand or table. Run the loose ends of the ropes through the sections of rope between the loops, criss-crossing from front to tail. Tie a secure knot, and the harpsichord is ready to go. Pick it up and put it in the station wagon or whatever

vehicle you are using. The instrument is usually transported on its bottom or on its spine. In a smaller vehicle it can ride on its cheek, suitably padded (pay particular attention if the registers protrude from the cheek of your Flemish harpsichord), with the tail resting over the back of the passenger's seat.

4. Disassemble the stand or table. Screw all bolts back into their holes; that way you cannot leave them behind or lose them. Put the screwdriver or stand tool in your pocket, for the same reasons.

5. Now, what do you do with all those parts to the stand? The best solution is to have a separate padded bag or cover that will accommodate all the parts. Give this some serious consideration if you move your harpsichord a lot. (A stand bag is simply a necessity if you have a fancy stand or table, with gilding or some special sculpting.) You may even be able to make something suitable yourself, since it does not have to be as sturdy as the harpsichord cover. Otherwise, wrap the individual sections in blankets and band the bundle with masking tape or large, heavy rubber bands. Wrap the music rack in a terry towel or blanket, too.

6. Do not forget to bring the tool kit with all its contents. Things *always* go wrong at crucial moments like this.

7. With everything packed and ready to go, check to be sure that some corner of the instrument is not digging into some part of the transporting vehicle. If it shows some tendency to do that, pad that corner with a pillow or with a section of thick foam rubber.

8. When you reach your destination, reverse the procedure: first bring in the stand parts and assemble the stand. Put the stand tool in the tool box, where it will be handy when it comes time to disassemble. Now bring in the harpsichord, set it on the stand on its spine, undo the rope, and turn the instrument right side up and set it on the stand.

9. Normally the cover is removed at this point, but you have moved your harpsichord into a new environment and it is going to start to shift and change. If you have tuned the harpsichord at eight, brought it to church at nine, and are going to play for a service at ten, it may be better to leave the cover on until time to play. Otherwise, get the cover off and let the instrument start to get used to its new environment. The sooner it does its changing, the sooner you can do the necessary adjusting. However, there may be another problem that overrides the environmental factor, and that is security. If you think there is the slightest chance that people might start banging on your in-

strument or that some violinist might put his case on top of your instrument (they do it with pianos all the time), then keep the cover on and the Devil take temperature and humidity.

The harpsichord is a unique and amazing instrument. It is one of the most graceful looking, beautifully decorated, wondrous-sounding and long-lived music-making tools bequeathed to us by our ancestors. For this reason alone our harpsichords deserve our care and protection. But beyond that, the antique harpsichords have shown us that, with care, harpsichords can go on making music for centuries. Rather than dim their glory, the years seem only to add luster to their tone. Judging from the best of the antiques, they never seem to stop improving. There are few other musical instruments of which this can be said.

Nobody *owns* a fine harpsichord. It is not a product to be consumed and, after a number of years, discarded. We are, instead, its caretakers, charged with ministering to it during our lifetime. When we are gone, it will be in someone else's care. It is a responsibility that we undertake when we purchase the instrument. It is my fervent wish that this book will help us fulfill that responsibility.

Epilogue

The Well-Regulated Harpsichord

1. The keyboards are visually even. The gaps between keys are consistent. The keys are all the same height.

2. The keyboards have appropriate and uniform dips.

3. There is no unnecessary action noise.

4. The harpsichord has a touch that is even to both the hand and to the ear. Notes do not feel harder or easier, nor do they sound louder or softer, than their neighbors.

5. The registers are appropriately balanced in sound.

6. There is no unnecessary motion in the pluck, the stagger, or the coupler.

7. The strings are all damped properly. There are no dampers damping strings they are not supposed to damp.

8. The jacks all rise and fall in their registers without binding.

9. The jacks pluck cleanly and reliably. There are no hangers. All the tongues work properly and repeat with consistency.

10. The harpsichord invites you to make music on it. Properly regulated, and properly approached, it will reward you with all the legatos, sforzandos, crescendos, and diminuendos that the harpsichord is not supposed to be able to make.

Notes

INTRODUCTION

1. Owners of clavichords will be well served by this book, since almost all the non-structural problems a clavichord can have are found in its action, which is even simpler than that of a harpsichord. The forte-piano's action, on the other hand, although not nearly as complicated as that of the modern piano, is very different from that of the harpsichord. Some matters treated in this book, such as easing sticking key levers or changing strings, will apply to the fortepiano but that instrument really needs a book of its own.

2. I wish I could say that I invented the *kaboom switch*, but it comes from David Kater, *Epson FX-80 Printer: User's Manual* (Torrance, Calif.: Epson America, 1983), xix.

3. These comments are not intended to be critical. That was the way harpsichords were built before the modern classical instrument, and the firms mentioned performed the invaluable service of reintroducing performers and listeners to the sound of the instrument. There is no denying that many of those earlier instruments, particularly the smaller ones, were literally pieces of junk, but then, so are some harpsichords built today. Although the revival instruments were a necessary step in reestablishing the principles of the classical instruments with which this book is concerned, there is no reason why the best of them cannot be taken on their own terms.

4. Wolfgang Zuckermann, *The Modern Harpsichord* (New York: October House, 1969), 201. Zuckermann's book landed on the harpsichord world like a bombshell, clearly showing, on page after page, the superiority of those instruments constructed on classical principles over the revival harpsichords, with all their "improvements." It is still worth reading—for its humor, if nothing else—but it is badly out of date and in this sense often inaccurate and misleading. It should be consulted as a historical document rather than as a useful shopper's guide. It should also be noted that Zuckermann considered all harpsichords built around the time of his book as "modern," while I am using that term to refer only to contemporary instruments built on classical lines.

CHAPTER I

1. Frank Hubbard, *Three Centuries of Harpsichord Making* (Cambridge, Mass.: Harvard University Press, 1967), 225–26, draws on several eighteenth-century sources for an interesting description of jack making.

2. The clavichord effect is described in Arthur Benade, *Fundamentals of Musical Acoustics* (New York: Oxford University Press, 1976), 356. Information on transients may also be found in Benade, 153–56.

3. Discussion of the metallurgy of strings and their breaking points can be found in: Friedemann Hellwig, "Strings and Stringing: Contemporary Documents," *The Galpin Society Journal* 29 (1976): 91–104; and W. R. Thomas and J. J. K. Rhodes, "Harpsichords and the Art of Wire-drawing," *Organ Yearbook* 10 (1979): 126–39. An excellent monograph on the subject is Cary Karp, *The Pitches of 18th-Century Strung Keyboard Instruments, With Particular Reference to Swedish Material* (Stockholm: SMS-Musikmuseet, 1984). A potentially important source, not yet published at this writing, will be J. Scott Odell and Martha Goodway, "The

Metallurgy of Harpsichord Strings," in vol. 2 of *The Historical Harpsichord*, ed. by Howard Schott (New York: Pendragon Press, 1986). Less formal articles on the metallurgy of strings, too numerous to cite, can be found in the various issues of the *Fellowship of Makers and Restorers of Historical Instruments Quarterly*.

4. For several views on the workings of the soundboard see Norville Fletcher, "Analysis of the Design and Performance of Harpsichords," *Acoustica* 37 (1977): 139–47; Michael Spencer, "Harpsichord Physics," *The Galpin Society Journal* 34 (1981): 2–20; and Edward Kottick, "The Acoustics of the Harpsichord: Response Curves and Modes of Vibration," *The Galpin Society Journal* 38 (1985): 55–77.

5. For a detailed experimental study of soundboard vibration see Kottick, "The Acoustics of the Harpsichord."

6. Ibid., 63.

CHAPTER 2

1. Any discussion of the harpsichord this short tends to distort and oversimplify its history. The reader will find that the following references, taken together, will present a more complete and accurate account.

For many years now, Frank Hubbard, *Three Centuries of Harpsichord Making* (Cambridge, Mass.: Harvard University Press, 1967), has been the standard source, and deservedly so. Although now somewhat out of date, it is still the best introduction to the history of the harpsichord. Raymond Russell, *The Harpsichord and the Clavichord*, 2nd ed. rev. (New York: W. W. Norton, 1973), contains basic information on the national styles of instruments and decoration. His material, although informative, is also out of date, and a certain amount of it is now considered to be incorrect. Nevertheless, it is still useful, for its eighteen appendixes and its 103 photographs of instruments, if nothing else. Wolfgang Zuckermann's *The Mod-*

ern Harpsichord (New York: October House, 1969), has a section devoted to the history of the harpsichord. Franz Josef Hirt, *Stringed Keyboard Instruments*, bilingual reprint of the 1955 German ed. and the 1968 English trans. (New York: Da Capo Press, 1981), includes a highly idiosyncratic historical section, but it also has pages of marvelous pictures and all sorts of interesting and esoteric information. John Paul, *Modern Harpsichord Makers* (London: Victor Gollancz, 1981), talks about construction as well as matters such as wire and acoustics in his historical section. Despite its all-inclusive title, the book consists mainly of essays about their own work by nineteen English harpsichord makers.

For the most reliable information on the history of the harpsichord, the reader should consult the appropriate articles in *The New Grove Dictionary of Musical Instruments*, 3 vols., ed. by Stanley Sadie (London: Macmillan, 1984). This work is a compilation of the articles on musical instruments found in *The New Grove Dictionary of Music and Musicians*, ed. by Stanley Sadie (London: Macmillan, 1980), but many of them, such as the article on "Harpsichord" (*Musical Instruments*, vol. 2, 164–99), have been revised or expanded.

One should also want to consult Donald Boalch, *Makers of the Harpsichord and Clavichord*, 2nd ed. (Oxford: Oxford University Press, 1974), which is an alphabetical listing of all known makers along with some biographical data and information about their extant instruments, including disposition, number of keyboards, former owners, and present location. Boalch's book is a monumental life's work; nevertheless, it is acknowledged to contain many errors, and its publisher, Oxford University Press, has announced the production of a third edition under the editorship of Charles Mould (see *The Galpin Society Journal* 38 [1985]: 163).

Readers interested in the history of harpsichord decoration will want to look closely at Sheridan Germann, "Regional Schools of Harpsichord Decoration," *Journal of the Ameri-*

can Musical Instrument Society 4 (1978): 54–105. Those whose interest in decoration extends to its symbolism should see Thomas McGeary, "Harpsichord Decoration: A Reflection of Renaissance Ideas about Music," *Explorations in Renaissance Culture* 6 (1980): 1–27.

2. The manuscript is a Latin treatise on instruments by Henri Arnaut, astronomer and physician to Phillip the Good. See G. Le Cerf and E.-R Labande, eds., *Instruments de musique du XVe Siècle: les Traités d'Henri Arnaut de Zwolle et de divers anonymes* (Paris, 1932).

3. See Edmund Bowles, "A Checklist of Fifteenth-Century Representations of Stringed Keyboard Instruments," in *Keyboard Instruments: Studies in Keyboard Organology, 1500–1800*, ed. by Edwin Ripin (Edinburgh: Edinburgh University Press, 1971), 11–17, plus 31 plates.

4. Like so many other elements of Italian harpsichord building in the sixteenth century, there is a lot of conflicting information about stringing. The clearest exposition of the available evidence can be found in Denzil Wraight's section on sixteenth-century Italian harpsichord building in the article, "Harpsichord," in *Grove Musical Instruments*, 2:171–72.

5. Ibid., 169, 170.

6. As discussed in chapter 1, the impedance of the bridge is also an important factor governing this element of tone quality. For further information on the relationship between bridge and soundboard, see Edward Kottick, "The Acoustics of the Harpsichord: Response Curves and Modes of Vibration," *The Galpin Society Journal* 38 (1985): 55–77.

7. For a general survey of clavicytheria see J. H. Van der Meer, "A Contribution to the History of the Clavicytherium," *Early Music* 6 (Apr. 1978): 247–59. For more descriptive information see Michael Thomas, "The Upright Harpsichord," *The English Harpsichord Magazine* 2 (Apr. 1979): 84–92. For a list of extant clavicytheria, see Peter Bavington, "Provisional Check-List of Surviving Clavicytheria," *Fellowship of Makers*

and Restorers of Historical Instruments Quarterly 39 (Apr. 1985): 50–54.

8. Two books by Peter and Ann Mactaggart not only tell you how it was done, they also tell you how to do it: Laying and Decorating Harpsichord Papers (Stonington, Conn.: October House, 1982); and Painting and Marbling Harpsichord Cases (Welwyn, Herts.: MAC & ME, 1983). See also Germann, "Regional Schools."

9. For a listing of mottoes known to have been used on harpsichords and a discussion of their significance, see Thomas McGeary, "Harpsichord Mottoes," Journal of the American Musical Instrument Society 7 (1981): 5–35.

10. See G. Grant O'Brien, "The Stringing and Pitches of Ruckers Instruments," in Colloquium: Ruckers Clavecimbels en Copieën . . ., ed. by J. Lambrechts-Douillez (Antwerp: Ruckers Genootschap, 1977), 48–71.

11. See G. Grant O'Brien, "The Numbering System of Ruckers Instruments," Brussels Museum of Musical Instruments Bulletin 4 (1974): 75–88.

12. See William R. Dowd, "A Classification System for Ruckers and Couchet Double Harpsichords," Journal of the American Musical Instrument Society 4 (1978): 106–13.

13. See Richard T. Shann, "Flemish Transposing Harpsichords—An Explanation," The Galpin Society Journal 37 (1984): 62–71; and his "Ruckers Doubles: A Survey of the Theories," Fellowship of Makers and Restorers of Historical Instruments Quarterly 41 (Oct. 1985): 69–75. See also Nicholas Meeùs, "Ruckers Doubles: the 'Sixth Hypothesis,'" Fellowship of Makers and Restorers of Historical Instruments Quarterly 42 (Jan. 1986): 50–55.

14. For an appreciation of the double virginal, see John Koster, "The Mother and Child Virginal and its Place in the Keyboard Instrument Culture of the Sixteenth and Seventeenth Centuries," in Colloquium, (1977), 78–96.

15. See Edwin Ripin, "French Harpsichords Before 1650," The Galpin Society Journal 20 (1967): 43–47; and Michael Thomas, "Early French Harpsichords," The English Harpsichord Magazine 1 (Oct. 1974): 73–84. Several seventeenth-century French harpsichords have been uncovered in the last few years, and this school may yet emerge as one of the dominant styles, as important as the Italian or Flemish traditions.

16. See Dowd, "A Classification System," 108.

17. Ibid.

18. The most famous of these "rebuilt" new harpsichords is the 1743 by Jean Goujon, now in the Paris Conservatoire. See Russell, The Harpsichord and the Clavichord, plates 21–23.

19. For an exhaustive discussion of the extant instruments of the Blanchet and early Taskin workshops, see William Dowd, "The Surviving Instruments of the Blanchet Workshop," in vol. 1 of The Historical Harpsichord, ed. by Howard Schott (New York: Pendragon, 1984), 17–107.

20. For further information see Germann, "Regional Schools."

21. For an account of harpsichord decoration in Paris in the eighteenth century, see Sheridan Germann, "Monsieur Doublet and his Confrères," Early Music 8 (Oct. 1980): 435–53; and 9 (Apr. 1981): 192–212.

22. See Thomas McGeary, "Early English Harpsichord Building: a Reassessment," The English Harpsichord Magazine 1 (Oct. 1973): 7–17; 30. McGeary points out that English harpsichord building in the seventeenth century was highly individualized, in no way constituted a "school," and had little to do with the eighteenth-century English harpsichord. See also Charles Mould, "An Early Eighteenth-Century Harpsichord by Thomas Barton," The English Harpsichord Magazine 1 (Apr. 1974): 36–38.

23. There is evidence that Tabel built quite a few harpsichords in London before his death in 1738, but only one remains. For an account of that instrument, see Charles Mould, "The Tabel Harpsichord," in Ripin, Keyboard Instruments, 59–65.

24. For a detailed discussion of the distinctions between Flemish and English virginals, see John Koster, "The Importance of the Early English Harpsichord," The Galpin Society Journal 33 (1980): 45–73.

25. Hubbard, Three Centuries, 150–51.

26. See Grove Musical Instruments, 3:172–73.

27. Boalch, Makers of the Harpsichord and Clavichord, 194–202.

28. The second and third of these points were first suggested by Germann in "Regional Schools." Both are more fully explored in her extensive article, "The Mietkes, the Margrave, and Bach," in Bach, Handel, Scarlatti: Tercentenary Essays, ed. by Peter Williams (Cambridge: Cambridge University Press, 1985), 119–48.

29. The date of this instrument is usually given as 1770 or sometimes 1710, but a recent restoration revealed the date to be 1750.

CHAPTER 3

1. For a short discussion of harpsichord "building" in the nineteenth century, see P. Sween, "The Nineteenth-Century View of the Old Harpsichord," The English Harpsichord Magazine 2 (Apr. 1979): 92–95.

2. For a defense of the revival harpsichord, written literally at the moment of its demise, read Hanns Neupert, Harpsichord Manual, trans. from the third (1955) German ed. by F. E. Kirby (Basel: Bärenreiter, 1960).

3. It is interesting to read Frank Hubbard's own words in this regard. See his "Reconstructing the Harpsichord," in vol. 1 of The Historical Harpsichord, ed. by Howard Schott (New York: Pendragon Press, 1984), 1–16.

4. I am indebted to R. K. Lee, the first apprentice to Hubbard and Dowd, for this intriguing concept.

CHAPTER 4

1. Every so often a short article on buying a harpsichord appears. For

one of the latest, the shortest, and the best, see Edgar Hunt, "On Choosing a Harpsichord," *The English Harpsichord Magazine* 3 (Oct. 1983): 97–98.

2. Even as late as eleven years ago the situation was quite different. See Ruth Nurmi, *A Plain and Easy Introduction to the Harpsichord* (Albuquerque, N.M.: University of New Mexico Press, 1974), 6–12.

3. See John Barnes, "The Specious Uniformity of Italian Harpsichords," and Friedemann Hellwig, "The Single-Strung Italian Harpsichord," both in *Keyboard Instruments: Studies in Keyboard Organology, 1500–1800,* ed. Edwin Ripin (Edinburgh: Edinburgh University Press, 1971), 1–10, 29–40.

4. See Derick Adlam, "Restoring the Vaudry," *Early Music* 4 (July 1976): 255–65.

5. Charles Burney, *The Present State of Music in France and Italy* (London: T. Becket, 1771), 38. Although he was delighted with the appearance of an enlarged Ruckers he was shown in Paris, Burney gave faint praise to its tone ("more delicate than powerful"), and he dismissed its touch as "very light, owing to the quilling, which in France is always weak."

6. For a cautionary lesson in copying, see the anecdote related in Michael Thomas, "Further Thoughts and Notes," *The English Harpsichord Magazine* 1 (Apr. 1977): 234–35.

CHAPTER 6

1. William Dowd, *A Short Maintenance Manual for William Dowd Harpsichords* (Boston: William Dowd, 1984), 22.

2. Ibid.

3. Builders of Zuckermann kits will recognize that this low-tech method is the one now recommended in the construction manuals. The no-tech procedure was the one previously suggested. Ibid., 22, also describes the no-tech method.

CHAPTER 7

1. William Dowd, *A Short Maintenance Manual for William Dowd Harpsichords* (Boston: William Dowd, 1984), 11; Eric Herz, *Maintenance and Tuning of Harpsichords* (Cambridge, Mass.: Eric Herz, 1976), 13.

2. My own experience with crow quill has been limited. Much of what I say here I have learned from John Bennett, chief voicer at the Zuckermann shops, and from information given to me by Robert Greenberg. Both have had considerable experience with crow quill.

3. There are exceptions, for dispositions such as lute stops, where two sets of jacks are intended to pluck the same set of strings. Obviously, the strings cannot be damped by one set of jacks at the same time that they are being played by another set.

CHAPTER 11

1. Sheridan Germann puts it something like this: some argue that since eighteenth-century owners did not seem to concern themselves about these matters, neither should we. But the eighteenth-century harpsichord lived in the relatively stable European climate that normally ranged from about 30 to 85 degrees Fahrenheit in temperature and from about 40 to 60 percent in relative humidity. In Iowa our temperatures normally range from −20 to 95 degrees Fahrenheit, with from 5 to 95 percent humidity. The instruments were designed neither for the North American climate nor for central heating. Either we alter the design of the harpsichord to compensate for the climatic differences (exactly what many of the revival builders tried to do earlier in the century), or we control temperature and humidity. The latter is easier and musically less dangerous.

2. William Dowd, *A Short Maintenance Manual for William Dowd Harpsichords* (Boston: William Dowd, 1984), 8.

CHAPTER 13

1. Much of the information on the subject of temperament has been written by experts for experts. The work that first awakened the interest of twentieth-century musicians in temperaments other than equal was J. Murray Barbour, *Tuning and Temperament,* 2nd ed. (East Lansing, Mich.: Michigan State College Press, 1953). Barbour's evolutionary approach related all older temperaments to equal temperament, which he considered to be an ideal end product.

Two more recent works that take an opposing view and, in addition, attempt to provide practical instruction in tuning the older temperaments, are Owen Jorgensen, *Tuning the Historical Temperaments by Ear* (Marquette, Mich.: Northern Michigan University Press, 1977); and Herbert A. Kellner, *The Tuning of My Harpsichord* (Frankfort am Main: Verlag Das Musikinstrument, 1980). Jorgensen later brought out a thirty-six page handbook called *The Equal-Beating Temperaments* (Raleigh, N.C.: The Sunbury Press, 1981). Despite the title, the book is not about equal temperament. A similar handbook is G. C. Klop, *Harpsichord Tuning* (Raleigh, N.C.: The Sunbury Press, 1974).

For a more complete history of temperament than the short version given here, see the article by Mark Lindley on "Temperaments," in *The New Grove Dictionary of Musical Instruments,* 3:540–55.

2. See Edward L. Kottick, review of Mark Lindley, *Lutes, Viols and Temperaments* (Cambridge: Cambridge University Press, 1984), in *American Lutherie* 2 (June 1985): 52, 53.

3. Some of this material has appeared in print in somewhat different form. See Edward L. Kottick, "The Truth about Temperaments," *The Guild of American Luthiers Quarterly* 12 (June 1984): 10–16.

4. Although it has been known for many years that it is not so, it is still believed by many. One of those stories that will not die, it probably will

linger as long as it continues to be found in standard reference works. The article on temperament in the *Harvard Dictionary of Music*, ed. by Willi Apel, 2nd ed. rev. and enlarged (Cambridge, Mass: The Belknap Press of Harvard University Press, 1969), 835, 836, insists that equal temperament was the inevitable consequence of the use of the more remote keys. To be fair, the article on temperament in the new edition— *The New Harvard Dictionary of Music*, ed. by Don M. Randel (Cambridge, Mass: The Belknap Press of Harvard University Press, 1986), no longer makes this statement. But Donald Grout, in his *A History of*

Western Music, 3rd ed. (New York: W. W. Norton, 1980), 377, continues to state that the use of equal temperament was a corollary to the development of the "systematic use of key relationships." And a book just out, Anita T. Sullivan, *The Seventh Dragon: the Riddle of Equal Temperament* (Lake Oswego, Ore.: Metamorphous Press, 1986), perpetuates the myth that Bach's *Well-Tempered Clavier* was intended to display the powers of equal temperament. Up until recent years the German title of Bach's monumental work was translated as "The Well-Tempered *Clavichord*," but people finally seemed to have gotten the idea that

the word *clavier* was a generic term for keyboard instruments.

5. This is the approach taken by J. Murray Barbour.

6. Eric Herz, *Maintenance and Tuning of Harpsichords* (Cambridge, Mass.: Eric Herz, 1976), 39.

7. William Dowd, *A Short Maintenance Manual for William Dowd Harpsichords* (Boston: William Dowd, 1984), 19; Herz, *Maintenance and Tuning of Harpsichords*, 31; Jorgensen, *The Equal-Beating Temperaments*, 10.

8. "Bach's Keyboard Temperament," *Early Music* 7 (Apr. 1979): 236–49. Barnes's temperament is a slightly modified Werckmeister III.

Index